Corporate Responsibility and Political Philosophy

This book argues for the inclusion of the corporation as an integral element of political philosophy. It begins with a historical evaluation of the corporation as a constituent of political society. It shows how Adam Smith, Hegel, and Marx conceived the role of the corporation in relation to the state, the market, and civil society before moving on to the rejection of the corporation as a genuine moral and political agent by Rawls and Habermas. The next chapter of the book presents the corporation as a collective that possesses political and moral agency. The author outlines four distinct political philosophies of corporate responsibility: the Aristotelian conservative–virtue ethical conception; the market liberal theory; the social liberal theory of corporate citizenship and political corporate social responsibility (CSR); and Marxist-inspired critical theories. It is argued that the social liberal theory provides a better justification compared to its rivals. The third and final group of chapters applies the social liberal conception – called the social liberal corporation – to important contemporary issues, including human rights in global supply chains, financial and digital firms, sustainability, and climate change. *Corporate Responsibility and Political Philosophy* will appeal to political philosophers, political theorists, and applied ethicists as well as scholars in other disciplines working on issues related to business ethics, organizational ethics, sustainability, and CSR. As it provides a comprehensive introduction to corporate responsibility, it is also relevant to sustainability professionals who seek an overview of the theoretical debate on corporate responsibility.

Kristian Høyer Toft earned his PhD in political philosophy at Aarhus University (2003) and was a visiting scholar in philosophy at Columbia University, the University of Pittsburgh, and the University of Reading. He has published articles about climate justice, human rights, and corporate responsibility in international journals, for example, The *Business and Human Rights Journal* and *Energy Research & Social Science*. He held positions as a postdoctoral researcher in bioethics at the University of Copenhagen (2006–2007) and assistant and associate professor at Aalborg University in applied philosophy (2011–2019) and is currently a guest researcher at the Sustainability Centre at the Copenhagen Business School (2020).

Routledge Research in Applied Ethics

Media Ethics, Free Speech, and the Requirements of Democracy
Edited by Carl Fox and Joe Saunders

Ethics and Chronic Illness
Tom Walker

The Future of Work, Technology, and Basic Income
Edited by Michael Cholbi and Michael Weber

The Ethics of Eating Animals
Usually Bad, Sometimes Wrong, Often Permissible
Bob Fischer

Self-Defense, Necessity, and Punishment
A Philosophical Analysis
Uwe Steinhoff

Ethics and Error in Medicine
Edited by Fritz Allhoff and Sandra L. Borden

Care Ethics and the Refugee Crisis
Emotions, Contestations, and Agency
Marcia Morgan

Corporate Responsibility and Political Philosophy
Exploring the Social Liberal Corporation
Kristian Høyer Toft

For more information about this series, please visit: www.routledge.com/Routledge-Research-in-Applied-Ethics/book-series/RRAES

Corporate Responsibility and Political Philosophy

Exploring the Social Liberal Corporation

Kristian Høyer Toft

Routledge
Taylor & Francis Group
NEW YORK AND LONDON

First published 2020
by Routledge
605 Third Avenue, New York, NY 10017

and by Routledge
2 Park Square, Milton Park, Abingdon, Oxon OX14 4RN

First issued in paperback 2022

Routledge is an imprint of the Taylor & Francis Group, an informa business

Publisher's Note
The publisher has gone to great lengths to ensure the quality of this reprint but points out that some imperfections in the original copies may be apparent.

Library of Congress Cataloging-in-Publication Data
A catalog record for this book has been requested

ISBN 13: 978-1-03-240045-7 (pbk)
ISBN 13: 978-1-138-06554-3 (hbk)
ISBN 13: 978-1-315-15962-1 (ebk)

DOI: 10.4324/9781315159621

Typeset in Sabon
by Apex CoVantage, LLC

Contents

Tables

Preface and Acknowledgements

Can corporations be morally responsible members of society, similar to how ordinary people can be? This book aims at answering this question by means of political philosophy.

Having studied political philosophy, I find the political role of corporations an intriguing subject matter. This is particularly so because, as demonstrated in Chapter 2, John Rawls argues that corporations are not an issue relevant to justice; hence, political philosophers should not take corporations too seriously. By coincidence, when I entered the research field of business ethics and corporate social responsibility (CSR) in 2008 (the year of the global financial crisis), the very idea that corporations are not only private firms, but also public and political actors, was already being extensively debated by theorists of corporate citizenship and political CSR. I also noticed that the research topic was, and still is, essentially and politically contested. The motto for newcomers seems to be: Either you are with the corporations or you are against them.

This book, however, aims at a less binary view of the corporation. It therefore offers an introductory overview of the different approaches, or *conceptions*, to use a term from political philosophy, to corporate responsibility. These are found in theories of conservative virtue ethics, market liberal libertarianism, democratic views of republicanism, corporate citizenship and deliberation, as well as critiques of current business ideology. I believe that each political view on the corporation has something important and relevant to tell us; however, if looking for a constructive and critical defence of corporate responsibility, I conclude that the social liberal conception is the most promising. Hence, the book is also a proposal for the *social liberal corporation*, a term that I use for categorizing the corporations that take on a political role for the common good in society based on a social liberal outlook. I take the theories of corporate citizenship and political CSR to be the basis for the social liberal corporation. The proponents of those theories do not themselves communicate their positions as explicitly social liberal, although in the case of corporate citizenship there is reference to T. H. Marshall, and political CSR relies much on Habermas's deliberative democracy. Moreover,

John Rawls's political philosophy and his concern with social justice is a comprehensive defence of modern social liberalism. Even though Rawls resists including corporations in the scope of a theory of justice, this book nevertheless challenges Rawls on this point by insisting on a political theory of the firm.

Thus, I take the liberty of grouping those, and other, approaches together in the catch-all orientation of the social liberal corporation. One reason for proposing the *social liberal corporation* as a term is also to intervene in the debate about the destiny of the welfare state and liberal democracy. Too often, business ethics and CSR are insulated from wider political currents. But the call for corporate responsibility only makes real sense when seen in the societal context. The pressure on, and potential weakening of, the nation state due to globalization processes leaves unsolved serious problems of welfare, social security, health, education, taxation, privacy, human rights, the environment, and climate change. It is a key insight and also a contested claim in corporate citizenship and political CSR theories that corporations can and should provide solutions to those problems. The claim is contested because, empirically, it is uncertain that business corporations, as private agents, are capable of providing public goods. Furthermore, for obvious reasons, we might not want private actors and big corporations to fill the vacant space in situations of government failure.

However, if the division of political labour in a future society also requires a constructive contribution from corporations in collaboration with the state and civil society, a plausible theory on corporate responsibility is needed to provide guidance. The standard response – that we must regulate the corporation – is surely the well-founded approach as long as market failures persist. But considering that the law often lags behind and the state's jurisdiction and powers are limited, it seems insufficient to maintain Milton Friedman's dictum that the sole corporate responsibility is to increase the profits within the limits of the law and ethical custom. Hence, the notion of the social liberal corporation is suggested to reconfigure thinking about corporate responsibility in society. And, in this book, this is done by exploring the notion of corporate responsibility in the context of political philosophy.

Even though I am the sole author, the book is an outcome of a collective process facilitated by the university "whose very name derives from the Latin term for corporation, universitas" (Avi-Yonah 2005, 772). I have benefitted much from discussions with philosophy students at Aalborg University. In fact, the students who voluntarily chose (I hope) to work on the topics of this book not only gave me new insights but also provided reasons to persevere with a research topic somewhat odd to most philosophers. I am therefore grateful to Claus Brink Mortensen, Sebastien Bouchara, Kasper Schmidt, Andreas Beyer Gregersen, Jens Christian Nielsen, Jesper Bach Christensen, Jakob Thrane Mainz, Emil

Laue Jacobsen, Marco Mosbæk Olsson, Jesper Fleckner Gravholt, Lasse Frandsen, Lasse Mølgaard Nielsen, Lisa Buus Nielsen, Anne Sivesgaard Jensen, and Morten Rønde Rasmussen.

Professor Antje Gimmler has given continued support to the writing of this book within the Applied Philosophy research group. And, on a more informal level, she invited her former Marburger fellow philosophy student, Guido Palazzo, to visit Aalborg University in November 2012 – a fortuitous coincidence for me. Guido has since been a source of inspiration and given feedback on papers and a draft of this book. He also generously shared his knowledge about political CSR during a visit to Lausanne in the summer of 2014.

Professor Finn Arler supported my research on corporate responsibility and climate change in the research project "Ethics and Energy" funded by the Independent Research Fund Denmark (Humanities). Chapter 11 is an outcome of this project.

I also owe much to a number of excellent academic researchers in the field of corporate responsibility and philosophy.

I am grateful to Steen Vallentin for accepting the invitation to teach a class of mine in 2013. He also wrote a great introductory book on CSR in Danish (*Afkastet og anstændigheden – Social ansvarlighed i kritisk belysning*, 2011) – the structure of my book is partially inspired by his review of the CSR field as conflicting political views – hence, I seek to go further and identify the political theories underlying the conflicts.

I am also grateful to Jeremy Moon for literature suggestions and for making it possible for me to join the Sustainability Centre at the Copenhagen Business School as a guest researcher. Jeremy, Camilla Sløk, and Lisa Herzog came all the way to Aalborg to teach and discuss corporate ethics. Lisa Herzog also arranged a workshop, "Between Ethics and Efficiency? The Political Theory of Corporate Governance," at TUM, in Munich in December 2016. Participating in this workshop gave me new ideas for the book, and I then realized that the topic of corporate responsibility had started to attract attention from a number of brilliant younger philosophers.

I am also indebted to Jacob Dahl Rendtorff for his enthusiasm and helpfulness through several collaborations on corporate responsibility projects.

I am grateful for the fine and informal talks about corporate responsibility and related issues that I have had with fellow philosophers Jørn Sønderholm, Claus Strue Frederiksen, Christian Olaf Christiansen, Jes Lynning Harfeld, and Hans Fink on various occasions and, also for an invitation from Raffaele Rodogno to present the early idea of a draft for this book at the Research Group for Ethics, Legal and Political Philosophy at Aarhus University in October 2015.

Parts of the book were presented in early drafts at conferences, where I received copious and helpful feedback, especially with respect to

Chapter 7 on political CSR at the EGOS conference 2017 at Copenhagen Business School.

Parts of Chapter 11 on corporate environmentalism, concerned with the carbon majors and human rights, were presented at the 4th Workshop on Business Ethics in 2017 in Brussels, arranged by Florian Wettstein and Pascal Dey. Florian has been helpful with another publication on this topic in the *Business and Human Rights Journal*.

For good friendship and interesting talks about philosophy over the years, I am grateful to Rune Jahn, Henrik Barsøe Jensen, Morten Kjær Jensen and Anne Flemmert Jensen.

In the process of proofreading, Julie Murray, Ashley Kim Stewart, Mia Juul Bolduc, Claire Neesham, and Andreas Beyer Gregersen have been helpful. Financial support for proofreading was generously granted by the Centre for Applied Philosophy and the Centre for Ethics in Practice (the Obel Foundation).

I am also grateful for the support given by Andrew Weckenmann, the editor at Routledge.

Any shortcoming or mistake is, of course, solely on my part.

The greatest debt, however, I owe to my family – Mette, Hedvig, Harald, and Sigrid. They have had to tolerate my mental and at times physical absence during the prolonged process of writing this book, not to mention the other papers and articles that subtracted from family time. I hope they will not hold it against me later because this was my own choice and ambition and certainly, as some philosophers would say, "no fault of their own".

I dedicate the book to them but also to my parents, Finn and Eva, and my two brothers, Anders and Peter, because they all knew and know what it means to live a family life close to a family firm.

Copenhagen, 6 December 2019

Reference

Avi-Yonah, R. S. (2005) The cyclical transformations of the corporate form: A historical perspective on corporate social responsibility. *The Delaware Journal of Corporate Law*, *30*(3), 767–818

Introduction

Corporations as the Missing Link in Political Philosophy

The aim of this book is threefold: first, to give an overview of how business firms fit into the broader landscape of political philosophy; second, to explore the prospects of a coherent political philosophical account of corporate responsibility; and third, to defend a particular conception of the business firm and corporate responsibility – the social liberal corporation.

The terms *corporation*, *firm*, *company*, or *enterprise* are used interchangeably. When relevant, the corporation is taken to signify the larger company or group of companies or firms, such as multinational or transnational companies or firms. The term *firm* refers to the legally defined agent, although the literature also uses it synonymously with *corporation* and *company* (cf. Orts & Craig Smith 2017; Avi-Yonah 2005). The *company* typically refers to the particular products, goods and services, and branch of industry it belongs to, for example, an energy company. The *enterprise* is a more neutral term and can refer to all of the above meanings. The current philosophical literature in analytical political theory tends to use the *firm* to a greater extent than the other terms – I therefore use the terms in the context of those referred to throughout the book.

The book has a focus on private and profit-driven organizations as these are the two features typically associated with the business organization. The idea that business firms can be reduced to simply private and profit-driven organizations is, however, contested by the notion of the social liberal corporation. Basically, it is argued that business firms *should* respect and contribute to the common good of society, which is taken as an abstract ideal (not reducible to private goods). This should be obtained through a balancing of the need for profit with other important concerns, such as those of the environment and basic rights of citizens. The view defended is a *normative view* spelled out in the language and categories of political philosophy. In some respects the view will overlap with actual firms; in other respects it may be too idealistic and thereby become a constraining ideal for real firms and governmental regulators to comply with or aspire to. The present project seeks to place the idea of the corporation in the framework of political philosophy as it has been perceived in the philosophical tradition and in the more recent literature on business ethics and corporate responsibility. There is a need for clarifying and creating a space for the corporation in political philosophy, a need that is evidenced by the current growth in research publications addressing this issue. Isabelle Ferreras (2017) has epitomized this development in a call for a *political theory of the firm*.

The three aims of the book – overview, exploration, and defence of the social liberal corporation – are interrelated because they all reflect a turning point in the current philosophy of the business firm. I here follow Hegel's view that philosophy "is its own time comprehended in thoughts" (Hegel 2011/1821, 21) because to get a grasp of the current philosophical thinking on the business firm, it is necessary to also widen the historical lens and revisit selected thinkers of the 19th century, Adam Smith, G. W. F. Hegel, and Karl Marx, because they, each in their own way, have provided the philosophical templates for the corporation, more or less, still at work today. Notwithstanding their differences, they all considered the corporation as part of public society; Smith saw in the corporation a liberating institution from feudal society, Hegel used the corporation to mediate between citizens and the state to ensure representation, and Marx saw the corporation as a site for concerns of exploitation and social justice, although he was also sceptical about liberal justice. The period of classical liberalism and its philosophical reactions operates with the now contested concept of the common good of society. The corporation should be of benefit to society and was therefore authorized by the state as a "franchise of the government" (Ciepley 2013). However, in the 20th century, liberal thinkers such as Jürgen Habermas and John Rawls exclude the corporation from the public domain and acknowledge it as a "private association" with the right to execute corporate authority over its employees. From this point onwards the corporation is to an increasing extent seen as a private enterprise, and its purpose is no longer in the service of the common good, but rather it should serve the private interests of shareholders and maximize profits (Friedman 1970; see Chapter 5). The firm is thus seen as a mere *nexus of contracts* and as a means to reduce "transaction cost" on the market. The liberal argument for this retreat to privacy assumes that promoting private interest will eventually turn into public goods, alluding to Mandeville' (1732) slogan that "private vices" are "public benefits".

Today it is less obvious that business firms are for the common good; rather, the opposite is often taken as a given. Elizabeth Anderson critiques the 21st-century corporation as an example of *private government* (Anderson 2017) due to the wide range of unconstrained authority management has over its employees in private business organizations. What is going on inside of private organizations is to be considered justified as a right to privacy. This has given rise to a debate concerning where to draw the public-private distinction in the case of the corporation, in particular with regard to workplace democracy (Ciepley 2013; Landemore & Ferreras 2016). The topic of workplace democracy and the relationship between the firm, democracy, and justice are key concerns as already made clear by Robert Dahl (1985). However, even though this topic is key to current debate over corporate responsibility, this book does not address the complexities involved in matters of "workplace democracy" besides the brief mention in the section on Rawls in Chapter 2.

The 20th-century notion of the insulated private company is now challenged by demands that exert a pressure on the traditional primacy of the shareholder. Now, the stakeholders are increasingly seen as relevant parties in corporate decision-making, that is, those parties who are affected by or could affect the corporation (Freeman 1984). Stakeholders want the corporation to respond to and care for issues of the environment, such as climate change and pollution, and a longer list of issues includes meaningful work, human rights, sustainable innovation, discrimination, poverty, global taxes, privacy protection on the internet, and structural issues of the global economy. The point to derive is that such issues cannot easily be dealt with by traditional means of public regulation and state governance, typically, because the problems are global issues far beyond the reach and jurisdiction of the nation state or, because there is a lack of political will to solve the problem through regulation within the state. Business firms therefore see an opportunity to provide solutions where the state fails and cannot deliver. Responsible corporations also see such a situation as a call for moral action. The governance vacuum following the absence of the state here elicits both moral and economic reasons for business corporations to act – and oftentimes the normative and the instrumental conflates. Theories of corporate citizenship (Crane et al. 2008) and political CSR (Scherer & Palazzo 2007), for instance, take this as an empirical economic given (a business opportunity) but also as a reason for why business firms ought to take responsibility (see Chapters 6 and 7).

The Emergence of the Social Liberal Corporation

This development in practice and theory is taken as a cue to hypothesize the emergence of the *social liberal corporation*. Hence, corporate citizenship theory and political CSR are key examples of social liberal theories designed to fit the corporate realm. This is so because they both have roots in social liberalism. Corporate citizenship theory refers to the social liberal T. H. Marshall's work on citizenship rights (Crane et al. 2008, 6), and political CSR theory refers to Jürgen Habermas's theory of deliberative democracy, which can be seen as referring to the social liberal tradition (Scherer & Palazzo 2007). Both theories also emphasize political participation as a key aspect of corporate responsibility and hence are social liberal *republican* theories of the corporation in society.

In my interpretation of the social liberal corporation, the philosophical heritage also includes thinkers such as G. W. F. Hegel (1770–1831), John Stuart Mill (1808–1873), John Dewey (1859–1952), and John Rawls (1921–2002). The sort of liberalism alluded to by the term *social liberalism* is often titled *modern liberalism* to distinguish it from *classical liberalism* (Ryan 1998). Moreover, social liberalism is merely one strand of modern liberalism, but characteristic is its commitment to government regulation of the market with the aim to compensate for unfair inequalities produced by an unregulated market. Social liberalism shares with classical liberalism the view that the individual should freely realize one's full potential and liberate oneself from oppression. In Rawls's words, one should have sufficient (primary) goods to be able to realize a personal *life plan* (Rawls 1971). Hence, the state avoids hindering individual freedom, but it should also encourage and support citizens' aspirations for self-realization. Social liberalism shares with classical liberalism the support to property rights and freedom of the market as a means to create welfare in society. Adam Smith saw the market as a liberator and as an example of the means for how individual human rights could be secured. But social liberalism is less optimistic compared to classical liberalism about the unregulated market's ability to secure and realize liberty. It therefore shares with socialism and Marxism, and even with Hegel and Adam Smith, the insight that the market also creates poverty and unfreedom. But social liberals call out for reform of the market and do not believe in the Marxist prescription for revolution and abolition of private property as the proper means to overcome market failure.

The point is that social liberalism aims at compensating for market failures in the capitalist system (cf. Heath 2014). This middle position can be difficult to retain in periods of time when the dualism between unregulated markets and a planning economy is considered as the only option available. Moreover, there are degrees and varieties of social liberalism, some of which are more libertarian or socialist in their orientation. And, if the point of view is, for instance, libertarian, there is a tendency to perceive social liberalism on par with socialism and vice versa.

This leads to the key point of a defence for the social liberal corporation, that it might well be the only viable option for a general and coherent argument in support of corporate responsibility. This is so because both market liberals (libertarians) and critical Marxists either reject or are sceptical about the idea that corporations can (the Marxists) or should (the libertarians) be (socially) responsible. Milton Friedman's (1970) dismissal of CSR is emblematic of this conviction as the sole "responsibility of business is to increase its profits". On the other hand, Marxist-inspired criticism of corporate responsibility is also dismissive but for different reasons than market liberals. Market liberals tend to dismiss corporate responsibility, beyond the managers' fiduciary responsibility to shareholders, because duties of corporate responsibility that extend beyond shareholders' interests are to be considered on a par with a hidden taxation of the corporation. Thus, corporate responsibility is competing with shareholders' interest for profit and therefore should be dismissed. Marxists, however, are against the idea of corporate responsibility because corporations cannot be moral agents, but even worse, the notion that a corporation can be socially responsible is an ideological cover-up for exploitative capitalism. Hence, Marxists will argue that the relevant focus is the capitalist system and not its local incarnation of the business firm, which is comparable to a profit-generating machine with no place for morality. Such critiques result in the notion that business ethics is a self-defeating oxymoron.

Because the social liberals disagree with the market liberals and the Marxists about what is a desirable and feasible way of resolving market failures, they welcome both public and private initiatives – whereas libertarians prefer private and Marxists public initiatives to resolve market failures. Only the social liberals (broadly construed) will concede that business firms both can and ought to be a means to realize social liberal ideals. This is typically done in tandem with non-corporate actors like the state or civil society. Hence, the corporation is a political actor on par with other players in society, even though it is also and at the same time a private one. This double identity creates an internal tension in the social liberal corporation that makes it particularly fit for times when the public-private distinction is in dispute. But it also creates a tension that might ultimately threaten the coherence and hence existence of the organization.

As will be argued in Chapter 4, conservative and some of the virtue ethical conceptions of corporate responsibility are also supportive of corporate responsibility and share the positive outlook with the social liberal. However, such approaches are mostly formulated in opposition to modern society and excessive capitalism; for example, in particular in the communitarian versions, the view is anti-globalist, against large-scale production and industrial divisions of labour.

The reason then for why it is a *social* liberal corporation and not simply a liberal corporation is because it responds to a longer list of social concerns, such as social justice, social rights, and claims to health and educational services. But also concerns associated with social liberal citizenship such as political rights pertaining to democracy and even concerns for the environment can be included on the list as, for instance, witnessed in debate over environmental justice and rights. The social liberal corporation might in some instances take on some of the duties of the state to administer and secure citizens' rights (Matten & Crane 2005), and it might provide public goods, such as education, health care, and infrastructure, where the state fails to deliver (Scherer & Palazzo 2011). The typical role of the social liberal corporation is, however, to *collaborate* with state and civil society to provide public goods. It is not aiming to crowd out the state's authority to govern; rather, it typically supports the state, when legitimate, in solving public problems that the state cannot solve on its own. Therefore the social liberal corporation is not a mere symptom of neoliberalism, which aims at privatizing public and state institutions. Rather, the social liberal corporation can be seen as a response to neoliberalism because the social liberal corporation emerges as a consequence of decades of neoliberal outsourcing of public activities from the state. In the era of neoliberalism (while admitting that this term evokes contestation), the big corporations take over state functions, and corporate elites are increasingly influencing the state system. The consequence of corporate elites' prolonged and excessive influence therefore constitutes a threat to democracy (Crouch 2004). Thus, the social liberal corporation is a double-edged sword that operates in the service of the state, but it also emerges in the wake of neoliberalist privatization and marketization. This makes it difficult to trust notions such as corporate citizenship and political CSR that the social liberal corporation relies on (Fleming & Jones 2013). Sometimes the critique is expressed in the saying that corporations are socially liberal about values but fiscally conservative. Hence, the modern corporation is forced to be politically correct to avoid offending customers and the general public, but when the chips are down, it remains as conservative as always about the priority of the financial bottom line. Hence, it is liberal as long as it does not cost any money. Certainly, this is not the view I would hold with regard to the social liberal corporation – my reading of the literature indicates that liberal values could easily entail a trade-off with profit maximization.

Thus, the private corporation is increasingly considered to be part of politics where the state fails or processes of neoliberal politics outsource functions of the state to private corporations.

Recent literature, however, contests the claim that the nation state has lost its power in the process of globalization. In fact current notions of CSR are reminiscent of former state–firm collaborative models, that is, paternalism and trusteeship (Djelic & Etchanchu 2015). CSR therefore is the latest example of state-led initiatives in a longer series of capitalist corporate-state models of governance. Hence, the nation state continues to set the regulatory framework for corporate activities (Schrempf-Stirling 2016), and it thereby facilitates and mandates CSR (Knudsen & Moon 2017). The notion of the social liberal corporation is therefore compatible with some recent revision of current theorizing in corporate citizenship and political CSR, conceding that the state is not absent or weak but rather highly present and active in framing and promoting corporate responsibility.

Another issue that challenges the view that the nation state is weakened is seen from the resurgence in the nationalist and populist currents gaining traction globally. With their expressed distrust in the system – sometimes termed the *liberal world order* – they have sparked an ideological crisis of liberalism and thus the large business corporation is especially distrusted. A shared premise among disbelievers in the liberal world order is a tendency to conflate liberalism into one crude notion of liberalism as neoliberalism. Hence, the social liberalism of welfare states is considered on a par with neoliberalism in the term *competition state*. In fact, the now dwindling support for the social-democratic European welfare state once seen as a protection of the working class is by critics considered to be in the service of neoliberalism and the creation of the growing precariat of the labour market.

A possible explanation for the conflation is that social liberals in political power since the 1990s have also implemented large degrees of market liberal policies (e.g., the third-way of the UK Labour government) to the extent that in political practice, only margins separate the social and the market liberal versions of liberalism.

Therefore, the social liberal corporation can also be seen as a response to the crisis of social liberalism in politics due to the tendency of a convergence or conflation between social and market liberalism. If the state fails at providing for social liberal governance, the ideology of social liberalism can be safeguarded by non-state organizations to give expression to a longing for this kind of governance.

The Corporation in Political Philosophy

This book, however, does not aim to provide answers to the macro-scale political and social questions relevant to the empirical facts of the social liberal corporation. Rather, it offers an overview, exploration, and defence of the social liberal corporation with a focus on political philosophy. This is primarily motivated by the fact that the corporation is a contested issue, even to the extent that corporations are neglected and absent in political philosophy.

The traditional division of labour between moral philosophy addressing the individual level and political philosophy that concerns the macro level of society, that is, the state or some higher-level political entity such as civil society or international society, is deeply entrenched (Heath 2014; Mäkinen & Kasanen 2016; Herzog 2018).

The link between the level of the individual and the macro organizations of society in the form of mediating institutions is often neglected in political philosophy and therefore the meso level, where the corporation is situated is a *missing link* in traditional political philosophy. The political theory of the firm is compensating for this lacuna in traditional political philosophy.

However, the history of political philosophy is abundant with thinking about the nature and proper structure of how society should be organized. For instance, Plato's ideal state should be organized according to a principle mirroring the three parts of the human psyche: desire, will, and reason. Hence, the state should have a class of working people, craftsmen and traders, reflecting the lower part of the psyche, the desire. The guardians, equivalent to the police and military, reflect bravery and the will. In the top of the social architecture one finds the leaders, the philosopher kings as Plato envisaged, who represent reason as an aspect of the psyche. Other organizing principles to mediate between the individual and political levels of the state are found in the social contract tradition grounded by Thomas Hobbes, John Locke, and Jean Jacques Rousseau and renewed by John Rawls. Sheldon Wolin (2004) refers to this vein of thinking as the *age of organization* in political theory.

The point to draw out from this is that what is missing is an elaborate philosophy on the nature and social role of the *meso* level organizations.

An exception is Hegel's *Philosophy of Right* (2011/1821), which contains a more detailed prescription for the role of corporations in society, and this is why the present book takes its historical starting point with the time of Hegel and his contemporaries (see Chapter 1). Later, John Rawls focussed on the main institutions of the basic structure of society as the objects of concern for a theory of justice (1971/1999). However, he does not say much about the actual design of those institutions, and he is vague in the description of where the business corporation is placed in the institutional architecture (see Chapter 2).

A key aim of the book is therefore to contribute to clarifying what role the business corporation can have in the general societal architecture according to current trends in political philosophy (cf. Heath et al. 2010).

The main approach taken is to address the question of how political philosophy relates to business ethics and to argue for a positive "cross-fertilization" between the two subjects (Moriarty 2005).

Proponents of an analogy between the firm and the state will argue that political philosophy is relevant to understanding business ethics and the corporation. This position is exemplified by Landemore and Ferreras (2016) in the case of workplace democracy.

Opponents, however, claim that the business organization should be seen as free-standing and in need of its own method and theory (Phillips & Margolis 1999). Or, as Alexei Marcoux has argued, business ethics "is in the thrall of normative political philosophy" rendering it irrelevant to the practice of businesspeople (2009, 21). Business ethics is already too idealistic for practitioners to benefit from, and what is needed is a more realistic sort of business ethics relieved from the burdens imposed by idealistic political philosophy.

This debate raises the question: Should philosophical theorizing about the corporation pursue ideal theory similar to the one found in John Rawls's theory of justice? Rawls assumes that the rule of law is institutionalized and that citizens will comply with ideals of justice. In situations where such ideals are not complied with, as in states governed by non-liberal law and despotism, Rawls retreats to "non-ideal" theory.

According to Rawls, in circumstances where non-ideal conditions prevail, the aim of political philosophy continues to be a promotion of ideal theory, that is, the sort of liberal core principles that well-ordered states are built on (Rawls 1999).

There might be ideals appropriate for the corporation that do not fit the state and *vice versa*. The task of business ethics approached as a sort of political philosophy would be to propose ideals with a sense for the particular business context. Businesses are organizations driven by the logic of the profit motive, and this makes them distinct and removes them from the image of public organizations driven by multilateral political logics.

High-minded theorizing does not work in the business context, it is argued, so it is better to help corporations to do better from where they are. Much hinges on this discussion over what sort of ideal theory, if any, is relevant to corporate responsibility.

The view adopted here on the ideal versus non-ideal theory debate with regard to the business firm is pluralistic. This means, first, that real-world domains are plural and, second, that a plurality of normative theories is relevant to the business firm. With the aim of giving an overview and exploring the political theory of the firm, pluralism therefore is considered a necessary starting point. However, with regard to defending the social liberal corporation, I also want to signal that even though pluralism is the starting point for this exploration, the end result is different. Not any given empirical context or normative theory will qualify. The political, cultural, and economic contexts should be compatible with social liberal ideals, I would argue, and thereby I base the argument on an assumption that such ideals are significant *per se*. This approach of course also introduces some circularity in the defence of the social liberal corporation, given that social liberalism is considered "significant" and morally important already. I acknowledge this because I find it difficult to avoid having any moral and political presuppositions when exploring corporate responsibility. However, I also do not believe that the argument is redundant for two reasons. First, the key argument for the social liberal corporation is based on the fact that competing approaches are dismissive about the idea that corporations should be morally responsible. So that is a negative argument in favour of the social liberal view. However, I also base the argument on the assumption that core liberal values, such as personal autonomy and basic rights, are significant. Lisa Herzog (2018), in her book *Reclaiming the System*, refers to such values as basic and thus significant for guiding the morality of corporations. My addition to Herzog's view would be to add social justice and concern for the environment to the list of basic values relevant for a social liberal theory. My aim here is not to make a separate argument for social liberalism besides those found in current theory of corporate citizenship and political CSR but instead to take those positions and demonstrate how they support social liberalism. Hence, I also base my argument on the assumption that the list of public concerns raised against the corporation, mentioned previously, provides empirical support to the need for the social liberal corporation.

The idea is to insist on the claim that the business corporation is an inherent part of society and that its purpose is to deliver the goods and services that society needs in a morally responsible and politically legitimate way (cf. Ulrich 2008). The business firm cannot be carved out of a field of study insulated from the rest of society, which is often the case in approaches of applied ethics, which are less context sensitive.

The main structure of the book consists of three parts: first, the philosophy of the corporation historically and systematically; second, corporate social responsibility theory; and finally, contemporary issues.

The first part contains three chapters: The first is a *historical* philosophical perspective on the corporation represented by Adam Smith, G. W. F. Hegel, and Karl Marx, followed in Chapter 2 by a critical presentation of John Rawls's and Jürgen Habermas's positions on the corporation. They maintain a traditional liberal separation of the state and the market, resulting in a marginalized and neglected concern for the corporation. Then in Chapter 3 there follows a reading of recent theory of corporate moral agency, which is needed to provide an account of how corporate responsibility is plausible, if at all, and how it relates to the social liberal corporation. In all chapters of Part I, I highlight how each theory and thinker can be related to the notion of the social liberal corporation. I argue that the notion is also found in aspects and features of the works of Smith, Hegel, and Marx as well as in Habermas and Rawls. Thus, the historical readings show that the social liberal corporation is not "coming from nowhere" because it has a grounding in the thinking we have inherited from the past.

In Part II of the book the focus is on major and influential theories of corporate responsibility. I have selected those most relevant for a political philosophy discussion. Hence, five chapters on corporate responsibility follow: first a chapter on the Aristotelian conservative-virtue ethical conception, then Chapter 5 on the market liberal theory, and Chapters 6 and 7 on the two social liberal theories – first the republican corporate citizenship theory, followed by the deliberative democratic approach of political CSR. Then, finally Chapter 8 is about the Marxist-inspired critical theories on corporate responsibility. Chapters 6 and 7 therefore in combination provide the theoretical basis for my proposed notion of the social liberal corporation. Hence, I do not intend to go much beyond what those two theories already state, although I group them together under the label of the *social liberal corporation*. So, my contribution lies in the reading of the literature with the aim of giving justification for a claim to the social liberal corporation. I also argue that this is better than the rival theories of corporate responsibility in the sense that it supports a positive understanding of corporate responsibility, given that corporations are politicized and should live up to moral demands pertaining to basic rights and other concerns such as the environment and social justice.

Finally, in Part III there follows a critical discussion of contemporary issues of corporate responsibility, starting in Chapter 9 with problems of the global supply chains and exploitation in the sweatshop. Chapter 10 considers digital and financial firms and the final chapter, Chapter 11, has a focus on corporate environmentalism with a purview to climate change. The contemporary issues are all considered from the perspective of the social liberal corporation – how can it respond to the problems raised. The book ends with a brief conclusion about the limits of, and prospects for, the social liberal corporation.

References

Anderson, E. (2017) *Private government: How employers rule our lives (and why we don't talk about it)*. Princeton: Princeton University Press

Avi-Yonah, R. S. (2005) The cyclical transformations of the corporate form: A historical perspective on corporate social responsibility. *The Delaware Journal of Corporate Law*, *30*(3), 767–818

Ciepley, D. (2013) Beyond public and private: Toward a political theory of the corporation. *American Political Science Review*, *107*(1), 139–158

Crane, A., Matten, D., & Moon, J. (2008) *Corporations and citizenship*. Cambridge: Cambridge University Press

Crouch, C. (2004) *Post-democracy*. Cambridge: Polity Press

Dahl, R. A. (1985) *A preface to economic democracy*. Berkeley: University of California Press

Djelic, M-L., & Etchanchu, H. (2015) Contextualizing corporate political responsibilities: Neoliberal CSR in historical perspective. *Journal of Business Ethics*, *142*(4), 641–661

Ferreras, I. (2017) *Firms as political entities: Saving democracy through economic bicameralism*. Cambridge: Cambridge University Press

Fleming, P., & Jones, M. T. (2013) *The end of corporate social responsibility – Crisis and critique*. London: Sage Publications Ltd.

Freeman, E. R. (1984) *Strategic management – a stakeholder approach*. Cambridge: Cambridge University Press

Friedman, M. (1970) The social responsibility of business is to increase its profits. *The New York Times*, September 13

Heath, J. (2014) *Morality, competition and the firm*. Oxford: Oxford University Press

Heath, J., Moriarty, J., & Norman, W. (2010) Business ethics and (or as) political philosophy. *Business Ethics Quarterly*, *20*(3), 427–452

Hegel, G. W. F. (2011/1821) In Allen W. Wood (Ed.), *Elements of a philosophy of right*. Cambridge: Cambridge University Press

Herzog, L. (2018) *Reclaiming the system: Moral responsibility, divided labour, and the role of organizations in society*. Oxford: Oxford University Press

Knudsen, J. S., & Moon, J. (2017) *Visible hands: Government regulation and international business responsibility*. Cambridge: Cambridge University Press

Landemore, H., & Ferreras, I. (2016) In defense of workplace democracy. *Political Theory*, *44*(1), 53–81

Mäkinen, J., & Kasanen, E. (2016) Boundaries between business and politics: A study on the division of moral labor. *Journal of Business Ethics*, *134*(1), 103–116

Mandeville, B. (1732) *The fable of the bees or private vices, public benefits*, 2 vols. With a commentary by F. B. Kaye. Indianapolis: Liberty Fund, 1988, vol. 1. http://oll.libertyfund.org/titles/846

Marcoux, A. M. (2009) Retrieving business ethics from political philosophy. *Journal of Private Enterprise*, *24*(2), 21–33

Matten, D., & Crane, A. (2005) Corporate citizenship: Toward an extended theoretical conceptualization. *Academy of Management Review*, *30*(1), 166–179

Moriarty, J. (2005) On the relevance of political philosophy to business ethics. *Business Ethics Quarterly*, *15*(3), 455–473

Orts, E. W., & Craig Smith, N. (Eds.) (2017) *The moral responsibility of firms*. Oxford: Oxford University Press

Phillips, R. A., & Margolis, J. D. (1999) Toward an ethics of organizations. *Business Ethics Quarterly*, *9*(4), 619–638

Rawls, J. (1971/1999) *A theory of justice*. Revised edition. Cambridge, MA: Harvard University Press

Rawls, J. (1999) *The law of peoples*. Cambridge, MA: Harvard University Press

Ryan, A. (1998) Liberalism. In R. E. Goodin & P. Pettit (Eds.), *A companion to contemporary political philosophy*. Oxford: Blackwell

Scherer, A. G., & Palazzo, G. (2007) Toward a political conception of corporate responsibility: Business and society seen from a Habermasian perspective. *Academy of Management Review*, *32*, 1096–1120

Scherer, A. G., & Palazzo, G. (2011) The new political role of business in a globalized world: A review of a new perspective on CSR and its implications for the firm, governance, and democracy. *Journal of Management Studies*, *48*, 889–931

Schrempf-Stirling, J. (2016) State power: Rethinking the role of the state in political corporate social responsibility. *Journal of Business Ethics*, 1–14

Ulrich, P. (2008/1997) *Integrative economic theory – Foundations of a civilized market economy*. Cambridge: Cambridge University Press

Wolin, S. S. (2004) *Politics and vision – Continuity and innovation in western political thought*. Expanded edition. Princeton: Princeton University Press

Part I

The Corporation in Liberalism and Corporate Moral Agency

1 The Corporation and Free Markets in Classical Liberalism and Its Critics

This chapter is a reading of Adam Smith (1723–1790), G. W. F. Hegel (1770–1831), and Karl Marx (1818–1883) and the role of the corporation in society and the market in the 18th and 19th centuries. This is a period of both industrialization and liberal political revolutions within the rising nation states. Pivotal is the freedom to pursue private interests in the market. The modern corporation, as we know it, is emerging, and the period experiences a transition from the small-holder corporation of the guilds and craftsmen to big industrial factory firms. Moreover, as David Ciepley (2013) has pointed out, the corporation first appears as a "franchise of the government" because the government provides legal permissions to run the corporation, and at the same time the corporation is also a creature of the market because it is seen as a vehicle for liberating individuals from the old feudal order. In Adam Smith's works, the focus is the joint-stock companies that he criticizes. However, Smith basically sees the corporation as a means to make production more effective. The idea of a division of labour is driven by expansion of the market and the needs it seeks to satisfy. The example of the factory where each worker contributes his share to produce a pin described in the *Wealth of Nations* (1776) is instructive. Hegel adopts Smith's idea of the emancipatory potential of free markets, which he titles the "system of needs", but he also seeks to connect citizens' freedom in the marketplace with the idea of the state and its institutions as a necessary condition for realizing political freedom. Hegel's notion of the corporation is a version of the socially embedded organization in which the private and public are united and mediated through the state. Marx, finally, launches a criticism of liberal market ideas, emphasizing that workers under capitalism are exploited and alienated and that capitalism as a system is doomed due to its internal contradictions. Marx's focus is clearly the system level of capital and the means of production to which the corporation *per se* is secondary. However, indirectly, Marx's main oeuvre on economics, *Capital* (1867), contains inherent contradictions between the free market and the not-so-free organization of production. Marx is asking why the worker is free to sell labour on the market, but when working in the factory, the worker loses freedom. Hence, the worker is denied the essence of the liberal revolution – the right to pursue individual freedom. In the space of the corporation, the feudal order is therefore preserved.

The point of a comparative reading of Smith, Hegel, and Marx in regard to unravelling the idea of corporate responsibility, the main theme of this book, is that they provide the historical backdrop for much of the modern understanding of the corporation. In terms of political theory, these three thinkers each represent different "ideologies", that is, the positions associated with market liberalism or libertarianism (Smith), social liberalism (Hegel), and socialism (Marx). This is, of course, a rather crude categorization because Smith also defended public education and social security, Hegel was clearly also a conservative about political institutions in his critique of the terror of the French Revolution, and Marx was not entirely content with socialism. Also relevant for current thinking is that they all grappled with how to reconcile markets, civil society, and the state or, in the Marxian understanding, the classes.

At the same time, it is also difficult if not misleading to look for the source of current notions of corporate responsibility in the philosophical literature of the 18th and 19th centuries. Basically, none of these philosophers mention corporate responsibility as a term, which is not surprising because the concept was coined much later in the 20th century (see, e.g., Christiansen 2015). However, the inherent meaning of corporate responsibility rendering the business firm responsible for its impact on society, or assessing the value of the corporation as a provider of goods or a problem solver in society, is not foreign to the thinking of Smith, Hegel, and Marx. In fact, the corporation is a key topic for these thinkers, but the concerns go by other names and also mirror a different historical context.

From the Manufacturer to the Industrial Organization

The period of around 90 years covering the publication of Smith's *Wealth of Nations* (1776) to Hegel's *Philosophy of Right* (1821) and Marx's first volume of *Capital* (1867) marks a significant development in the political institutions of society. The breakdown of feudalism and departure from absolutist monarchism in the wake of the French, the British, and American revolutions created the institutional background for emancipation of individuals to "pursue their happiness" in society and on the market. The institution of the market is a liberating force, functioning as a level playing field for individuals to exchange goods, to "truck and barter" as Smith would say (2000, 14). This view of the market is mirrored in the cosmopolitan ideal of *doux commerce*, which later proved constructive in promoting co-operation and partnership among trading nations. According to classical liberalism the market is even seen as an institution that realizes the natural or a human right (Muthu 2008, 206) to pursue personal freedom, mirrored in both Smith's and Hegel's recognition of the market. They are, however, also aware that the market can be skewed to the interests of the few and mighty, for instance, in the case of monopolies and state-granted privileges to corporations. The market is not perfect, but it is instrumental in granting liberties to individuals as citizens in the emerging nation states, and liberal democracy is therefore historically linked to market liberalism. The optimistic view of the market as a liberating force, however, changes. Hegel acknowledges that a particular group of citizens lose on the market because they cannot find proper labour to sustain a household. With the advent of industrial factories and large-scale production, this marginalized group grows into a *rabble* (Hegel 1821, §244 on the "Pöbel"). Hegel's dialectic way of "sublating" (Aufheben) contradictions of the system reaches an impasse because the rabble cannot be sublated, that is, integrated into the system of society by getting proper jobs. The rabble, in fact, contradicts the positive story of the new market society that will elevate all its citizens to prosperity. To Marx, the sad fact of the rabble, which he names the "Proletariat" or the "reserve army" of workers, is that the market fails to cater for all. The developmental storyline of the period running from Smith to Marx shows a remarkable turn from sheer optimism to grave pessimism in the belief of what the market can bring to society. So what happened during this period to prompt such a drastic change of view?

Elizabeth Anderson (2017) diagnoses the advent of industrialism as the cause of the turn. To Smith the agents on the market are mostly small groups of merchants and individual manufacturers exchanging with equals. To Marx it has become clear that big business corporations now run industry and dominate the market, meaning that there is unequal access to possible benefits of the market. In particular, according to Marx, the labour market has resulted in a general exploitation of the working class, who have no alternative but to sell their labour to make an income. So the ideal view of the market held by classical liberalism was shattered by the advent of industrialization, which ultimately resulted in the differing views of the market that continue to exist today. The market liberal will insist that there is nothing wrong with the market as such; rather, it is external forces, in particular the state, that have made it imperfect. Marxists, conversely, tend to see the market as inherently effective and rational, and thus agree with classical liberalism, but they believe that the market is harmful to the majority of humans because it represents a commodification of human labour that can be exchanged for a price that does not correspond to the actual labour invested by the worker. Social liberals accept that markets are a vehicle for human liberty and wealth creation, but they also concede that markets are never perfect and therefore need to be regulated or instilled with an ethos of "responsibility". Conservatives tend to also be critical about markets and in agreement with Marxists; they prefer a retreat back to local and reciprocal exchange in the community where the goods are produced and used – basically a critique of the modern organization of the division of labour. Admittedly, these descriptions are nothing new, but I restate them because they have had considerable impact on how we currently perceive the prospects for corporate responsibility.

The next sections will focus on the political role of the corporation in the works of Smith, Hegel, and Marx to set the stage for the search for foundations of the social liberal corporation.

The sections will show that a balanced liberalism of a social liberal kind is at work here as Smith is positive about small merchants and manufacturers *but* critical about monopoly. Hegel envisages a significant role for the corporation to *mediate* between citizens and the state. Marx is critical about industrialized production *but* positive about pre-modern localized production. Hence, his view of the cooperative as an alternative to capitalist firms is explored.

Adam Smith: Free Markets and Colonial Monopoly

Adam Smith is a recurrent source of reference for research on CSR. In particular, Milton Friedman, the godfather of modern market liberal critique of CSR, refers to Smith's idea of an *invisible hand* when emphasizing that the only responsibility of business is to increase its profits and not see to the public good (*Capitalism and Freedom* 1962, 133; see also Chapter 5 for a discussion of Friedman). Other market liberals favour Smith as an authority who can back up their views on corporate responsibility. For instance, Porter and Kramer (2011, 17) in introducing their "shared value" concept allude to Smith's invisible hand of an undisturbed market:

> Creating shared value represents a broader conception of Adam Smith's invisible hand. It opens the doors of the pin factory to a wider set of influences. It is not philanthropy but self-interested behavior to create economic value by creating societal value. If all companies individually pursued shared value connected to their particular businesses, society's overall interests would be served.

Hence, Smith is here taken to represent the value of self-interest as a means to create public wealth. Indeed, this is the reading most commonly associated with the market liberalism that Smith endorses. However, this reading is also disputed by several commentators of Smith who claim that he did not endorse an unconstrained self-interest. Indeed, the entire debate over Smith has resulted in what has been called the "Adam Smith problem", alluding to the fact that Smith's position was incoherent about the value of selfishness in the market (Herzog 2013, 20–21). The incoherence appears in the allegedly incompatible views found in the two main works of Smith, the *Wealth of Nations* and the *Theory of Moral Sentiments*. The first propagates unrestrained selfishness, it is assumed by the popular reading, and the latter an altruist morality often overlooked because the work is less famous. The contradiction is real insofar as the two works are in some tension on the view about balancing selfishness and altruism. A few famous quotes from Smith will show why the "Smith problem" is a commonly held view of the internal incoherence of his position.

In the *Wealth of Nations* (15), he contends:

> It is not from the benevolence of the butcher, the brewer, or the baker, that we expect our dinner, but from their regard to their own interest. We address ourselves, not to their humanity but to their self-love, and never talk to them of our own necessities but of their advantages.

The reciprocity found in the marketplace is therefore founded on self-regard rather than any altruistic concern. Furthermore, this quote, which is often used to illustrate the utter pointlessness in asking for businesses to be morally responsible, is supplemented with the equally famous quote about the collective effects of promoting self-regard. This is the metaphor of the invisible hand (ibid. 485):

> [The man of commerce] generally, indeed, neither intends to promote the publick interest, nor knows how much he is promoting it. . . . By directing industry in such a manner as its produce may be of the greatest value, he intends only his own gain, and he is in this, as in many other cases, led by an invisible hand to promote an end which was no part of his intention. Nor is it always the worse for the society that it was no part of it. By pursuing his own interest he frequently promotes that of the society more effectually than when he really intends to promote it.

However, these quotes are then confronted with the opening sentence of the *Theory of Moral Sentiments*, which sets a quite different tone (Smith 2009, 13):

> How selfish soever man may be supposed, there are evidently some principles in his nature, which interest him in the fortune of others, and render their happiness necessary to him, though he derives nothing from it except the pleasure of seeing it.

Commentators have argued that only a superficial reading of Smith would give rise to the perception of incoherence. Our morality is conditioned on the ability to view our own sentiments and interest at "a certain distance" by invoking the *impartial spectator* in us (Smith 2009, Introduction, xx). We have an interest in other peoples' interests and the ability to take ours, and their interests, into consideration. Therefore, the dilemma of choosing between self and another's interest dissolves, and hence the "Adam Smith problem" is also dismissed. Patricia Werhane (2000, 186) also critiques the libertarian reading of Smith on the grounds that it mistakes his views of the free market with Herbert Spencer's libertarian view of the night watchman theory of the state and the mistaken interpretation of free markets as analogue to the Darwinian "survival of the fittest" (a phrase that Spencer and not Darwin proposed). The idea that self-interest prevails in Smith's *Wealth of Nations* is a misreading, so according to Werhane,

> [o]ur natural desire to cooperate motivates us to work together by dividing and specializing our labor. It also motivates us to barter, where the appeal to self-interest of others as well as to their good will in honoring the exchange results in "mutual and reciprocal" gains.
> (Werhane 2000, 194)

The free market is also not unconstrained; rather, it presupposes, according to Smith, that the government provides a legal context that ensures that buyers and sellers are meeting on a level playing field (ibid. 195). And, the role of government is also beyond the minimalism often ascribed to Smith because he argues that some level of free education must be offered to the youth (Smith 2000, 779).

To get a more concrete impression of how Smith viewed the corporation, besides these general normative views of the market and personal morality, his writing on the pin factory and the East India Company in the *Wealth of Nations* is helpful. In Chapter 1 on the subject of "the division of labour", he describes how this type of modern production can increase the efficiency in the manufacturing of pins. In this pin factory ten men can produce up to 48,000 pins in a day due to the division of labour, whereas if they "had all wrought separately and independently . . . they certainly could not each of them have made twenty, perhaps not one pin in a day" (ibid., 5). However, besides praising the efficiency from the division of labour, Smith is also aware that this kind of production can be burdening to the workers. Smith does not use the word *alienation*, but he precursors Marx (Lamb 1973) in his description of deleterious effects of the division of labour on workers:

> In the progress of the division of labour, the employment of the far greater part of those who live by labour, that is, of the great body of the people, comes to be confined to a few very simple operations; frequently to one or two. But the understandings of the greater part of men are necessarily formed by their ordinary employments. The man whose whole life is spent in performing a few simple operations, of which the effects too are, perhaps, always the same, or very nearly the same, has no occasion to exert his understanding, or to

> exercise his invention in finding out expedients for removing difficulties which never occur. He naturally loses, therefore, the habit of such exertion, and generally becomes as stupid and ignorant as it is possible for a human creature to become.
>
> (Smith 2000, 839–840)

The division of labour, it appears, can stunt the imagination and future intellectual development of workers who have to spend their working days focusing on a few repetitious operations. According to Smith it is not the corporation that should be blamed for running its factories this way; rather, the responsibility to compensate falls on the government, and the means to compensate are mainly publicly supported education programmes (ibid. 840; cf. Herzog 2013, 123). However, even though the manufacturer as corporation is not blamed for the alienation of the worker, Smith can be said to provide the premise for an argument that has some uptake in current debates on workplace democracy and hence corporate responsibility (Anderson 2017).

The second example of immediate relevance to corporate responsibility that Smith discusses is the colonialist corporation. What is striking about colonialism is the emergence of big multinational business companies growing to the size of nation states and acting like a sovereign with its own army to defend and expand its commercial interest. Adam Smith devotes an entire chapter in the *Wealth of Nations* to the issue of colonialism and globalization of trade and here provides a vivid presentation of the British East India Company showcasing the inefficiency and bureaucracy of the company. The philosopher John Stuart Mill was employed in the company and found "office duties an actual rest from the other mental occupations which I have carried out simultaneously with them", thereby reflecting Smith's view that the joint-stock company is ineffective and management does not work in the interest of the owners (Micklethwait & Wooldridge 2005, 44).

According to Muthu (2008) Smith provides two narratives of the international trading company. The first is a "progressive set of changes from savage to barbarian to civilized, and finally to commercial societies" (ibid. 193), whereas the second is a "tragic account" of "a historical narrative in which the right of commerce is not realized, but instead corrupted and turned toward destructive and irrational ends throughout the globe" (ibid. 194).

Smith critiques big international colonialist companies because they hamper the potential wealth creation of free markets by their excessive power and political influence that curtails the equality among nations necessary for free markets to exist. He has no trust in the benefits from the political role of big companies. Rather they are the "worst of all governments" (ibid. 201) that any country could have. Moreover, he finds it "absurd" to believe that the big companies by themselves will ever be responsible enough to promote freedom of trade:

> Accordingly, the idea that European states, merchants, and multinational firms would somehow reform themselves, as a result of adopting more enlightened ideas of the kind that Smith himself sought to propagate in WN, was, in his own view, a fanciful hope.
>
> (ibid. 204)

The problem with the international trading companies is the privileges offered by the state, which gives them monopolist status. Smith therefore argues in favour of anti-trust laws to avoid monopolies (Smith 2000, 501–502). Moreover, he is critical about the joint-stock company because management is separated from ownership, and this can then result in irresponsible behaviour on the part of managers. He therefore foresees modern discussion about the principal-agent problem:

> The directors of such companies, however, being the managers rather of other people's money than of their own, it cannot well be expected, that they should watch over it with the same anxious vigilance with which the partners in a private copartnery frequently watch over their own. . . . Negligence and profusion, therefore, must always prevail, more or less, in the management of the affairs of such a company.
>
> (ibid. 800)

The problem with the big firms is the inherent logic of their financing, their political partnership with the state, and their immense influence that curtails free markets. Hence, this picture of international trade, which is the "tragic account" that Smith provides, contributes to the corrective reading of him as less libertarian than commonly portrayed.

What can then be derived from this sketch of Smith's position on morality and the market with relevance for corporate responsibility? Surely, libertarians like Friedman, Porter, and Kramer have celebrated the invisible hand metaphor and used it as leverage against government regulation and against the idea of CSR. Corporate responsibility, according to the libertarian understanding, is not compatible with the assumption that the promotion of private interests will result in increased public goods. This boils down to the idea that the market should not be planned or intended to conform to a particular design but left alone as a *spontaneous order*. Invoking corporate responsibility is, therefore, to impose onto the market a certain design where business firms offset the market mechanism and thereby curtail the market's propensity to seek a "natural" equilibrium between supply and demand at a certain price level. However, even though this reading of Smith is obvious and justified if taking the quote from the *Wealth of Nations* about the invisible hand, it is less obvious that Smith would reject the idea of corporate responsibility on these grounds. Because he also argues for equality and mutuality in the exchange on the market, and the moral significance of imposing an impartial spectator to judge market outcomes, he does not appear to be a defender of laissez-faire capitalism. Also considering the critique he leverages against the big joint-stock colonialist companies, a moderate form of libertarianism seems the most warranted reading of Smith.

Then what view on corporate responsibility can be retrieved from the works of Smith? This is difficult to say, and therefore the adoption of Smith's moral theory to current CSR can also be disputed (Szmigin & Rutherford 2013).

Even those who admit that Smith is a more nuanced philosopher than the libertarian reading assumes are hesitant to expose consequences for corporate responsibility. One possible answer is that it is an anachronism to seek answers about corporate responsibility in an 18th-century thinker like Smith. He does not have the modern conception that a corporation can also be considered a moral agent. However, he provides a template for understanding the role of the corporation in society, the benefits it produces, and also the harms it can inflict. A balanced view of a cautious social liberal orientation can thus be gleaned from Smith's work on the corporation. At least, this is the conclusion I draw from the previous discussion.

Hegel and the Mediating Corporation

As mentioned, Hegel is an admirer of the free market and refers in his *Philosophy of Right* to Adam Smith and the new theories of political economy in his description of the market, which he calls "the system of needs" (Hegel 2011, 127, §189). The market is part of civil society (*Bürgerliche Gesellschaft*), which also contains the administration of justice and the corporations. Hegel's writings are famous for being difficult, if not impossible, to read. However, in his *Philosophy of Right* he is relatively straightforward compared to his earlier works, although also in this work he structures the substance with a dialectical method resulting in a tripartite framework of concepts. Hegel is one of the first philosophers to take a historical approach in philosophy, assuming that history is best described as a series of related events realizing a potential. Freedom is the inherent purpose of human society, and Hegel shows a developmental history evolving from an abstract idea of freedom as negative right (protection of property) to an inner notion of freedom as freedom of conscience, which he calls *morality*, to the fulfilment of freedom as *ethical life* within political institutions of a free society in the state (*Sittlichkeit*). Hegel is a conservative insofar as he acknowledges the importance of tradition in the development of institutions of a state system, its judiciary, and its estates and family traditions. However, he equally values personal liberty, the freedom of the market and the freedom citizens can enjoy in civil society as publicly engaged. Institutions are in Hegel's view vehicles that can realize freedom in concrete living. Hence, Hegel is critical about abstract freedom, a freedom of principles that takes no notice of reality and tradition. The outcome of such freedom can ultimately be seen in the terror of the French Revolution. Even though Hegel is sympathetic to the surge for freedom that drove the civil revolts, he is equally appalled by the cynicism that these revolts were capable of in turning over the old regime.

Corporations must be seen in this wider context of Hegel's system because their function is to mediate between the arbitrariness of the market and the governance of the state (Ross 2008, 57). Corporations provide a concrete social space for citizens to find an identity based on their profession and work. Corporations thus protect citizens from poverty, and without the corporation a person will find it difficult to sustain a meaningful existence as a "recognized" citizen (ibid. 271f, §253). In fact, one of the main purposes of the corporation is to take care of the lower classes and ensure that the worst-off are also integrated into the professions. When the corporation fails at this, the chance of contributing to the rabble has increased. This has sparked debate over whether Hegel considered poverty and the rabble as unavoidable collateral damage of the free market in civil society or whether he in fact thought that the rabble could be avoided. The Marxist reading of Hegel will showcase the places where Hegel admits that poverty is an inescapable fact of the bourgeois society (Ruda 2011, 21). However, more charitable readings will emphasize that corporations have the potential to integrate to the degree that the rabble is avoided (Avineri 1995). Axel Honneth in his *Freedom's Right* (2014, 9) defends the charitable reading of Hegel by emphasizing the "neglected potential of already existing institutions", here alluding to the system of guilds, estates, and corporations.

Moreover, the corporation, according to Hegel, also provides education for the young so that they too can be participants in the corporation, which as such becomes an ethical institution; Hegel refers to *Bildung*. This sense of belonging in a meaningful community that provides direction and development in life is offered by the corporation. So, Hegel argues that what the family is to the individual in private life, the corporation is to the individual in public life – the corporation is "a second family to its members" (ibid. §252).

The corporation is an association of organizations of the trade and industry estate (ibid. 270, §250). It is therefore not the exact same as the "corporation" referred to by much of the modern literature and our common understanding of the corporation as an individual business firm operating to maximize profits. To Hegel the business firm is just one organizational unit of the corporation. Hence, according to Ross

(2008, 56–57) the corporation is different from its modern sibling in three regards: first, it is not a single business, but it represents "the interests of all of the members of a specific kind of industry". Second, the corporation is not managed to maximize profits but to "balance the need for professional stability with the needs of society for that which the industry contributes". And third, Hegel does not acknowledge the strict "dichotomy between state regulation of an industry and self-regulation within the corporation" because the corporation is the concrete realization of the state.

The corporation, according to Hegel, then is more about political representation and social autonomy from the state than about competition and gaining wealth. The latter are features of the market, but to ensure that these liberties are not merely accidental, and that individuals are being atomized in civil society, the corporation is invoked to recapture the social bond based on the institutional foundation that work and the professions provide. Avineri (1995, 163) points out that Hegel's corporation is a precursor to the modern political party as it offers both a public identity and political influence in matters of the state. Hegel is sceptical about democracy and in fact advocates monarchism. However, he also advocates political representation through the estate and its corporations. Looking to the British model of political representation and bi-cameralism, Hegel proposes an upper house composed of the nobility and a lower house with elected members from the corporations. In the assembly decisions are made by deliberation, and hence, it is wrong to say that Hegel is an anti-democrat (ibid. 164). The deliberative model for corporations to participate in civil society on political matters has gained renewed attention by the proponents of "political CSR" (see Chapter 7). And the idea of worker inclusion in the management of the corporation is echoed in current debate over workplace democracy.

Furthermore, the model of the corporation that Hegel offers is resonating in the later *corporatism* of European welfare states (Esping-Andersen 1990). The corporatist welfare model is mainly found in middle Europe, and it emphasizes the key role of the business corporation to offer social securities and pensions to the worker. This is opposed to the liberal model found in the UK and the USA, which offers a minimal level of social security and demands no contribution from firms. The social-democratic welfare model of Scandinavian countries is liberal also but offers universal and high levels of social security. Hence, only the corporatist model requires firms to contribute their share to social security. This type of division of labour between the public and the private permeates the core of current debate over corporate responsibility. So, the message to take from Hegel's account of the corporation is that it offers a model of striking a balance between liberal and conservative views of the role corporations should have in society. Assuming that the "natural" approach is a liberal one that constrains the scope of responsibilities as "private" from the outset falls short of taking into consideration the complexity involved in the issue of corporate responsibility. Perhaps Hegel's modified liberal approach can explain why his thinking on the corporation has had limited uptake in current theorizing on CSR. This approach can be seen as social liberal in orientation but with a conservative acknowledgment of the importance of social and political institutions. Hence, Hegel's position provides a useful point of reference for later discussion throughout this book (especially in Chapter 7).

Marx, Production, and Cooperatives

In the Marxist tradition one finds the most critical views of the corporation and often an outright dismissal of the idea that corporations can be morally responsible agents at all. However, the dismissal relies not so much on a preconception of the corporation as particularly incapable of moral agency. Rather the view is that the corporation is a salient part of the capitalist system, maybe even the main culprit in the instance of a big multinational corporation (MNC), and therefore corporate responsibility is considered a self-refuting idea, an oxymoron. The Marxist tradition has had a huge influence on the widespread scepticism towards business providing a vocabulary and a theoretical framework that explains why corporations cannot be trusted. The more recent criticism of corporate responsibility is addressed in Chapter 8. Here follows an introduction to Marx's views of the corporation.

The corporation as a specific unit of concern features only marginally in the Marxian oeuvre, and he does not have any conception of corporate responsibility, as such, unless the extensive elaborations over labour, capital, exchange, production, exploitation, and alienation are considered as an analysis of the corporate inventory. In a way, Marx is actually extremely occupied with the production process of the factory and therefore is the first to provide a modern theoretical elaboration of the corporation's inner organizational life. However, he presents this analysis as a general analysis of capitalism, as such, and therefore his interest is not confined to production in the corporate realm but instead the wider political economic capitalist system. Hence, this is also why Marxists are preoccupied with macro-level structural and systemic mechanisms and less with more limited, meso-level organizational questions.

As Shaw (2009, 567) notes, corporate social responsibility is irrelevant to Marxism because "the moral or immoral behavior of individual firms and managers – distracts attention from capitalism's systemic flaws and the need to replace it with an altogether different and better socioeconomic system".

One major reason why Marx is insisting on taking the macro level into account is because of the violence committed against the majority of people in the transition from feudalism to bourgeois society. He claims that the "[a]ccumulation of capital, its historical genesis" is a "transformation of slaves into wage-labourers – the expropriation of the immediate producers, of private property based on the labour of its owner" (Marx 1867, 927). Hence, capitalists steal the property from small-scale producers like farmers and artisans and thus make them dependent on seeking work to make a living in the factory. For instance, the land is expropriated from small holders to be used for industrial production, what is now called *land grabbing* (ibid. 930).

This transition is essentially driven by the dynamics of the division of labour that also leads to moving the productive powers from the countryside to the cities, that is, from the farm to the factory. Hence, capitalism rests on a basic injustice of stealing the means of production from the individual producers who used to be self-reliant, turning them into dependent workers. The right to one's own production is reminiscent of Kantian autonomy and Locke's labour theory of value. Marx does, however, agree with Smith that the division of labour is an efficient means to increase general wealth, just as he also considers market exchange in general to be beneficial. However, taking the wider capitalist context into consideration, the division of labour and the allegedly free market become threats to the majority of people, the class of people who are not owners of capital, the proletariat (ibid. 736). The proletariat are exploited and alienated because they are bereft of their products and they receive less wages in comparison to the contributions they make through their labour. In fact, the worker is reduced to a means of production and thus wage labour is commodified, which is incompatible with treating the worker as a dignified human autonomous being, "[h]ence the rule of the capitalist over the worker is the rule of things over man, of dead labour over the living, of the product over the producer" (ibid. 990). The purpose of capitalism is to transfer any means of value creation into capital. The surplus value, that is, profits, are created by labour, according to Marx (as well as to Locke and Smith), hence the worker is exploited by the logic that drives capitalism because any profits derived rely on wage labour "stolen" from the worker. And the reason why profits are derived from exploited workers is due to the "original sin" of expropriating the means of production from small-scale producers. Otherwise, there is nothing inherently bad about selling labour on the labour market for a wage. Freely consenting workers can sell their work time and competence at a certain price that the capitalist agrees to. However, according to Marx, the logic of wage labour relies on the illusion or ideology that there are "freely consenting workers" because the logic of the labour market is that work is scarce and the workforce is competing to get work, resulting in redundancy of workers and giving rise to the *reserve army* of day labourers that eventually can turn into the rabble.

So, in Marx's view there is a contradiction between the freedom associated with the market and the political freedom granted to members of the civil society and, conversely, the unfreedom experienced by workers.

This leads Marx to move the analysis from the outcome of production, the goods sold and distributed on the market, to the conditions of production in the factory:

> Let us therefore, in company with the owner of money and the owner of labour-power, leave this noisy sphere, where everything takes place on a surface and in full view of everyone, and follow them into the hidden abode of production, on whose threshold there hangs the notice "no admittance except on business". Here we shall see, not only how capital produces, but how capital itself is produced. The secret of profit-making must at last be laid bare.
>
> (ibid. 279–280)

Here it becomes clear that the realm of the corporation is considered a "hidden abode of production" that needs to be revealed: The capitalist ideology of free labour contracts and workers' rights cover up the fact that "capital produces", so the analysis needs to reveal what capital has hidden.

Marx's coauthor on several of his books, in particular *The Communist Manifesto* in 1848, Friedrich Engels, was a son of a factory owner and textile manufacturer in Manchester. He knew from his own work as a factory manager about working conditions in industrialist companies. Together they were politically engaged in the labour movement and acquainted with socialist activists. It is worth considering the empirical grounding of their conception of the corporation and the insights they might have had of real life in the factories, considering that both belonged to the bourgeoisie. The misery of the workers' conditions in the industrial factories was, however, common knowledge. The poet William Blake, for example, described steam factories as "satanic mills", and it can be no coincidence that Marx and Engels recommend in the *Manifesto* the abolition of child labour in the factory.

Marx was also critical about the sheer size of the big corporations because the power of the "Asiatic and Egyptian kings . . . has in modern society been transferred to the capitalist, whether he appears as an isolated individual or, as in the case of the joint stock companies" (ibid. 452). The big, modern industrial corporation is therefore also a bureaucratic monster led by "an army of managers" (ibid. 450).

However, what alternatives did Marx perceive to the joint-stock company and the exploited factory workers? First, it is disputed whether Marx even had a normative theory of justice. According to Rainer Forst (2017) it is clear that Marx did not have a theory of justice of how goods should be distributed in a more equal manner such as the egalitarian theory of John Rawls (see Chapter 2). Rather, his theory, if at all about justice, is about the institutions that produce goods and how wage labour is "unfairly" exploited. But, there is no explicit positive theory or standard to provide guidance about justice found in Marx. Instead the entire work of Marx is an elaborate showcase of the inner logic and contradictions permeating capitalism. This leads to a perennial debate about Marxism and critical theory: What is the aim of theory? Is it to negatively reveal what ideology is hiding and suppressing or to provide a positive and normative theory about alternatives to capitalism?

Marx is surely mostly focussed on revealing the logic of capitalism, but he does also have positive views of communism as an alternative to capitalism. For instance, with the abolition of capitalist private property, there are no more problems of scarcity because as it is noted in *The Critique of the Gotha Programme* of 1875, goods are distributed according to the principle "from each according to his abilities, to each according to his needs". Within this communist future the division of labour ceases to alienate the worker as it does in the production process known from capitalism. The worker is emancipated to pursue his or her own interests and determine how to lead his or her life. The romantic inspiration becomes most explicit in this famous quote from *The German Ideology*:

> For as soon as the distribution of labour comes into being, each man has a particular, exclusive sphere of activity, which is forced upon him and from which he cannot escape. He is a hunter, a fisherman, a herdsman, or a critical critic, and must remain so if he does not want to lose his means of livelihood; while in communist society, where nobody has one exclusive sphere of activity but each can become accomplished in any branch he wishes, society regulates the general production and thus makes it possible for me to do one thing today and another tomorrow, to hunt in the morning, fish in the afternoon, rear cattle in the evening, criticise after dinner, just as I have a mind, without ever becoming hunter, fisherman, herdsman or critic.
>
> (Marx & Engels 1846, 54)

Hence, autonomy and self-determination are the key issues, and therefore the question arises of what sort of co-operation is compatible with communist production? Some level of division of labour is needed to ensure a satisfactory level of production. Marx is not entirely clear about what sort of co-operation is the best vehicle to ensure worker's autonomy. On the one side co-operation among workers is "brought about by the capital that employs them" (Marx 1867, 449). On the other side, if abolishing capitalist production and hence "the concentration of the means of production, it also excludes co-operation" (ibid. 927). Therefore, Marx concedes that capitalism is a necessary historical phase that must be surpassed before the "association of free men" (ibid. 171) can emerge after a long history of capitalist rule (ibid. 173).

The allusion to the association of free men has by some commentators been taken as Marx's supporting worker-owned cooperatives as an alternative to the capitalist privately owned corporation. However, this is a disputed issue in the literature. First, Marx, in the third posthumously published volume of *Capital*, was not that critical about the joint-stock company as one might assume because "[c]apitalist joint-stock companies as much as cooperative factories should be viewed as transition forms from the capitalist mode of production to the associated one" (Jossa 2005, 5). The joint-stock company is an example of collective ownership, so it is contradicting the capitalist preference for individual ownership, according to Marx. And, therefore it can be perceived as a "transition" from capitalism to free association and communism, supposedly.

However, Marx also seems to praise co-operatives, at least those owned by the workers themselves. In a footnote in the first volume of *Capital*, he praises Robert Owen's co-operatives (Marx 1867, 635). But, according to Shaw (2009, 575), Marx saw co-operatives as isolated experiments that "were harbingers of a socialist future, but not a vehicle for transforming capitalism into socialism". Jossa (2005, 12) agrees that Marx first had confidence in workers owning co-operatives as a possible means of transition to socialism, but later on he seems to have lost this confidence due to "the collapse of many producer cooperatives between 1860 and 1870".

Moreover, in the tradition following Marx, there is a division between supporters of local worker cooperatives and supporters of a centralized planning economy (Jossa 2005, 4). At least, this tension is still found within debates about organizing production in the communist society following the revolution. Should Marxists be explicit about the plan they have for the future of production in a communist society – the positive vision following the logic of Marx in *Capital*? Or should Marxists be silent on this issue leaning towards the negative critique also permeating *Capital*, allowing for freedom of the emancipated to decide on this issue? There is no clear answer to be found in Marx's writing about this.

Marx is the *locus classicus* for current critical thinking about the corporation, but as has become clearer, his thinking is also more nuanced than the bold critique one might assume. In his work one finds templates for how to think about the corporation today, not least his views on exploitation and the importance of not leaving the productive unit, the corporate factory, out of the normative philosophical equation. Even though Marxist thinking is about the importance of the systemic level, it is also clear that Marx is keen on observing what is going on inside the corporation. And, his views about collectivism and co-operation, be it in the joint-stock company or the workers' co-operative, provide food for thought for current thinking about corporate responsibility.

Even though the corporation is not the main concern of Smith, Hegel, or Marx, it is clear that they have each given much thought to how corporations can support the general good of society as well as how they can be obstructive. Most debates over corporations and economics in the 18th and 19th centuries tend to focus on the market as the key topic. However, such focus also overlooks the significance of corporations in the main political philosophies of the period. What is missing in the period is the idea that a corporation can be a unified moral agent as will be discussed in Chapter 3 and further explored in later chapters. However, this lacuna is not necessarily a shortcoming because the thinking of Smith, Hegel, and Marx also testifies that the corporate arena is infused with deeply normative concerns. These concerns are addressed in the context of 20th-century political philosophy in the next chapter on Rawls and Habermas.

References

Anderson, E. (2017) *Private government: How employers rule our lives (and why we don't talk about it)*. Princeton: Princeton University Press

Avineri, A. (1995) *Hegel's theory of the modern state*. Cambridge: Cambridge University Press

Christiansen, C. O. (2015) *Progressive business: An intellectual history of the role of business in American society*. Oxford: Oxford University Press

Ciepley, D. (2013) Beyond public and private: Toward a political theory of the corporation. *American Political Science Review*, *107*(1), 139–158

Esping-Andersen, G. (1990) *The three worlds of welfare capitalism*. Princeton: Princeton University Press

Forst, R. (2017) Justice after Marx. In *Normativity and power: Analyzing social orders of justification*. Oxford: Oxford University Press

Friedman, M. (2002/1962) *Capitalism and freedom*. Chicago: University of Chicago Press

Hegel, G. W. F. (1821/2011) *Elements of the philosophy of right*. Edited by Allen W. Wood. Cambridge: Cambridge University Press

Herzog, L. (2013) *Inventing the market*. Oxford: Oxford University Press

Honneth, A. (2014) *Freedom's right: The social foundations of democratic life*. Cambridge: Polity Press

Jossa, B. (2005) Marx, Marxism and the cooperative movement. *Cambridge Journal of Economics*, *29*(1), 3–18

Lamb, R. (1973) Adam Smith's concept of alienation. *Oxford Economic Papers*, *25*(2), 275–285

Marx, K. (1867/1990) *Capital, volume 1*. London: Penguin Classics

Marx, K., & Engels, F. (1846/2007) *The German ideology*. London: Lawrence and Wishart

Marx, K., & Engels, F. (1848/2014) *The communist manifesto*. In M. Zwolinski (Ed.), *Arguing about political philosophy*. 2nd edition, 295–308. New York: Routledge

Micklethwait, J., & Wooldridge, A. (2005) *The company: A short history of a revolutionary idea*. London: Phoenix

Muthu, S. (2008) Adam Smith's critique of international trading companies: Theorizing "Globalization" in the age of enlightenment. *Political Theory*, *36*(2), 185–212

Porter, M., & Kramer, M. (2011, January–February) Creating shared value: How to reinvent capitalism – and unleash a wave of innovation and growth. *Harvard Business Review*, *89*(1–2), 62–77

Ross, N. (2008) Hegel on the place of corporations within ethical life. In M. Painter-Morland & P. Werhane (Eds.), *Cutting-edge issues in business ethics. Issues in business ethics*, vol. 24, 47–58. Dordrecht: Springer

Ruda, F. (2011) *Hegel's rabble*. London: Bloomsbury

Shaw, W. H. (2009) Marxism, business ethics, and corporate social responsibility. *Journal of Business Ethics*, *84*(4), 565–576

Smith, A. (1776/2000) *The wealth of nations: Introduction by Robert Reich*. New York: The Modern Library

Smith, A. (1790/2009) *The theory of moral sentiments*. Introduction by Amartya Sen. 6th edition. London: Penguin Classics

Szmigin, I., & Rutherford, R. (2013) Shared value and the impartial spectator test. *Journal of Business Ethics*, *114*(1), 171–182

Werhane, P. H. (2000) Business ethics and the origins of contemporary capitalism: Economics and ethics in the work of Adam Smith and Herbert Spencer. *Journal of Business Ethics*, *24*, 185–198

2 Excluding the Corporation From the Political

Rawls and Habermas

In the 20th century, two philosophical views of the corporation prevail in particular: the classical liberal view inherited from Adam Smith and the critical Marxist view. Market liberalism's central assumption is that the state and the market are separate spheres. The strict, principled separation of the market and the state is adopted by liberal political philosophy in the 20th century. This chapter considers two influential social liberal political thinkers, John Rawls (1921–2002) and Jürgen Habermas (1929–), and how they conceive of the corporation. The corporation is marginal as a topic to both thinkers, which is also representative of the tendency to exclude the corporation from political philosophical thinking in the 20th century. The reason for choosing social liberal thinkers and not libertarians or neo-Marxists is first due to the fact of the huge influence in political philosophy of both Rawls and Habermas. Rawls is often applauded as the philosopher who turned the tide towards ethics and political philosophy in the 20th century and singlehandedly reasserted political philosophy as an honourable discipline for serious academics to specialize in. Second, because this book aims at defending a social liberal view of the corporation, Rawls and Habermas are key points of reference – not least because they both deny any role for the business firm within the scope of their normative theories and therefore challenge the idea of the social liberal corporation. Finally, it is fair to prioritize social liberal thinkers because other political philosophies are considered and discussed in later chapters that comprise Part II.

A general outcome of the liberal separation of the state and the market is that the corporation is relegated to a construct of the private market and cannot be seen as a franchise of the state nor as eligible for normative assessment, thus leading to difficulties for a political theory of the firm.

Within the limits of the law, it is permissible for a firm or an individual consumer to pursue moral aims, but this is voluntary only according to the liberal thesis that Rawls and Habermas subscribe to. So, how can their theories be turned into defences for a social liberal view of the corporation when they both deny that corporations are moral creatures? In this chapter, the common understanding – that Rawls's and Habermas's theories are in tension with a normative conception of the corporation – will be restated.

In later chapters (Chapters 6 and 7 on corporate citizenship theory and political CSR) the positive theory of the social liberal corporation is presented and discussed. Even though the theory of political CSR is suggested to be a Habermasian one (Scherer & Palazzo 2007), it is not a version compatible with Habermas's own views portrayed in this chapter but rather a theory that "tweaks" and applies Habermas's theory to the case of corporate responsibility. Because the discussion of Habermas is continued when treating political CSR, this chapter focuses primarily on Rawls.

To summarize, Rawls's and Habermas's comprehensive social and political theories cannot be dealt with in all their depth and complexities, and a full account of their impact on political philosophy is also left out. So, there is a focus on how they perceive the corporation within their own philosophy and less on the widespread debate about their views of markets and corporate responsibility.

Rawls

It is a contested issue whether Rawls's theory of justice, construed for the basic social, legal, and political institutions of society (the judiciary, the state administration, and the legal system), can or ought to be applied to the corporate domain. Many commentators on Rawls agree that the corporation is excluded from the sphere of justice because it does not belong to the basic structure, most of all because it is a private voluntary association and not a legally regulated institution of the state. Only indirectly are corporations affected by the basic structure as this is a background framework that sets up constraints on private life in the corporation. This mirrors the liberal division of labour where the state administers law and order and ensures that justice is upheld, where corporations and individual citizens can be free to do as they please within this constraint. This also means that the burden of securing the common good is the state's job. Certainly, this understanding seems warranted by Rawls's stipulated definition of the fit between the principles of justice and the basic structure of society and how private corporations are not eligible for justice:

> There is no reason to suppose ahead of time that the principles satisfactory for the basic structure hold for all cases. These principles may not work for the rules and practices of private associations or for those of less comprehensive social groups. They may be irrelevant for the various informal conventions and customs of everyday life; they may not elucidate the justice, or perhaps better, the fairness of

> voluntary cooperative arrangements or procedures for making contractual agreements.
>
> (Rawls 1971/1999, 7)

Rawls also makes it clear that the principles of justice reached for relevance to domestic society (the nation state level) do not have direct import for the local level of private interaction and association, for instance, *within* the family, the labour union, the university, the church, *and the firm* (Rawls 2001, 10). But, the principles of justice can regulate private institutions from the *outside*, "while churches can excommunicate heretics, they cannot burn them" (ibid. 11). So, justice sets up certain *constraints* on private institutions but does not determine what the "suitable principles of local justice" for internal governance are (ibid. 12). Although free to pursue its own ends when it acts on the market or employs people, the business corporation should also comply with the law (Rawls 1971/1999, 241). To ensure that justice is upheld in society, business firms are regulated to compensate for the inequality that they otherwise cause in the pursuit of economic interest. In other words, the negative externalities from private business are taken care of by the state. From this viewpoint, Rawls does not assign any moral responsibility to the private corporation, and as Singer (2015) remarks, he could support the libertarian view of the firm as a moral-free nexus of contracts. However, this is too hasty a conclusion because principles of justice might be worked out to fit with private associations also, perhaps in a modified form. Rawls argues that principles of justice (justice as fairness) "starts with domestic justice – the justice of the basic structure. From there it works outwards to the law of peoples and inward to local justice", and he continues: "No attempt will be made here to deal systematically with local justice" (Rawls 2001, 11). So, Rawls is not denying that justice has relevance to private associations like the corporation, but rather he remains neutral or agnostic about the matter.

In other parts of his work he opens the door for including the business corporation into the sphere of justice. He argues that private organizations are to be regulated in accordance with a "property-owning democracy" (POD), where the ownership of wealth and capital is distributed "to prevent a small part of society from controlling the economy, and indirectly, political life as well" (ibid. 139). In a POD, workers may own and control firms, as in the co-operative, as long as the principles of justice are not violated. In fact, Rawls concedes that worker co-operatives might well be a key instrument to ensure the realization of his principles of justice:

> [W]ould worker-managed firms be more likely to encourage the democratic virtues needed for a constitutional regime to endure? If

> so, could greater democracy within capitalist firms achieve much the same result? I shall not pursue these questions. I have no idea of the answers, but certainly these questions call for careful examination. The long-run prospects of a just constitutional regime may depend on them.
>
> (Rawls ibid. 178–179)

Rawls contrasts the POD with a capitalist welfare state in which the distribution of wealth and income can be unequal and hence in breach of the difference principle, saying that inequalities are "to be to the greatest benefit of the least-advantaged members of society" (ibid. 43). Rawls is not making it clear what precise consequences the POD has for the internal governance of the corporation, besides his concession to workplace democracy. Hence, attempts have been made to argue on the basis of Rawls's premises for workplace republicanism as a means to ensure the primary good of the basis of self-respect (Hsieh 2005).

Applying the Principles of Justice to the Corporate Sphere

Perhaps surprisingly in view of the Rawlsian abstinence with regard to talking about the private business corporation, several attempts have been made to apply Rawls's political philosophy to the corporation. In particular the core aspect of *A Theory of Justice*, the contractual setup – the original position – has been applied as a justification for prioritizing the corporation's stakeholders (Freeman 1994, 416; Child & Marcoux 1999; Cohen 2010; Fia & Sacconi 2018). The idea is to follow the guidelines Rawls offers for how to reach principles of justice from an impartial viewpoint. Hence, participants (here managers and stakeholders) should imagine a thought experiment where they are deprived of knowledge (they deliberate behind a *veil of ignorance*) about their position and the rights and goods they might hold after justice is settled. In Rawls's original position framed to work for "you and I", that is, citizens who mutually recognize each other as free and equal, principles are to be reached for the distribution of goods within the basic structure of society only. The outcome here is two principles: The first is the principle of liberty according to which everyone has an equal right to liberty as long as it is compatible with the same liberty for all others. This principle concerns freedom of expression, property rights, and also democratic freedom to participate in politics. The second principle of justice is reached in the original position behind the veil of ignorance and is about equality. This principle has two parts: The first states that offices and positions are to be open to all "under condition of fair equality of opportunity" (Rawls 2001, 42). And the second principle is the *difference principle*.

Now, some of the principles that Rawls argues would be reached make sense in the context of a political society but less so in a private local and corporate context. For instance, it makes sense to argue that the political liberties cannot be denied to employees, even though there might be contractual agreement to limit freedom of speech as, for instance, in the case of confidential material that could be harmful to the corporation if revealed to competitors. And, the same goes for property rights: A corporation cannot expropriate employees' private property. However, it is less obvious how principles of justice concerning inequality can make sense in the corporate context. First, participants might find it even more difficult to accept the veil of ignorance and embrace impartiality if they conceive of themselves as agents of the market. As market agents they are to look out for their own interests and take others' interests into consideration only if this is compatible with maximizing their self-interests. Rawls admits this by acknowledging citizens as *rational* in their deliberations behind the veil of ignorance. And, citizens are also taken to have a sense of justice and a capacity for fairness or what Rawls calls being *reasonable*. The ability to approach politics from a perspective of the common good or a reciprocal relationship to other citizens is fundamental to the *political conception* of justice in a pluralist liberal society (Rawls 1996). So, even if Rawls does make concession to egoism, he also assumes that altruistic features characterize individuals in his setup. This assumption can of course be disputed as suitable for the corporate sphere. Moreover, the principle of distributive justice and the concern for equality expressed in Rawls's second principle seems less in tune with corporate reality. Internally in the organization the principle of equality of opportunity is balanced with a principle of merit, ideally, or more to the point positions are distributed on all sorts of grounds such as collusion or being an excellent networker. Workplace culture can be a competitive jungle and far from the ideals liberals prefer. However, the principle of equal opportunity and open positions that Rawls argues would be reached in the original position does in fact also regulate private organizations as members of liberal society – it is illegal to discriminate on grounds of gender, race, or religion. More problematic is the difference principle stating that inequalities are justified only if those who are worst off benefit. First, what is the measure of inequality here? In Rawls's theory the measure is so-called primary goods like basic rights and liberties, income, and wealth and the social basis of self-respect (ibid. 58–59) – goods that are needed to live a full life as a free and equal citizen and to realize one's life plan. But how should a distribution of primary goods within the corporate sphere be perceived? This is not so clear, even though I would argue that in the corporate sphere in a liberal society, working life has an immense impact on the chances of realizing one's life plan. Another argument could, however, be made in favour of applying the difference principle to the corporation. This is the argument that Rawls also uses in the political context of the basic structure, stating that the most talented employees will have an incentive to work harder if they can earn higher wages. This extra effort makes the corporation more successful and financially richer, which means that working conditions and perhaps wages for the lower echelon of employees become better. This is the "trickle-down" argument. So, what, if any, is the morally relevant difference between the political and the corporate context within this argument? In principle nothing because all employees, managers, and owners of a corporation are in fact allowed, due to their right to contract freely, to reach such a conclusion and use the difference principle to distribute goods and rights within the corporation. In reality, the fact that CEOs' remuneration has risen based on the assumption that this will create incentives for increasing stock value and not because this will improve the situation of the worst-off in the organization, the ideal of equality held by Rawls is quite far from corporate reality. The more principled counterargument is that a corporation does not distribute the wider list of rights and goods that Rawls associates with his principles of justice; only a government can ensure that citizens are acknowledged as free and equal members of society.

The Basic Structure Argument and the Corporation

As mentioned, Rawls is deliberately vague about the limits of the basic structure. The literature following *A Theory of Justice* offered several points for critical reappraisal. For instance, it was argued that Rawls relied on an abstract model of moral reasoning and that he had too little sense of politics as embedded in a particular culture and tradition – a point particularly highlighted by communitarians. However, among the critics were those who agreed with Rawls about his liberal ideals and the importance of the principles of justice for reaching a just society. Such critics, however, in particular disagreed with Rawls about the scope of justice. In the current phase (2019) of Rawlsian debate regarding the scope of the basic structure and the reach of justice, the conclusion seems to be that on the one hand, Rawls was right that if principles of justice as demanding as those he suggested were to be realized, some scope restriction to domestic society is justified – in particular on grounds of ensuring feasibility and uptake in society by citizens and institutions. This scope restriction is often stated as the *basic structure objection* (Blanc 2016) raised against those who require that Rawlsian justice should also be applied to institutions below and above domestic society. On the other hand, the critics challenging the Rawlsian scope restriction have also succeed in demonstrating problematic limits in Rawls's theory. Susan Moller Okin (1989) convincingly demonstrates how inequality in the family is harmful to women and therefore should be seen as a clear case relevant to justice in the Rawlsian sense. Thomas Pogge (2010), a student of Rawls, together with Charles Beitz were the first to challenge Rawls's limits of distributive justice and the neglect of applying the difference principle to the international sphere. Moreover, at the individual level G. A. Cohen (1997) has challenged Rawls's argument for scope restriction-based incentives by arguing for an egalitarian ethos as opposed to Rawls's view of institutions of the basic structure. According to Cohen the *site* of justice can be permeated by the difference principle as a principle of solidarity that motivates individuals when they act morally. Cohen thus rejects Rawls's moral psychology, and the feasibility constraints that Rawls adheres to, in his promotion of the egalitarian ethos. Citizens can freely choose to act so that they maximize distributive justice according to the requirement to provide for the worst-off without external incentives such as an increased wage. This debate between Cohen and the pro-Rawlsians, who raise the basic structure objection to the feasibility of Cohen's proposal, still takes for granted the Rawlsian commitment to some version of ideal theory. Cohen even claims that Rawls is too empirical in his reference to general facts of social science and moral psychology, thus Cohen argues that a theory of justice should not be fact sensitive in the clarification of what ideals are defensible as norms of justice. Thus, this is to some extent an internal family dispute about the finer grains of what Rawls said and not least what he ought to have said given his initial starting point.

With regard to clarifying further whether or not, and how, the corporation is part of or associated with the basic structure, there is renewed attention to Rawls's relevance to business ethics. It is surprising that after at least 30 years of debating the scope of justice and the nature of the basic structure as seen from the discussions about the family, individuals, and international society, so little has been done to clarify the status of corporations – at least, not until recently, and then mostly by scholars dedicated to discussing the general outline of how political philosophy has relevance to business ethics and CSR (Phillips & Margolis 1999; Heath et al. 2010; Mansell 2013; Whelan 2012). However, the debate has been extended further with Abraham Singer's "There Is No Rawlsian Theory of Corporate Governance" in *Business Ethics Quarterly* (2015). Singer launches a general critique against all attempts to use Rawls in business ethics: "As political philosophers have become more interested in business ethics, this tendency has melded with a predisposition that Anglophone political philosophers brought with them: an over-reliance on Rawls" (Singer 2017, 16). This temptation to use Rawls as an authority in business ethics is doomed to failure (Singer 2015, 75), according to Singer, and mainly due to Rawls's commitment to a *political conception* of justice as proposed in his later work *Political Liberalism* (1996). Hence, the distinction most significant to excluding the corporation from the basic structure is the one between a "political conception" and a "private association". In *A Theory of Justice*, the conception of justice as fairness was metaphysical and contractualist and could be conceived of as a comprehensive liberal doctrine, according to Rawls in *Political*

Liberalism. In *Political Liberalism*, Rawls distances himself from his earlier presentation of the possible metaphysical and morally comprehensive reading of justice as fairness (as in his *Theory* of 1971) and now instead opts for a "thinner" and non-metaphysical liberal conception of justice, the political conception that bases itself on the appeal to citizens as free and equal with a sense of justice (Rawls 1996). This move is made to compromise with the pluralism of morals and religion in liberal society and hence to seek a consensus beyond the significant differences dividing people on issues of religion and morality. Hence, Rawls foresaw or hoped that across the plurality of cultures and religions an overlapping consensus on core liberal values (the political conception as a freestanding non-metaphysical view) would emerge. This move would also consider and acknowledge communitarian criticism of Rawls's earlier, more comprehensive liberal theory as not sufficiently grounded in real, historical political culture. Hence, the thin political conception of seeing people as free and equal is not a construction from the world of political ideas but something that people living in real liberal democracies would recognize as their own values (Rawls 1996). Even if the early theory could perhaps have allowed corporations into some sphere of the basic structure, now, in the later theory's appeal to a political conception, the door is irreversibly closed to corporations. At least this is what Singer argues, and thus another argument is added to earlier critiques of Rawlsian business ethics as incompatible with Rawls's own views. If the state is a legitimate legal coercer, it must be based on values that all "reasonable" people (liberal or not) would endorse. And, Singer does not think that a liberal moral view that includes the corporation is compatible with what reasonable people would see as acceptable. This is because such a view is a comprehensive moral view that would divide people, and certainly the libertarians would be repelled. To explain this argument, Singer (2015, 76) appeals to Abizadeh's (2007) proposal for criteria that Rawls(ians) should use to define the limits of the basic structure.

Accordingly, three criteria characterize the vast terrain of the debate: the basic structure must 1) consist of a fair *system of co-operation* that distributes benefits and burdens to the participants, 2) the basic structure of society has *pervasive impact* on the lives of citizen right from the start (and there is no exit from it because immigration will place one in another basic structure), and finally 3) must be a *legally coercive system*.

Those who want to challenge Rawls's narrow limiting of the basic structure to include only domestic society, like, for instance, Moller Okin does when she argues that justice is relevant to the internal sphere of the family (mainly the inequality between genders), and Pogge does when appealing to the global structure of institutions that harm the poor, and Cohen does with personal morality, appeal mostly to criterion 2 and the fact that institutions create a structural power over and pervasive impact on people's lives. Clearly corporations, especially the big MNCs, have a huge impact on many people's lives, regardless of whether or not citizens are employed in them or not.

Considering the *pervasive impact* of corporations on peoples' lives (Rawls 1971/1999, 82) and the fact that corporations are a significant part of the *system of co-operation* that produces goods for distribution (ibid.), it is likely that the Rawlsian position could support notions of corporate responsibility. Furthermore, because MNCs comprise the pillar of international trade and regulation, according to Thomas Pogge (2010), Martha Nussbaum (2007), Onora O'Neill (2001), Nien-he Hsieh (2004), and Iris Marion Young (2006), the exclusion of the corporation from the purview of global justice can be challenged, even on liberal grounds. But in the debate on global justice, Rawls relied heavily on the framework of the political conception established in political liberalism. In the *Law of Peoples* (Rawls 1999) he therefore does not allow for corporations to be part of framework.

However, if all three criteria need to be satisfied to be genuinely Rawlsian, then corporations cannot be said to satisfy criterion 3 of being a legally coercive system. Perhaps in some sense, corporations are clearly aspects of the *system of co-operation* being productive organizations and thus satisfying criterion 1. Singer deducts that the Rawlsian commitment to a political conception strictly excludes the corporation from satisfying criterion 3, regardless of how the other criteria fare. Blanc (2016) in a reply to Singer argues that there are plenty of examples of how corporate governance is legally coercive, and Welch and Ly argue that corporations are best seen as part of the system of co-operation (see Singer 2017 for his response).

I will not intervene, for now, in this debate, apart from stating that I agree with those who argue that because corporations have such an impact on peoples' lives (right from the start), thus satisfying the second criterion of the basic structure, and in fact also can be seen as key to the system of co-operation in the first criterion, it seems problematic to characterize corporations as irrelevant to Rawlsian justice. Given that Rawlsians have made such efforts to transfer justice to other non-domestic spheres, why not also take the corporation and the corporate sphere into account as well? Hence, I submit that it would be possible to modify or sidestep the third criterion of legal coercion in a theory of corporate responsibility and justice.

For the purpose pursued here of justifying the social liberal corporation, it is therefore premature to discard Rawls as a possible ally, even accepting the restrictions on use that Singer recommends.

So, here follow some suggestions as to how Rawls can be of use in clarifying the features of a social liberal corporation in a liberal society.

Rawls and the Social Liberal Corporation

As mentioned with regard to Rawls's remarks on the "property-owning democracy" (Rawls 2001), corporations and the means of production (wealth and assets) should be part of a scheme ensuring a just distribution among citizens. He allowed for worker-owned and controlled cooperatives as long as such a construction would follow the principles of justice, hence a socialist planning economy would not be possible, although a liberal socialist would be. Rawls's later "restatement" of his theory in 2001 concerning the institutions of the welfare state and the means of production, reflects a turn towards conditions of justice before distribution (*ex ante*; O'Neill 2008) away from the focus he held in his earlier work on the just distribution of the outcome of production (*ex post*). Hence, this could be seen as an *institutional turn* in Rawls's work reflecting the importance already assigned to institutions in *A Theory of Justice*, where one of the first sentences is: "Justice is the first virtue of social institutions, as truth is of systems of thought" (Rawls 1971/1999, 3).

Rawls presupposes that the basic institutions can be designed to ensure justice, while also considering that in non-ideal circumstances such institutions are absent or defective. In the *Law of Peoples* he "assume(s), as in the domestic case, that, unless fair background conditions exist and are maintained over time from one generation to the next, market transactions will not remain fair, and unjustified inequalities among peoples will gradually develop" (Rawls 1999, 42, footnote 52). So, what consequence will a failure of background conditions (a weak basic structure) have for the dispute concerning corporations? Blanc and Al-Amoudi (2013, 515) argue that the decline of the Western welfare state over the last 30 years due to the forces of globalization "dilutes the conditions for participation in an economic life compatible with people's life projects, thereby threatening the self-respect of the worst-off". Furthermore, they argue that the declining welfare state (basic structure) "prompts a restructuring of non-democratic work organizations" moving the "social bases of people's self-respect and moral powers" from the welfare state to corporate institutions.

Rawls does not consider the withering away of the welfare state in liberal democracies and therefore also does not consider whether his concession to workplace democracy in the "property-owning democracy" could be a solution to this problem. And, given that he conceded that "justice does not by itself favor either form of regime", and "which system is best for a given people depends upon their circumstances, institutions, and historical traditions" (Rawls 2001, 248), it is possible that he would have condoned corporate institutions taking on the securing of citizens' primary goods, when the welfare state is in decline. According to Hussain (2012), Rawls's idea of citizens having a sense of justice can be promoted in the corporate setting.

The insight to take from these explorative readings of Rawls's later work is that arguments can be extracted to support the notion of the social liberal corporation, a type of corporation that compensates for the failure of the state to secure basic rights and interests of its citizenry.

So, even if the corporation does not fit into the basic structure as Rawls envisaged it, it can still be argued that Rawlsian justice (the two principles) can be realized in some modified form in circumstances where the basic structure of state institutions fails. Whether corporate institutions are the appropriate institutions to rely on needs further examination and will be explored further in the remainder of the book.

Habermas

The influence of Habermasian thinking in the business ethics literature is slightly different from how Rawls has been debated despite the fact that they share the broadly social liberal approach to political philosophy and are often seen as defenders of social justice and the welfare state. The main difference regards that Rawls is widely discussed within the philosophical-oriented business ethics community (e.g., in the *Business Ethics Quarterly*), whereas Habermas has had a huge influence mediated by proponents of *political CSR*, which concerns the broader aspects of CSR and is also published in the mainstream of business ethics literature of a more transdisciplinary and empirical nature compared to the narrower philosophical perspectives associated with Rawls. This is not least because Habermas, due to his work in social systems theory, is also influential in social theory, sociology, and the social sciences.

Just as Rawls developed his theory over the years, Habermas also developed his theory from the early focus on systems theory and communicative action (1987) to the later post-metaphysical theory of deliberative democracy (1994, 1996). Famous is his discourse ethics from the 1980s stating that an ethical dialogue should strive towards universality by neutralizing unequal powers among participants in a *domination-free* ideal speech situation (Habermas 1996, 481) by accepting the *force of the better argument* (ibid. 103). This ideal speech situation Habermas later applies and modifies to real politics in a comprehensive theory of deliberative democracy. Deliberative democracy, according to Habermas, seeks to be squarely situated between a communitarian and republican conception of democracy that relies on membership of the political culture and tradition and the liberal conception that imagines democracy as a free market in which each individual citizen can cast a vote and thus individual preferences are aggregated into a collective legitimate political decision (Habermas 1994). The Habermasian political theory, although also explicitly sociological in its orientation, is comparable to the Rawlsian in its outspoken commitment to Kantian deontology in light of its universalist aspiration, thus setting it in opposition to consequentialist ethical and teleological perfectionist approaches. Hence, the core of discourse theory (D) is: "Just those action norms are valid to which all possibly affected persons could agree as participants in rational discourses" (Habermas 1996, 107). Thus, consensus is the criterion of validity (and legitimacy in the political realm) based on reasons and arguments and not on bargaining based on power relations and individual interests. In this respect there is a clear affinity to Rawls's social contract of the original position stripping participants of empirical knowledge to obtain conditions for an impartial decision procedure in which only abstract arguments count in the search for principles of justice. The Kantian heritage is found in the commitment to moral autonomy and the internal connection between morality and practical reason made explicit by Habermas in a norm-based, linguistic, and action-coordinating decision procedure.

System and Lifeworld Readings of the Corporation

Now, with regard to corporations and corporate responsibility, two aspects are striking in Habermas's work. The first is his distinction between the system and the lifeworld (1987), and the second is whether corporations can participate legitimately in deliberative democracy (1996). Despite the system aspect being downplayed in his later theory to a focus on law, these two aspects are internally connected and provide the conditions for agency in deliberative democracy. Basically, the agents of the system (bureaucrats, consumers, and capitalists) are not proper agents of democracy, but rather they are found to be citizens living in the lifeworld of civil society. Hence, Habermas, on this rather crude reading, proposes a strict dualism between the system and the lifeworld, where the first is a "norm-free" sphere in which: "the capitalist enterprise and the modern administration are systemically independent units within norm-free subsystems" (Habermas 1987, 172). And, therefore the lifeworld is a sphere where solidarity and morality can thrive and from where moral norms originate.

Habermas takes his inspiration from Max Weber by picturing organizations, both public and private, as autonomous entities:

> The capitalist enterprise, detached from the family household of the entrepreneur, can serve as a historically significant example of the indifference between an organization and those who belong to it, when the latter are neutralized into "members." For a business enterprise, the private life-contexts of all of its employees become part of the environment. . . . Organizations use ideological neutrality to escape the force of traditions that would otherwise restrict the scope and the sovereign exercise of their competence to shape their own programs.
>
> (ibid. 308)

Thus, Habermas tends to provide a dualistic view of the system versus the lifeworld. However, the strict dualism is perhaps too crude a view to ascribe to Habermas because he perceives society as historically developing from a pre-modern society with little division of labour and hence no system or merely a simple one embedded in local social relations, into a complex and larger society of immensely comprehensive divisions of labour in production and administration. The lifeworld thus provides an ongoing basis for coherence and coordination of functional differentiation in the process where modern institutions of the market and the public administration expand. Modernity, due to its nature as large-scale division of labour and subsequent organizational complexity, requires markets and bureaucracies to develop and grow. Therefore, the law provides the formal bond necessary to bind together the lifeworld and the system in the process of functional differentiation and system growth. Thus, for the system and the law to be legitimate, it requires the rooting in and support of civil society. According to this reading, the lifeworld is the primordial space of norms and morality, and therefore the system is secondary (call this the historical reading). However, Habermas stresses that the system and the lifeworld are in a co-evolution, mutually dependent on each other to provide suitable conditions for a modern society to develop. The complexity of modernity in particular means that the individual citizen cannot have the sufficient overview and powers to be a responsible agent, hence the administration and the market take over and relieve the citizen of burdens from losing the ability to coordinate and have an overview of the consequences from acting on the market. For instance, being a consumer in the market does not require moral considerations because the state regulates the market and sets the citizen as consumer free to pursue his or her own interest. So, to be a modern citizen in the lifeworld, one needs regulated markets and public bureaucracies to relieve one from burdens of judgment (call this reading the co-evolutionary): "[P]ositive law becomes the guarantor of the calculability of private business activity" (ibid. 167) mediated through 'money' as a system of exchange (ibid. 171; Habermas 1996, 117).

In the co-evolutionary reading, the market and the state, although devoid of morality in their aspect of being "systems", still create the necessary conditions for modernity to develop without losing its coupling to civil society and the lifeworld, which bestows legitimacy.

The historical reading tends to be conservative and critical by emphasizing the uncoupling of the system and its colonializing expansion into the sphere of the lifeworld, calling for a dismantling of modern institutions to avoid pathologies of exploitation and alienation. This is so because "[t]he differentiation of a highly complex market system destroys traditional forms of solidarity without at the same time producing normative orientations capable of securing an organic form of solidarity" (ibid. 116).

This critical view of the inherent harmful tendency of the system certainly is at stake in Habermas's work; however, the co-evolutionary reading is a better theory of a well-functioning modern society and democracy. Just like Rawls, who presupposes a well-ordered society for his theory of justice, Habermas presupposes that civil society can "tame" and "democratize" the expansive tendencies of the market and the bureaucracy (ibid. 469). A balance of powers can be found in the dynamics of a co-evolution of the system and the lifeworld. The theory of communicative action and deliberative democracy together, can, according to Habermas, provide the layout for modernity in co-evolutionary balance.

But such ideal conditions do not necessarily obtain in an excessively capitalist market-driven economy, where big corporations tend to *colonize* the sphere of the lifeworld by commodifying human relations and aspirations, for instance, by inventing new products for needs people did not know they had. Moreover, as Scherer and Palazzo (2007) argue, the ideal situation in which the bureaucracy of the public administration and the market as systems ensure protection of rights and democracy cannot be taken for granted in the process of globalization, where the nation state is weakened. However, that non-ideal conditions might prevail is recognized by Habermas: "Today, the integrative capabilities of the state continue to diminish under the pressure of regional movements, on the one hand, and worldwide corporations and transnational organizations, on the other" (Habermas 1996, 465). And, this is regrettable because: "[s]tate sovereignty is undermined to the extent that powerful corporations are involved in the exercise of political authority without being legitimated for this and without submitting to the usual responsibilities incumbent on government authorities" (ibid. 433–434). Business corporations in those circumstances are expected to exert *political* power "directly by influencing the administration or indirectly by manipulating public opinion" (ibid. 175). However, later in 2009 Habermas maintains that nation states "remain the most important actors on the global stage", and "compared to the most economically influential MNCs, states enjoy the advantage being of monopolists of political power who control legitimate means of regulation and sanction" (Habermas 2009, 90–91). This dualistic reading that Habermas provides of the system–lifeworld dichotomy (to affect the exclusion of corporations from the sphere of legitimate democratic politics) is taken up by critics of political CSR (Whelan 2012, 726; Sabadoz & Singer 2017, 184).

But the prize for excluding corporations from the moral sphere of the lifeworld is paid when Habermas contradicts his own premise of the market as a "norm-free" zone of the system. The premise, for instance, makes it difficult to question the internal situation of working conditions within the corporation and to explore debates on workplace democracy, according to Timo Jütten (2013, 592). Moreover, Jütten shows how Habermas ends up in an impasse by commenting on a quote from Habermas about the moral blaming of corporations in the aftermath of the financial crisis:

> However, he [Habermas] seems adamant that the blame for the crisis should be squarely laid at the door of the political class, rather

> than the banks and other financial institutions. Why? [here follows the quote from Habermas 2009] "The speculators, too, were acting consistently within the established legal framework, according to the socially recognized logic of profit maximization. Politics turns itself into a laughing stock if it resorts to moralizing instead of relying upon the enforceable law of the democratic legislator. Politics, and not capitalism, is responsible for promoting the common good."
>
> (Jütten 2013, 588)

Hence, according to Jütten, the project of business ethics is an oxymoron, a *category mistake*, if committed to Habermas's dualistic view of system and the lifeworld (ibid. 595). But there is a possible way out of the impasse. Jütten shows how Habermas is also committed to what I have called the "co-evolutionary view" – a view that modifies the stern dualism between system and lifeworld thus incurring the inclusion of the corporation, or at least aspects of it, into the moral sphere.

It is true that according to Habermas (and the dualist view), agents get *detached* from their lifeworld when employed in a business (or public) organization that is ruled by a bureaucracy. However (according to the co-evolutionary reading), this does not mean that employees lose complete attachment to the lifeworld and the sense of justice obtained from there. Rather they continue to be moral persons and do not become mere robots or "cogs in the wheel"; according to Jütten, "[f]unctionalist imperatives constrain actors in the economic and bureaucratic systems, but they do not reduce actors' actions to purposively-rational, strategic attitudes" (ibid. 591). So, the kind of functionalism that Habermas proposes, according to Jütten, is not permeating (or colonizing) into the minds of persons working within the system. It only "functions" as an external *constraint* on their actions within the system. This interpretation Jütten finds justified in the text of Habermas (1987, 311): "The lifeworlds of members, never completely husked away, penetrate here into the reality of organizations". So, there are "moral resources" available to people making them able to carry a moral responsibility for their own actions as well as the consequences of their participation within organizations.

Such a reading makes Habermas's own moral engagement and criticism of corporate wrongs more coherent, although it also leaves the impression that Habermas is "at best ambivalent" (Jütten 2013, 594) about the moral status of corporations.

Deliberative Democracy and Corporations as Partners of Civil Society

The same ambivalence is also found with regard to the topic of corporations and deliberative democracy. Habermas pursues a state-centric theory where "will-formation" is centralized and formal (system-like), and "opinion-formation" is less formal and decentralized to the periphery (Mansbridge et al. 2012, 9). Hence, the dualism of the historical reading reappears in the relegation of the corporation to a place from outside the state.

However, the corporations belong to the market in Habermas's liberal view and do not have a particular status of their own. And they are therefore part of the system, being a market agency.

Corporations might be market-based organizations, but they can also be state- or worker-owned enterprises. And, given that it is possible to argue for political, state-like features and examples where the corporation acts in partnership with civil society organizations (nongovernmental organizations) to promote public goods (Scherer & Palazzo 2007), the question becomes pressing: Where are corporations placed vis-à-vis the state? At this point, the turn to deliberative democracy, which political CSR (ibid.) also refers to, challenges the dualistic view of the system versus the lifeworld held so persistently by Habermas.

Hence, in *Between Facts and Norms* (1996) Habermas introduces civil society, the sphere of solidarity, and part of the lifeworld to be a possible intermediary between the state and society writ large. He states that deliberative "democracy requires a realignment in the relative importance of the three resources from which modern societies satisfy their needs for integration and steering: money, administration, and solidarity" (Habermas 1996, 299). But the reason why civil society can counteract and realign both money and administration is because Habermas revises the theory of civil society to exclude the market from it and thereby renders it a forum for public deliberation on private and public matters different from the market. His revision of civil society is therefore in opposition to Hegel, as he included the *system of needs* into the civil or bourgeois society, the *Bürgerliche Gesellschaft*, and consequently he also opposes the Marxist tradition (ibid. 366). With this new revised version of *civil society*, it becomes less clear whether corporations, considered as quasi-political enterprises, are strictly excluded and prohibited from this sphere. This unclarity is evident in the following quote:

> Rather, its institutional core comprises those nongovernmental and noneconomic connections and voluntary associations that anchor the communication structures of the public sphere in the society component of the lifeworld. Civil society is composed of those more or less spontaneously emergent associations, organizations, and movements that, attuned to how societal problems resonate in the private life spheres, distill and transmit such reactions in amplified form to the public sphere. The core of civil society comprises a network of associations that institutionalizes problem-solving discourses on questions of general interest inside the framework of organized public spheres. These "discursive designs" have an egalitarian, open form

> of organization that mirrors essential features of the kind of communication around which they crystallize and to which they lend continuity and permanence. Such associations certainly do not represent the most conspicuous element of a public sphere dominated by mass media and large agencies, observed by market and opinion research, and inundated by the public relations work, propaganda, and advertising of political parties and groups. All the same, they do form the organizational substratum of the general public of citizens. More or less emerging from the private sphere, this public is made of citizens who seek acceptable interpretations for their social interests and experiences and who want to have an influence on institutionalized opinion- and will-formation.
>
> (Habermas 1996, 366–367)

So, given that the corporation cannot be reduced to "economic connections" (as in the nexus of contract view of the libertarian conception), but also carries features of being political, state-sanctioned, or simply morally responsible (and thus not reducible to a norm-free zone), it becomes difficult to conclude on the basis of Habermas's comprehensive definition of civil society, whether the corporation, or any aspect of it, can be a part of civil society. In contrast, the explicit reference to "noneconomic connections" in the quote can, of course, provide sufficient reason for not letting the corporation in as a member of civil society, as any transaction occurring in the corporate realm, by definition, must be of an economic nature. Certainly, the spirit expressed by the quote is clear enough, and Habermas surely did not imagine business firms to satisfy such criteria. Therefore, even if his theory does raise some doubts about the status of business firms, and also about the status of morality within organizations as part of the system (as the co-evolutionary reading shows), the conclusion must be that Habermas did not offer much guidance about how business firms, apart from being of the market, could fit into his political philosophy and even less about how, if at all, they could be morally responsible in any meaningful sense.

The conclusion of the present chapter on Rawls and Habermas is illustrative of the philosophical problems associated with seeing corporations as morally responsible agents and as excluded from the political philosophy as found in the mainstream of liberal thinking during the late 20th century. In fact, this exclusion, although it is certainly justified by its adherence to a liberal view of the market and firms, is in open contradiction to all talk about corporate responsibility now resonating at the beginnings of the 21st century.

So, assuming that Rawls and Habermas were both wrong, or at least should have said more, about their view on the corporation, where do we start to look for a revised theory? The next chapter presents a discussion of the idea that corporations are autonomous group agents qualified to be morally responsible for what they do. Hence, to explain how this is possible, the perspective turns from the outside view that Rawls and Habermas have towards an inside view of corporate moral agency.

References

Abizadeh, A. (2007) Cooperation, pervasive impact, and coercion: On the scope (not site) of distributive justice. *Philosophy & Public Affairs*, *35*(4), 318–358

Blanc, S. (2016) Are Rawlsian considerations of corporate governance illiberal? A reply to singer. *Business Ethics Quarterly*, *26*(3), 407–421

Blanc, S., & Al-Amoudi, I. (2013) Corporate institutions in a weakened welfare state: A Rawlsian perspective. *Business Ethics Quarterly*, *23*(4), 497–525

Child, J. W., & Marcoux, A. M. (1999) Freeman and Evan: Stakeholder theory in the original position. *Business Ethics Quarterly*, *9*(2), 207–223

Cohen, G. A. (1997) Where the action is: On the site of distributive justice. *Philosophy & Public Affairs*, *26*(1), 3–30

Cohen, M. A. (2010) The narrow application of Rawls in business ethics: A political conception of both stakeholder theory and the morality of markets. *Journal of Business Ethics*, 97(4), 563–579

Fia, M., & Sacconi, L. (2018) Justice and corporate governance: New insights from Rawlsian social contract and Sen's capabilities approach. *Journal of Business Ethics*, 1–24

Freeman, R. E. (1994) The politics of stakeholder theory: Some future directions. *Business Ethics Quarterly*, 4, 409–422

Habermas, J. (1987) *The theory of communicative action: Lifeworld and system, volume 2*. Cambridge: Polity Press

Habermas, J. (1994) Three normative models of democracy. *Constellations*, *1*(1), 1–10

Habermas, J. (1996) *Between facts and norms: Contributions to a discourse theory of law and democracy*. Cambridge: Polity Press

Habermas, J. (2009) Afterword: Lessons of the financial crisis. In *Europe: The faltering project*. Translated by Ciaran Cronin. Cambridge: Polity Press

Heath, J., Moriarty, J., & Norman, W. (2010) Business ethics and (or as) political philosophy. *Business Ethics Quarterly*, *20*(3), 427–452

Hsieh, N. H. (2004) The obligations of transnational corporations: Rawlsian justice and the duty of assistance. *Business Ethics Quarterly*, *14*(4), 643–661

Hsieh, N. H. (2005) Rawlsian justice and workplace republicanism. *Social Theory & Practice*, *31*(1), 115–142

Hussain, W. (2012) Nurturing the sense of justice: The Rawlsian argument for democratic corporatism. In M. O'Neill & T. Williamson (Eds.), *Property-owning democracy: Rawls and beyond*, 180–200. Oxford: Wiley-Blackwell

Jütten, T. (2013) Habermas and markets. *Constellations*, *20*(4), 587–603

Mansbridge, J., Bohman, J., Chambers, S., Christiano, T., Fung, A., Parkinson, J., Thompson, D. F., & Warren, M. E. (2012) A systemic approach to deliberative democracy. In J. Parkinson & J. Mansbridge (Eds.), *Deliberative systems*, 1–10. Cambridge: Cambridge University Press

Mansell, S. F. (2013) *Capitalism, corporations and the social contract: A critique of stakeholder theory*. Cambridge: Cambridge University Press

Moller Okin, S. (1989) *Justice, gender, and the family*. New York: Basic Books
Nussbaum, M. (2007) *Frontiers of justice: Disability, nationality, species membership*. Cambridge, MA: Harvard University Press
O'Neill, M. (2008) Three Rawlsian routes towards economic democracy. *Revue de philosophie économique*, *9*(1), 29–55
O'Neill, O. (2001) Agents of justice. *Metaphilosophy*, *32*(1–2), 180–195
Phillips, R. A., & Margolis, J. D. (1999) Toward an ethics of organizations. *Business Ethics Quarterly*, *9*(4), 619–638
Pogge, T. (2010) *Politics as usual: What lies behind the pro-poor rhetoric?* Cambridge: Polity Press
Rawls, J. (1971/1999) *A theory of justice*. Revised edition. Cambridge, MA: Harvard University Press
Rawls, J. (1996) *Political liberalism*. New York: Columbia University Press
Rawls, J. (1999) *The law of peoples – with "The idea of a public reason revisited"*. Cambridge, MA: Harvard University Press
Rawls, J. (2001) *Justice as fairness: A restatement*. Cambridge, MA: Harvard University Press
Sabadoz, C., & Singer, A. (2017) Talk ain't cheap: Political CSR and the challenges of corporate deliberation. *Business Ethics Quarterly*, *27*(2), 183–211
Scherer, A., & Palazzo, G. (2007) Toward a political conception of corporate social responsibility: Business and society seen from a Habermasian perspective. *Academy of Management Review*, *32*(4), 1096–1120
Singer, A. (2015) There is no Rawlsian theory of corporate governance. *Business Ethics Quarterly*, *25*(1), 65–92
Singer, A. (2017) Rawls well that ends well: A response to welch and Ly. *Business Ethics Journal Review*, *5*(2), 11–17
Whelan, G. (2012) The political perspective on corporate social responsibility: A critical agenda. *Business Ethics Quarterly*, *22*(4), 709–737
Young, I. M. (2006) Responsibility and global justice: A social connection model. *Social Philosophy & Policy*, *23*(1), 102–130

3 Corporate Moral Agency and Political Theory of the Firm

Another obstacle to taking corporations into account as genuine political and moral agents, besides reducing them to the amoral system or the norm-free market, as seen in Chapter 2, is the failure to qualify as moral agents. Responding to the rebuttal of corporate responsibility on the basis of the claim that corporations cannot be moral agents is the subject of this chapter. Assuming that criteria for being a moral agent requires abilities such as self-awareness, conscience, empathy, intentionality, and perhaps embodiment, it is difficult to explain how an organization or a collective of individuals could meet these criteria. The debate on collective responsibility with regard to corporate responsibility often takes its point of departure in Peter French's (1979, 211) claim that the corporations can be "full-fledged moral persons" (ibid. 215). He argues with a functionalist approach that the existence of a "corporate internal decision" (CID) structure is a necessary and sufficient condition to be accorded moral agency and intentionality (ibid. 215). Even though French provides a justification for the idea that corporations can be persons, his concept of the moral person is not to be mistaken for the legal person ascribed to the corporation in the context of law. In practice the question about whether or not a corporation can be a moral person is substituted with taking the corporation to be a legal person as a necessary prerequisite for contracting and matters of liability. And, for a business firm to promote an image as sustainable and socially responsible, it requires nothing more but reference to the legal construct "incorporated". However, the legal conception of the corporation also has limits. First, it does not give any clear answer to what corporate moral responsibilities are insofar as these are difficult to clarify on the basis of the law. Hence, corporate responsibility is sometimes assumed to be a particular kind of responsibility that goes beyond the law, meaning that in situations where the law is either not clear, nonexistent, or morally contestable or does not cover an issue (yet), a certain moral responsibility is needed to compensate for the incompleteness of the law. Thus, corporate responsibility cannot be exhausted by reference to the law but also needs clarification when the law is insufficient to provide answers. Corporations and real people share this situation, so in this regard corporations are no different from individuals. However, corporations consist of individuals and as such are different from individuals as they are collectives or groups. And, even if the legal construct of being incorporated is widely acknowledged as ascription of personhood to the corporation, it does not reflect any consensus on whether corporations as collectives or groups can be genuine moral agents – this is what Avi-Yonah (2005) calls the real entity conception of the corporation. The contested nature of the legal construct when it comes to the deeper moral discussion about corporate responsibility can be seen in the debate following the 2010 *Citizen United vs. the Federal Election Committee* case, in which the US Supreme Court acknowledged corporations as having an equal standing with ordinary citizens. The Citizen United were sued for having published a critical campaign video about Hillary Clinton in the election of 2008. The Supreme Court in its ruling assigned to corporations the constitutional right to freedom of speech of the First Amendment. Critics pointed out that corporations by nature cannot have the status of a citizen, and thus the ruling represented a regrettable slide towards giving the already powerful undemocratic corporations even more power and influence in politics. Robert Reich, professor at Berkeley, a former advisor to President Clinton and a fierce critic of corporate lobbyism, commented on the ruling of the Supreme Court with the provocative claim: "I'll believe corporations are people when Texas executes one" (Reich 2012).

So, the conclusion to draw is that a belief in the legal notion of incorporation does not preclude disputes about corporate moral agency. And, the idea of ascribing moral agency to corporations might well qualify to be a candidate for an "essentially contested concept" (Kusch 2014, 1593; cf. List 2018).

This chapter concerns the contested topic of corporate moral agency and will first introduce the broader aspects of the debate, then it will discuss a currently influential attempt to justify and explain corporate moral agency, and finally the chapter explores the possible relevance of corporate moral agency to the wider issue of CSR (as taken up in chapters of Part II). The latter gives reason to seek clarification about whether notions of corporate moral agency determine positions in the political theory of the firm – for instance, it seems reasonable to assume that libertarians will prefer an individualist reductionist view of corporate agency. This latter issue therefore also provides a link to the second section of the book that concerns theories of corporate responsibility in the business ethics literature. It is a major concern that there is no justificatory relation to be found between the level of the metaphysical aspects of corporate agency and the practical-ethical aspects of CSR. For instance, it is a widely held view that there is a discontinuity between the domains and that the practice of corporate responsibility does not depend logically or pragmatically on having a credible theory of corporate agency. It will be argued that it is better (makes CSR more credible) if we have a coherent and non-controversial notion of corporate moral agency compared to not having one. This and similar concerns are considered at the end of this chapter (see also the discussion in Chapter 7 on justification and pragmatism).

Introduction to the Debate on Corporate Moral Agency

To grasp the core of the dispute over corporate moral agency one needs first to see that the individualists and the collectivists share the assumption that it does make sense to ascribe moral responsibility to corporations. Kendy Hess calls this the "unrecognized consensus" (Hess 2017, 170). So, the dispute is not about *whether* firms have a corporate responsibility but rather about *how* to talk about it and provide a theoretical account of it. Those who deny that there is any corporate moral responsibility over and above the level of individual members of the organization – the individualists (e.g., Velasquez 1983) – will typically agree that in practice the corporation is responsible for the harms it might inflict on people or the environment. The dispute concerns how to distribute responsibility within the corporation, where individualists want to distribute it to the individual members in proportion to their share of the harm done. Conversely, collectivists will go further and also attribute responsibility to the corporate agent *per se*. So, even when no particular individual in the organization can be found guilty or responsible for some harm done, the corporation as an agent, according to the collectivist, can still be considered culpable. Philip Pettit (2007), in a defence of corporate responsibility, refers to the company owning the ferry *Herald of Free Enterprise*, which sank in 1987 in the English Channel and caused almost 200 people to drown. The official inquiry did not find any individuals to be blameworthy for the accident, although a "significant organizational sloppiness" was pervasive (ibid. 171). In situations like this it makes sense, according to Pettit, to ascribe responsibility to the corporate agent defending the slogan: "No incorporated agency without incorporated responsibility, and this, even when individual responsibility is diminished" (ibid.).

Such a formulation easily leads to the understanding that the corporate agent must have some sort of mysterious existence over and above the individual members. Perhaps as some kind of superhuman intelligence to be found in the corporate ontology, Hess calls such a view the "humunculus theory of firm behaviour" (Hess 2017, 170; List 2018). Or, the mystery of corporate agency could be seen as some sort of biological vitalism presenting the corporation as a living organism with a mind of its own that can determine and penetrate its thoughts downwards into the minds of individual members (List & Pettit 2011, 9). In fact, if collectives have a mind of their own independent of their members, this leads to far-out claims such as Schwitzgebel's (2015) that the "United States is probably conscious".

However, such allegedly controversial readings are not necessary according to Pettit (and also List & Pettit 2011) because corporate agency "supervenes" on the agency of individual members (ibid. 64ff). Clarifying what this means leads to the core of much current debate because there is disagreement about whether it makes sense to ascribe responsibility to a corporate agent in situations when individuals cannot be found sufficiently blameworthy (e.g., Rönnegard 2013). The theory of List and Pettit (2011) will be further introduced and discussed in the next section of the present chapter. Their theory has proved to be one of the most influential accounts in the current literature and therefore needs to be taken into consideration to understand the development of this research topic.

In the remainder of this section the general layout of the debate is in focus.

So, the general motivation driving the debate on corporate moral agency is often pragmatics. We not only need to perceive corporations to be responsible in situations where they are the cause of harm, but our language also makes us talk this way (ibid. 1). Language makes it natural to say sentences like "Royal Dutch Shell has a big share in causing climate change and therefore needs to clean it up" or "the Republican Party is guilty in the downfall of democracy because it is too tolerant of Trump's manipulation of the media". The daily news is full of examples of how corporate agents are either blamed for some act or are acting responsibly in some way that is then applauded. The moral phenomenology and the way our language works leaves us with the appearance that there are these "corporate persons" who do good or bad. The fact that language makes us talk about corporate entities that have no "real" existence is reminiscent of the medieval distinction between nominalism and realism (cf. Dewey 1926, 667). The problem with nominalist debunking of "corporate talk" is illustrated by List and Pettit in their book *Group Agency* (2011, 186; also cited by Kusch 2014, 1590):

> One reason why it is important to recognize the reality of group agents is that this lets us discern the true contours of the moral and political world we inhabit. . . . Swaddled in glib conviction that the only social agents are individual human beings, we can look right through the organizational structures that scaffold group agency and not see anything there. We can live in an illusory world in which the comforting mantras of individualist thought make corporate power invisible.

The question then is about how to make sense of moral talk about corporations and also acknowledge that the core of the dispute is *not* about whether corporations are morally responsible for their doings because all contenders in the debate, individualists and collectivists alike, subscribe to corporate responsibility. Rather, the disagreement is about whether corporate responsibility can be reduced to individual responsibility or not.

In the debate over corporate moral agency, there is also dispute about *what sort* of organization qualifies as an agent. Loosely coupled coincidental interaction among strangers may not qualify as these are mobs without any clear intention or decision procedure. What are the necessary and sufficient conditions for holding loosely organized groups morally responsible? Individualists tend to argue that regardless of the feasibility in satisfying such conditions for moral agency of the group, individuals will always be morally responsible for their actions (as far as they caused them and had sufficient information about consequences). However, collectivists would disagree about what are sufficient conditions. Even among collectivists caution is taken in cases where the group is not clearly defined. Iris Young, for instance, seeks to solve such a problem by proposing a "social connection model" to justify forward-looking and collective moral responsibility for examples of structural injustice (Young 2011). Addressing difficult cases where responsibility regards, for instance, matters of global justice and institutional structures where no one in particular is responsible, nor for that matter can do much on his or her own, corporate responsibility becomes relevant, Young argues. Only in collective political action is it realistic to address difficult structural problems of the global economy. This topic of responsibility for the global supply chain leading from the producer (in the sweatshop in this case) to the consumer is addressed in Chapter 9 of this book.

Another key topic in the dispute between the individualist and the collectivist on corporate moral agency is the question about the *fairness* in blaming individual members of the organization for corporate deeds. The proponent of individualism – the view that corporate responsibility must be reduced to individual responsibility to make sense – also argues that corporate responsibility is unfair to individuals because they might not have any share in the situation or they might have only a limited share (Velasquez 1983; Rönnegard 2013). John Hasnas (Orts & Craig Smith 2017, 103) argues that corporate responsibility leads to collective punishment of "the innocent" and this "is antithetical to the respect for the individual that lies at the heart of a liberal society". Interestingly, defenders of collective responsibility have not attempted to answer this concern. One possible and obvious answer would be that the responsibility for harms done by the organization is distributed to each member of the organization in accordance to the harms he or she caused. Distributing responsibility this way would still hold that even when the guilty individuals were found and attributed their share of the responsibility, the corporate unit could end up with the residual or the general responsibility (which the legal construction of the firm in fact acknowledges). However, such a solution would not be sufficient to the individualist because the residual responsibility ascribed to the corporate agent would still translate into a punishment of all, for example, a fine to be paid by the corporation. To compensate for the financial loss, the corporation would have to cut costs and perhaps have to lay off (innocent) employees (ibid. 99).

Another possible reply to the concern raised by Hasnas and other individualists is to argue that the alternative to not holding corporate agents responsible for anything they do (over and above individual faults) is seriously problematic on a consequentialist account. Conceding that the individualists' concern is based on a deontological view committed to the priority of individual rights (and rightly so), the consequences of not holding corporations accountable and responsible at all would be catastrophic. First, it would undermine the legal notion of corporate liability. Second, it would induce individuals to participate and do harm in their roles as members of corporations, in particular within larger corporations where action is complex and concerted. Third, it would require a revision of our language and our moral emotions that make us blame corporate agents. The latter might not be unfair, but it would require some sort of re-education of the populace that might not make sense and result in an atmosphere that censors speech. Finally, it seems to be too hasty to relieve corporations from any responsibility on the view that they are incompetent moral agents. As Pettit (2007, 176) points out it can have an edificatory effect to treat irresponsible collectives as if they were morally competent. Pettit uses the analogy of a teenager whose parents know that he or she will not act responsibly but nevertheless treat the teenager as an adult to encourage a development into being a mature moral person. If the analogy is justified in this respect, it makes sense to confer upon immature and immoral corporations the blame for their wrongdoings to establish a future path of organizational development where decision procedures and authority within the organization makes it prone to becoming responsible.

The point to draw, however, even if a credible account of corporate moral agency can be given, is that it also needs to have some good answers to the individualist concern. The suggested consequentialist argument and the argument from education are attempts to provide an answer to this concern about the illiberal harming of individuals by employing the notion of corporate moral agency in our moral life and moral language.

So far, the dispute over corporate moral agency has been introduced to include only two opposing positions: the individualist versus the collectivist. However, this is too crude to do justice to the finer grains and nuances. Tim Mulgan (2018) and Kendy Hess (2017) offer typologies that are helpful to get an overview. Mulgan points out that in the philosophy of mind relevant to the debate on corporate agency, individualists generally adhere to phenomenological accounts (awareness and embodiment), whereas collectivists prefer functionalist accounts that look for performance. Hence, individualists tend to have an internal perspective of the mind, whereas collectivists have an external approach (Mulgan 2018, 5). Besides these characteristics, Mulgan's typology proposes four positions in the debate on corporate moral agency (ibid. 3):

1. *Individualism.* Corporate groups are not agents of any kind. The only agents are individual human beings (and perhaps some other animals). All talk of corporate agency or personhood is metaphorical. Although we hold corporate groups "responsible" for legal or compensatory purposes, corporate groups themselves cannot bear genuine moral responsibility. It makes no sense to literally blame a corporate group.
2. *Minimal collectivism.* Some corporate groups are independent agents that act in the world, but none are moral agents or moral persons.
3. *Moderate collectivism.* Some corporate groups are moral agents, but none are fully fledged moral persons. Corporate groups enjoy some rights (e.g., property or contract) and can be held responsible for their actions. But they do not enjoy human rights.
4. *Extreme collectivism.* Some corporate groups are both moral agents and moral persons. They have the same moral status as human beings and enjoy analogous rights.

This typology is helpful because it makes it clearer where "the action is" because, according to Mulgan, the proponents of corporate responsibility are mainly situated in position 3, moderate collectivism. And, this moderate position should not be confused with the extreme version that ascribes personhood to a corporation. Much of the debate can be interpreted using this typology to avoid unnecessary use of strawman argumentation. Often, the proponents of collectivism are seen as implying extreme collectivism. For instance, John Hasnas (2018; see also Hindriks 2014) argues that if accepting List and Pettit's (2011) account of corporate moral agency, it follows that corporations are on an equal standing with ordinary citizens and therefore should have voting rights. Hasnas is not serious about drawing this consequence and instead uses the argument as a *reductio* against List and Pettit. However, even though it is possible that more follows by deduction from the account of List and Pettit than they are willing to accept, it is also possible that such "reductios" miss the point that collectivism comes in various degrees and that it is possible to argue for moral agency without falling prey to moral personhood in the sense that entails a standing equal to ordinary humans. In fact, List and Pettit make it clear that they do not think that corporations should have an equal standing with ordinary individuals. And, even though they do not make it explicit, it follows from their discussion of this issue that corporations should not have a right to vote (ibid. 181). In Chapter 6 the issue of corporations and voting is also considered.

In an attempt to reconcile the individualist and the collectivist positions, Kendy Hess (2017, 181–182) suggests that there are four positions at stake in the debate: atomism, individualism, holism, and dualism. She then argues that atomism and dualism are the "crazy/rabid versions of individualism and holism". The atomists (wrongly) think that individuals in organizations live in "splendid isolation". This sounds equivalent to former British Prime Minister Margaret Thatcher's dictum: "They are casting their problems at society. And, you know, there's no such thing as society. There are individual men and women and there are families" (The Guardian 2013). But even Thatcher admits that there are also families, so the atomist position is not credible. The dualist position on the other hand invokes the spooky idea of a ghost-in-the-machine metaphor of the corporate agent as completely detached from its individual members. So, according to Hess, the two credible positions that remain are individualism (where individuals interact socially and create institutional relations) and holism (where the corporate agent both has its own level of agency but at the same time relies on its members to exist). Hess therefore adds a dimension to Mulgan's typology by highlighting the extremes of the dispute that are strawmen attributed to opponents. The strawmen are always "lurking in the background of the debate" (Hess 2017, 182). Mulgan does not have "atomism" in his typology either, and extreme collectivism is not necessarily identical with "dualism". So, it is worth taking Hess's suggestions as a heuristic not to waste an effort to expose the opponent's position as entirely ridiculous, especially when in fact this is not the position held by the opponent.

Bearing in mind this general introduction to the (currently evolving) debate on corporate moral agency, the much influential position of Christian List and Philip Pettit, which provides a theoretical account based on functionalism, is presented and discussed.

The List–Pettit Account of Corporate Moral Agency: Functionalism

In this presentation it is impossible to give full justice to the comprehensive and far-reaching aspects of the List–Pettit theory on corporate moral agency. The aim is to present the key aspects relevant to justifying the claim of their position – that corporate moral agency is a coherent position. What is left aside are the intricate metaphysical, epistemological, and methodological aspects that concern the deeper foundations of the theory.

What characterizes the theory is its commitment to a functionalist conception of mind transposed to collective agency. Hence, the theory aims at avoiding the controversial extremes already alluded to, in particular that corporate agency must entail some sort of mysterious superego that completely transcends the group's individual members (List & Pettit

2011, 73). The commitment to functionalism means that if the performance of corporations can satisfy conditions for being a moral agent, it follows that it is possible for a corporate agent to be a moral agent (and person in a qualified sense; see ibid. Chapter 8). The functionalist theory is similar to the one French proposed in 1979 relying on certain internal decision procedures for moral agency to be possible. Basically, List and Pettit distinguish between loosely organized collectives, like the mob or the political movement, and structured entities like the firm, the party, or a committee. The latter are the focus of their theory. According to List and Pettit the following conditions must be satisfied to be a moral agent. In the following I will mainly refer to Pettit (2007, as his article is rephrased in Chapter 7, in List & Pettit 2011).

First, "There must have been grave matter . . . full knowledge of the guilt, and full consent of the will" (Pettit 2007, 174). This is spelled out in the following three conditions that corporations must satisfy to have moral agency:

1. They must have *autonomy* (and can make a value-relevant choice among options)
2. They can make a *normative judgment* (and have access to evidence required for making such judgments)
3. They must have a capacity for *self-control* (to choose among options)

Each condition is necessary for moral agency to obtain, but together they constitute sufficient reason. In particular condition 1 about corporate autonomy from its individual members is the main point that critics address, and List and Pettit also give this condition thorough consideration. The main thrust of their defence for arguing that corporations can be autonomous follows from social decision theory. They suggest that the reason why the corporate agent cannot be reduced to the aggregation of individual decisions is due to the fact that a majoritarian procedure like simple voting will produce inconsistency. The *discursive dilemma* is then used to illustrate this point.

Imagine that three employees are to decide on the corporate decision of a particular topic, for instance (to use Pettit's example, 2007, 197), of whether or not to buy a new safety measure in a worker-owned corporation to secure the workers from accidents. But in buying it the workers will have to forego a pay rise. The decision is taken by the workers themselves about whether or not this safety measure satisfies three requirements: Does it remedy a serious danger? Does it remedy effectively? And does it incur a bearable loss in pay? They take a vote, and in this stylized version of the decision procedure, three workers participate following a rule stating that worker A will endorse to buy the safety measure (and forego the pay rise) only if the three conditions are satisfied (see Table 3.1). In the sketched situation, worker A thinks that there is no serious danger to remedy, that it might be an effective safety measure, and that the loss in pay in bearable. So, one of the conditions does is not obtained (the serious danger condition), and therefore worker A cannot support the acquisition of the safety measure (and forego the pay rise). This approach is called the *conclusion-driven* approach because it derives its conclusion based on three premises. The other decision procedure is to vote for each condition (serious danger, etc.) at a time and calculate what the majority votes. Following this *premise-driven* approach the result, perhaps surprisingly, is different. Because the conclusion-driven approach gives the result that all three workers reject and say no unanimously, and the premise-driven approach gives the opposite result, that each issue (premise) gets a yes from the majority, there is inconsistency in the group decision. According to Pettit (and List) the premise-driven approach represents the group's decision, and the conclusion-driven approach the individualist viewpoint (see also Tollefsen 2015, 56–64).

Pettit asks us to imagine that the individually based, conclusion-derived approach was not used in this case, and only the premise-driven approach was used, so the group is ignorant about the fact that the conclusion-driven approach would have resulted in a rejection. Suppose then that some of the poorer workers' spouses complain about the decision to buy the safety measure and forego a pay raise. Pettit thinks that they can direct their complaint against only the group and not the individual workers because they would have made the opposite decision (if the conclusion-driven approach was used) and so are innocent and cannot be blamed for the decision. According to Pettit the reason why the corporate organization is responsible is because "[t]he corporate organization has routines in place whereby the chair is triggered to represent the group in announcing the decision for a pay sacrifice and in putting that decision into effect" (ibid. 198).

Now, this sounds as if the group follows some sort of deterministic algorithm that makes individual members innocent of corporate choices. However, in this situation it is possible that when the workers become aware that their decision might have detrimental consequences for some of their less well-off coworkers, they regret the decision and deliberate on how to change it and also change the procedure leading to this result. So, there is a chance of reverting decisions of the corporate system based on the feedback the organization receives from within and from its outside

Table 3.1 The discursive dilemma

	Serious danger?	*Effective measure?*	*Bearable loss?*	*Pay sacrifice?*
A	No	Yes	Yes	No
B	Yes	No	Yes	No
C	Yes	Yes	No	No

stakeholders (List & Pettit 2011, 62–63). The role of inflexible feedback mechanisms is the concern behind some of the criticism of the theory (Ciepley 2018).

Importantly, for the corporate decision procedure to be internally consistent, the members must together as a group form a "constitution" that prescribes how to reach a decision. This can be done by means of conducting a general vote, by authorizing subgroups, or by appointing an official to represent the organization (Pettit 2007, 180). The point is, however, that in the case of groups, collectives, and corporate agents, there will always be a need for some sort of procedure (and a relatively formalized explicit one) to satisfy the requirement of organizational autonomy. When the group deliberates over such decisions, they show to be epistemically capable agents satisfying condition 2 for carrying a capacity for "normative judgment". Corporations can assess the evidence available and make decisions on this basis. They resemble ordinary rational agents who can act on their desires for how they prefer the world to be in the future and make decisions based on credible beliefs about how the world is now.

The last condition for being a moral agent, according to List and Pettit, the capacity for self-control, is also argued to be possible for corporations to satisfy. In medieval clerical practice, corporate organizations were considered *persona ficta* (fictional persons), and therefore they could not be excommunicated (ibid. 188). The idea that organizational action must lead back to individual acts prevented the medieval philosophers (like Thomas Aquinas) to take corporate moral agency into account. List and Pettit argue against the idea of fictional persons by claiming that in fact *both* individuals *as well as* the corporate agent can be responsible. The members have "responsibility as enactors of the corporate deed, so far as they could have refused to play that part and didn't" (ibid. 192). But at the same time the group agent is the "ultimate, reason-sensitive planner at its origin" (ibid.). Hence, corporations also satisfy condition 3 by showing a capacity for self-control due to the symmetrical involvement of both members and the organizational whole, according to Pettit.

Objections to the List–Pettit Account

Objections have been levelled against the List–Pettit account of corporate moral agency. As already mentioned there is concern about whether corporations are sufficiently capable of assessing and responding to feedback from their stakeholders (Ciepley 2018). This amounts to an objection to List and Pettit's account of corporate moral agency and *deliberation* (Tollefsen 2015, 64). The functionalist account that List and Pettit defends seems too focussed on a formalized logical procedure that does not sufficiently consider the full scale of institutional, cultural, and moral qualities relevant to moral deliberation. Rönnegard & Velasquez

(2017, 136) complain that the method is too formalistic and that a decision procedure or "a code of conduct cannot be morally responsible". This objection is not surprising as the proponents of individualism do not accept the functionalism of corporate agency. According to Tollefsen (2015, 64) the voting procedure testifies to a preference for an individualist methodology inherent to List and Pettit's approach that ultimately undermines the holistic view of corporate agency.

However, the main objection regards the distinction between intrinsic and performative personhood that List and Pettit use to defend their functionalist view of corporate personhood (List & Pettit 2011, Chapter 8). The dispute can be explained by Mulgan's typology (presented previously) because it concerns whether or not the List–Pettit account is an example of moderate collectivism (where corporations have only a limited set of rights) or if it slides into extreme collectivism (granting human rights to corporations). This debate is ongoing as it was already found in the critical reception of French's notion of corporations as "full-fledged persons" (1979, e.g., Donaldson 1982, 22–23). French responded by acknowledging that corporations cannot be "persons" but only "agents" (Orts & Craig Smith 2017, 4). Recently, Hindriks (2014) in a response to List and Pettit has objected that it follows from their account that corporate persons logically possess "the right not to be enslaved, the right to life, or the right to vote", which he calls the "problematic trio" (ibid. 1582). Hasnas (2018), as mentioned, also contends that *if* corporations acquire the capacity for moral agency that List and Pettit argues, *then* it follows in a liberal democracy that corporations should have the right to vote. Kusch (2014) is also discontent with the notion of corporate personhood and value because it ignores the Kantian distinction between *person* and *personal property* and between *dignity* and *price* (ibid. 1598). The problem with List and Pettit's account, according to Kusch, is that it ignores the historical, sociological, and political context and therefore "ends up being descriptively inadequate and normatively empty" (ibid. 1599).

In taking stock of the objections raised against List and Pettit's work on corporate moral agency, I think it is possible to defend their account of personhood to the extent that they do not (want to) extend human rights to corporations (List & Pettit 2011, 180–182). So, I will assume that their position is capable of providing a reply to the critics who blame them for this. However, I think that the objections relying on the deficient account of corporate deliberation and its ability to process and act on information is more to the point (even if the deliberation and the personhood objections are interdependent). The general organization theory that emerges from the functionalist theory appears to be somewhat limited with regard to the wide dispute about what an organization is. And, it certainly seems ill-conceived to account for the possibility of moral deliberation (cf. Habermas 1994; Scherer & Palazzo 2007; Dubbink & Smith 2011; Sabadoz & Singer 2017). Considering that the research field of organization theory builds on the assumption that a plurality of paradigms or *metaphors* (Morgan 1997; Moon et al. 2005) are at hand for the researcher to embark on the study of organizations, it seems to be unnecessarily narrow to constrain the approach to functionalism, especially without providing an argument for why functionalism is the proper approach. A plausible reply that List and Pettit could give to this complaint is that their theory is not comparable to the empirically based theory of organization alluded to here. For instance, they conceive of their book as a contribution to "foundational research rather than empirical social science or applied political theory" (List & Pettit 2011, Preface viii). Adding to this line of defence, their contribution is in fact a much-needed corrective to the normatively underdeveloped field of organization theory. So, there is a need in the theory of organization to better understand how collectives, groups, and corporate agents of any kind can be considered morally responsible, if at all.

Corporate Moral Agency and the Social Liberal Corporation

This point leads to the focus of this book because in defending corporate responsibility, and the social liberal corporation as an example of a responsible unit, it requires that it is possible to have a credible conception of how corporate responsibility is possible. Otherwise, we are left with the problem of an unsurmountable discontinuity between the theory of organization and the theory of corporate responsibility (cf. Phillips & Margolis 1999; Heugens & Scherer 2010). One way out of this impasse is to aspire to justificatory neutrality or epistemic abstinence (Rawls 1994). Such a strategy is adopted by both corporate citizenship theory in its satisfaction with a metaphorical conception of citizenship (Moon et al. 2005) and political CSR in its appeal to anti-foundationalist Rortyan pragmatist "priority of democracy to philosophy" (Scherer & Palazzo 2007). Hence, both social liberal approaches take an explicit anti-metaphysical stance towards the foundational issue of corporate moral agency. I shall return to these stances and strategies in Chapters 6 and 7, but for now I contend that they are missing the point of justification – that pragmatics requires a theory of corporate moral agency to be credible. We need to make sense of corporate moral agency to make sense of corporate responsibility whether metaphysically loaded or not.

The concern however remains whether the functionalist version of corporate moral agency is the most promising way to overcome the divide between the descriptive-explanatory level and the normative level. The need for overcoming this divide is clear enough. For instance, in the literature on political CSR (discussed in Chapter 7), corporations should participate in politics by playing the role of being a democratically deliberative agent. But if so, what rights, if any, does the corporation have to participate in politics? Mulgan (2018, footnote 9) raises this question to show the relevance of providing a theory of corporate personhood. He goes further in a controversial defence of corporate moral agency by claiming that in the future we will depend on ascribing moral agency to corporations (and collectives of various sorts). This is because the future looks bleak: Climate change might endanger our liberal preference for individualism in a *broken future* where the "circumstances of justice" (Rawls 1971) are radically different from today's abundance of resources. Also, digital futures of artificial intelligence taking over from humans will require us to demand that corporations are reliable. Hence, according to Mulgan (2018, 10), we will have to downgrade "those criteria that corporate groups cannot possibly meet, such as ensoulment or embodiment" to reach a workable understanding of corporate agency. To Mulgan the question is whether or not we can find out what the criteria are for reliable corporate agency because this will turn out to be decisive in the future. In this regard he paves the way for functionalist and performative accounts of corporate agency because in the future it does not make pragmatic sense to work against corporate responsibility on the basis of individualist claims to the phenomenology and embodiment of human experience and consciousness. This is, of course, not equivalent to saying that the human perspective is downgraded or excluded; it means only that we will have to assure that we can hold corporations responsible (Herzog's 2018 notion of "reclaiming the system" is comparable in this regard; see also Dempsey 2013).

I think that the gist of Mulgan's proposal and its argument is very much to the point. My concern, however, and obviously many of the critics' concerns, with regard to the particular organization of the business firm, is that it is programmed for a unilateral purpose: making profits (Jensen 2002; Bakan 2004). In the functionalist framing, this means that the profit objective, as far as it dominates or constrains the corporate decision procedure to the detriment of ethical interest, will be an obstacle to reaching a credible theory of corporate moral agency (see Palazzo et al. 2012 about ethical blindness and the decision procedure).

I notice that Pettit (2017), in his latest contribution to the issue, explicitly acknowledges that his approach sets aside the differences between the corporate agent as a profit-seeking commercial organization and other corporate organizations such as "clubs, churches, universities, voluntary organizations, political parties and indeed political states" (ibid. 15). But is it justified to neutralize this key difference, in particular, if the aim is to give an account of corporate *moral* agency? I think not. It seems counterintuitive to neutralize the profit objective from the start as this feature captures the common concern about the viability in responsible business. In Part II of this book, addressing the political philosophies of corporate responsibility, different proposals for how to respond to the profit objective are suggested. This will provide suggestions for how to think about the nature of the business firm as a corporate moral agent and the prospects for the social liberal corporation.

References

Avi-Yonah, R. S. (2005) The cyclical transformations of the corporate form: A historical perspective on corporate social responsibility. *The Delaware Journal of Corporate Law*, *30*(3), 767–818

Bakan, J. (2004) *The corporation: The pathological pursuit of profit and power*. London: Constable

Ciepley, D. (2018) Can corporations be held to the public interest, or even to the law? *Journal of Business Ethics*, 1–16. doi: 10.1007/s10551-018-3894-2

Dempsey, J. (2013) Corporations and non-agential moral responsibility. *Journal of Applied Philosophy*, *30*(4), 334–350

Dewey, J. (1926) The historic background of corporate legal personality. *Yale Law Journal*, *35*, 655–673

Donaldson, T. (1982) *Corporations and morality*. Englewood Cliffs, NJ: Prentice Hall

Dubbink, W., & Smith, J. (2011) A political account of corporate moral responsibility. *Ethical Theory and Moral Practice*, *14*(2), 223–246

French, P. (1979) The corporation as a moral person. *American Philosophical Quarterly*, *16*(3), 207–215

The Guardian (2013, April 8) *Margaret thatcher: A life in quotes*. www.theguardian.com/politics/2013/apr/08/margaret-thatcher-quotes

Habermas, J. (1994) Three normative models of democracy. *Constellations*, *1*(1), 1–10

Hasnas, J. (2018) Should corporations have the right to vote? A paradox in the theory of corporate moral agency. *Journal of Business Ethics*, *150*(3), 657–670

Herzog, L. (2018) *Reclaiming the system: Moral responsibility, divided labour, and the role of organizations in society*. Oxford: Oxford University Press

Hess, K. (2017) The unrecognized consensus about firm moral responsibility. In E. W. Orts & N. Craig Smith (Eds.), *The moral responsibility of firms*, 169–187. Oxford: Oxford University Press

Heugens, P. P. M. A. R., & Scherer, A. G. (2010) When organization theory met business ethics: Toward further symbioses. *Business Ethics Quarterly*, *20*(4), 643–672

Hindriks, F. (2014) How autonomous are collective agents? Corporate rights and normative individualism. *Erkenntnis*, *79*(S9), 1565–1585

Jensen, M. C. (2002) Value maximization, stakeholder theory, and the corporate objective function. *Business Ethics Quarterly*, *12*(2), 235–256

Kusch, M. (2014) The metaphysics and politics of corporate personhood. *Erkenntnis*, *79*(S9), 1587–1600

List, C. (2018) What is it like to be a group agent? *Noûs*, *52*(2), 295–319

List, C., & Pettit, P. (2011) *Group agency – The possibility, design, and status of corporate agents*. Oxford: Oxford University Press

Moon, J., Crane, A., & Matten, D. (2005) Can corporations be citizens? Corporate citizenship as a metaphor for business participation in society. *Business Ethics Quarterly*, *15*(3), 429–453

Morgan, G. (1997) *Images of organization*. London: Sage Publishing
Mulgan, T. (2018) Corporate agency and possible futures. *Journal of Business Ethics*, 1–16. doi: 10.1007/s10551-018-3887-1
Orts, E. W., & Craig Smith, N. (2017) *The moral responsibility of firms*. Oxford: Oxford University Press
Palazzo, G., Krings, F., & Hoffrage, U. (2012) Ethical blindness. *Journal of Business Ethics*, *109*(3), 323–338
Pettit, P. (2007) Responsibility incorporated. *Ethics*, *117*(2), 171–201
Pettit, P. (2017) The conversable, responsible corporation. In E. W. Orts & N. Craig Smith (Eds.), *The moral responsibility of firms*. Oxford: Oxford University Press
Phillips, R. A., & Margolis, J. D. (1999) Toward an ethics of organizations. *Business Ethics Quarterly*, *19*, 619–638
Rawls, J. (1971) *A theory of justice*. Oxford: Oxford University Press
Rawls, J. (1994) *Political liberalism*. New York: Columbia University Press
Reich, R. (2012, November 16) *Why BP isn't a criminal*. http://robertreich.org/post/35848994755
Rönnegard, D. (2013) How autonomy alone debunks corporate moral agency. *Business & Professional Ethics Journal*, *32*(1–2), 77–106
Rönnegard, D., & Velasquez, M. G. (2017) On (not) attributing moral responsibility to organizations. In E. W. Orts & N. Craig Smith (Eds.), *The moral responsibility of firms*, 169–187. Oxford: Oxford University Press
Sabadoz, C., & Singer, A. (2017) Talk ain't cheap: Political CSR and the challenges of corporate deliberation. *Business Ethics Quarterly*, *27*(2), 183–211
Scherer, A. G., & Palazzo, G. (2007) Toward a political conception of corporate responsibility: Business and society seen from a Habermasian perspective. *Academy of Management Review*, *32*, 1096–1120
Schwitzgebel, E. (2015) If materialism is true, the United States is probably conscious. *Philosophical Studies*, *172*, 1697–1721
Tollefsen, D. P. (2015) *Groups as agents*. Cambridge: Polity Press
Velasquez, M. G. (1983) Why corporations are not morally responsible for anything they do. *Business and Professional Ethics Journal*, *2*, 1–18
Young, I. M. (2011) *Responsibility for justice*. Oxford: Oxford University Press

Part II

Corporate Responsibility and Political Philosophy

4 Aristotelian Organizations and Corporate Responsibility

Conservatism

This chapter presents conceptions of an organization that aim to challenge the main features of the modern conception, which sees the organization as a system (a bureaucracy) and also presupposes an individualist stance. The virtue ethics associated with Aristotelian approaches in this regard are *conservative* and *communitarian* in their critical outlook on modernity's giving priority to the individual (MacIntyre 1985; Solomon 1993, 71). They distance themselves from the commonplace ethics of modernity, such as utilitarianism and deontology, and instead opt for a resurgence of Greek antiquity's notions of personal character and judgment (Phronesis), often with a religious underpinning (McDowell 1979; Melé 2009). Hence, even though there are several good reasons for buying into the virtue ethical approach to business and corporate responsibility (as will be argued), it remains that the conservative aspects of virtue ethics fall short of providing a sufficiently satisfying account of modern (or even postmodern) notions of corporate responsibility. I am going to argue that virtue ethics and the Aristotelian conception of politics and metaphysics are helpful resources in the argument for corporate responsibility, in particular with regard to clarifying the internal communication and coordination of the organization. But the inherent anti-modern and conservative tendencies are shortcomings with regard to acknowledging the complex nature of modern institutions – and not least the liberal preference for safeguarding the individual that is a priority to the social liberal corporation.

The point of departure here is Robert Solomon's Aristotelian virtue ethical account of certain *business virtues* (1992) and Geoff Moore's reading of Alasdair MacIntyre on the practice–institution distinction transposed to the *virtuous corporation* (Moore 2005). A common feature of more recent Aristotelian organizational thinking is the preference for a bottom-up model of organizing. Person and character precede organizational ethics and take priority in the role of business in society, for example, the virtuous leader and employee are necessary conditions for a good organization to succeed. Moreover, the site of morality is local in close relationships among family members, friends, and collaborating citizens. No philosophy or theory – with scant sensitivity to local circumstance and the needs of the situation and applied from the outside of the organization – will work in this Aristotelian universe. As such, it provides a remedy for the defects of modern top-down or centralized governance models. Neo-Aristotelians, therefore, also tend to perceive the institutional framework of modern society that surrounds the practice of corporations as secondary to the inner moral life of the organization. For instance, MacIntyre and Moore believe that *practice* comes before *institution* in the sense that the virtues are related to practice and that the function of institutions is to uphold and support practice (Moore 2005, 676). This view can be argued to be in tension with the view of Aristotle, who saw the city-state – the *polis* – as pivotal to the development of the virtues, and thus life, in the organization (households) (Aristotle 1997, 1253a18). Humans are political animals (*zoon politikon*) first and foremost as engagement in politics is the distinctive feature of humans compared to other animals.

One of the most attractive, although also problematic, features of Aristotelian-inspired approaches and the sort of neo-Aristotelian business ethics that this chapter considers is the metaphysical language it allows. From a (neo-)Aristotelian viewpoint, it is meaningful, if not required, to talk about the *purpose* of an organization (the telos) and how it fits into the common good. Invoking an organic view of organizations in analogy to the life of living creatures makes it possible to overcome the machine metaphor present in much organizational theory, which avoids normativity in its striving for objectivity. The idea of an organizational ethics is controversial in organization theory, and there is a division of labour between business ethics and organization theory, in which the latter – if acknowledging norms in the organizational sphere – abstains from taking an explicit normative-prescriptive approach. Also, in much theory of CSR, norms and ethics are dealt with in a descriptive manner. However, according to the Aristotelians, there is no fact–value distinction, which makes it difficult to say that corporations can be morally responsible agents. There is no brute fact of the market or the organization that escapes morality, and thus corporations are, by definition, moral creatures. Such anti-modern, or what I would call conservative (with some qualification as they need not be committed to traditional anti-liberal values), stances allow the sort of language that is needed in giving a voice to concerns about the purpose of business, meaningful work, and a conception of how business is part of society.

Another feature of the conservative outlook that can be associated with virtue ethics is the kind of corporate *culture* it envisages (Solomon 1993). Where do the virtues thrive? In a sense, they are suppressed in an amoral bureaucracy, even though the public servant's role is to follow the rules (*decorum* or the law) and avoid allowing subjective opinions to interfere in their daily work as Max Weber envisaged the civil servant. As such, the ethos of the civil servant is an exposition of certain virtues of neutrality in judgment, objectivity, and respect for the law. However, virtues are, by definition, reflected in the culture of tradition, and the historic element is significant too (MacIntyre 1985).

Some of the oldest organizations in the world, are in fact, family businesses. The Japanese Kongō Gumi was a family-owned firm, with an impressive longevity of more than 1400 years going back to the year 578. The reason why family businesses survive so long, and are resilient in times of crisis, could be due to their long-term strategic planning. They tend to avoid seeking short-term profits over long-term goals. A major reason for this is caused by the fact that a key objective in a family business is to turn over the firm to the next generation (Bennedsen & Van der Heyden 2010). A publicly traded stock-owned company or a hedge fund has a kind of short-sighted governance that makes it obey fluctuations in the market, and investors demand a continual flow of high returns on investment. Hence, family businesses can be, although they are not always, examples of how conservative virtue ethics prefer a corporation to be. In the 1905 novel of Thomas Mann, *The Buddenbrooks*, the father and owner of the family company inculcates his successor: "My son [Thomas], attend with zeal to thy business by day, but do none that hinders thee from thy sleep at night". The allusion to the Kantian imperative is here translated into a care for the virtue of conducting business with prudence. In a family business, the family and the physical unit of the factory or the head office is situated in the same area. So, the life of the family depends on the corporation's reputation in the local community. This will exert a pressure on the family to respond to the surrounding community's expectations. For instance, if employees are laid off, they will oftentimes be neighbours to the family or perhaps parents to the friends of the children at school. Moreover, the first generation in a family business will typically also take pride in being seen as valuable and trustworthy members of the local community as this can be crucial for growing the business by gaining support from authorities, customers, and employees. Certainly, these favourable features of family businesses may change as the business grows and becomes detached from its local origin. However, research shows that family businesses might continue to have higher standards in corporate responsibility as they grow into huge multinationals, if the owner converts ownership to a foundation, compared to non-family-owned businesses (Ciepley 2018).

Sometimes, leaders and managers of the corporation, when new employees arrive, welcome them as members of the family. Such corporate cultures and metaphorical talk of a *corporate family* seem phony and potentially oppressive to the employees' right to freedom of thought. However, the family metaphor can also resemble aspects of virtue ethical outlooks on what an organization is and ought to be vis-à-vis places of belonging and sites of formation of personal identities with a deep commitment to mutuality and solidarity among the members of a corporation. Hence, Aristotelian organizations can be ideal sites for responsible corporations on that account, if the talk of family membership is taken literally to imply a true sense of solidarity among members of the business and if the corporate leaders can show a non-oppressive paternalistic concern for the well-being of the employees (if such a thing is meaningful in a modern liberal society).

In this chapter, I will therefore argue that we need virtue ethics to understand and also promote ethical, or responsible, cultures within the organization but that virtue ethics needs a liberal orientation to avoid the potential neglect of individual rights. This is so because it is a conservative and not a liberal philosophy of the corporation. In the first section, corporate responsibility is discussed, based on Solomon and Moore's contributions to the virtue ethics of business, in particular how it is possible to have an Aristotelian business ethics when most holders of Aristotelian conceptions of business, Aristotle himself included, are negative and dismissive of them. Subsequently, looking at the promising contribution that virtue ethics can make to promoting notions of responsible leadership in the handling of difficult moral dilemmas, the influential theory about the transformational leader is pivotal (Bass & Steidlmeier 1999) and argues that authentic leadership might be understood in a too instrumental fashion and could be harmful if virtues are not internalized in the leader's character (Skubinn & Herzog 2016). This leads to questioning how the lack of virtues can damage the internal communication and co-operation within the organization, as perceived by the virtue ethical theory of *epistemic injustice* (Fricker 2007). The lack of virtue in an organization can undermine corporate responsibility from below, and therefore one of the key strengths of virtue ethics is its ability to provide guidance for how to make organizations into responsible collectives. Finally, the chapter will conclude that virtue ethics is a helpful theory to promote social liberal ideas but that it also falls short in acknowledging the complex reality of conflicts within and outside the organization. Being sceptical, if not outrightly against modernity, comes at a price.

Aristotle and the Business Organization as a Site for the Virtues

Looking into the original writing of Aristotle in *Politics* (1997), it is obvious that he was not in favour of business because he dismissed *profits* in the exchange of money and goods. He distinguished between the economy of the household (*oikos*), which is based on nature, and the exchange of goods by means of money to make profits (*chrēmatistikē*).

> But business is twofold, as we said, one being proper to trading and the other to household management. The latter is necessary and

> praiseworthy but the one proper to exchange is justly blamed, since it is not according to nature but is a taking from each other.
> (Aristotle 1997, Book 1, 1258a34)

According to Aristotle, business as making profits or usury from lending money is "unnatural" and is equated to "taking from each other", which is exploitation (Solomon 1992, 321; cf. Flew 1976). Aristotle is the source of Christian ethics' condemnation of usury and the later critique of capitalism. The distinction between business as household management and business as exchange reappears in Marx's two concepts of use value and exchange value, where the latter is critiqued by Marx. Solomon claims that Aristotle simply gave expression to the aristocratic view that commerce is a lower kind of activity because, if one is already wealthy, one need not work to make money (ibid. 322). In the anecdotal department, Aristotle is less critical about making money, as in this story about Thales.

> There is, for example, the achievement of Thales of Miletus. For what he thought up was a business scheme. . . . They say that when he was being reproached, because of his poverty, with the uselessness of philosophy, he noticed from his study of the stars that there was going to be a good olive harvest. So while it was still winter, he got possession of a little money and put a deposit on all the olive presses in Miletus and Chios, paying out a small sum because no one was bidding against him. Then when the harvest season came and many presses were suddenly in demand all at once, he rented them out on whatever terms he chose and collected a great deal of money. Thus he showed that it is easy for philosophers to get rich if they want to, but that that is not what they have a serious interest in.
> (Aristotle 1997, 1259a6)

However, the story about Thales can be interpreted to show that philosophy as a theoretical activity, although devoid of immediate practical usage, has the potential – if turned towards practice – to become a means of creating wealth. The philosopher, though, prefers the higher form of living a life of theoretical contemplation, the *Bios Theoretikos* (Aristotle 1976, Book 10). Hence, a hierarchical order of human activities emerges from Aristotle's writings, which places business in the lower echelons compared to philosophy as human activity.

The Aristotelian suspicion about the virtues of business as exchange, which Solomon calls a "prejudice" (Solomon 1992, 322), reappears in current neo-Aristotelian thinking. For instance, Alasdair MacIntyre is critical about capitalism in general and the corporation as the proper site for virtues to develop (MacIntyre 2016; Moore 2005, 677–678). So, how is it possible to use virtue ethics and the political philosophy of Aristotle in the endeavour to theorize corporate responsibility?

Geoff Moore concedes that MacIntyre is against business in the sense that it is exploitative and in tension with virtues. However, Moore also argues that the theory of the relationship among virtues, practice, and the institution in MacIntyre's work can be used to understand corporate responsibility. This involves a reformist stance, as opposed to the allegedly revolutionary potential that can also be found in a capitalist critical account of virtue ethics (ibid. 679). Similarly, Solomon explicitly commits to a reformist stance in his polemical allusion to Marx: "[A]nd I do not see myself as the instrument of radical change, no matter how many such fantasies may be entertained in the college libraries and the reading room of the British Museum" (Solomon 1993, 7). To both Solomon and Moore, it is about cultivating a moral character that is realistic within the institution of capitalism (ibid. 6). Solomon goes a long way to explain how important it is to not impose an ethics from the academic ivory tower onto the business organization. And, businesspeople are experts in their own affairs, similar to those in other types of professions. So, it makes no sense to teach businesspeople about business ethics without understanding what the *practice* of business is about. Hence, Solomon argues that for instance, toughness can be a virtue in business if taken in the right way and should not be confused with insensitivity and a lack of empathy for others.

Now, Moore's usage of the virtue–practice–institution scheme taken from MacIntyre can show how it is possible to think of corporate responsibility from within the virtue ethical tradition (which is a plausible and fair reading of MacIntyre, according to Moore). According to MacIntyre, a practice is "any coherent and complex socially established cooperative human activity" (MacIntyre 1985, 187) that makes it possible for humans to obtain *internal goods*. Such goods are the types of pleasures that are associated with *eudaimonia*, the Aristotelian notion of happiness, which allows a person to flourish and realize his or her full potential. Practices are activities that are valuable in themselves, and serve no external purpose. MacIntyre suggests the game of chess as an example of a practice. Playing chess and developing skills to improve chess playing are inherent to the practice of chess. One enjoys playing it and being good at it (MacIntyre 1985, 188). The practice of chess is different from the institution of chess, which is an external social framework that can support chess playing, for instance, chess clubs. The institution provides so called external goods, which are funding, political support, protection, and reputation. The purpose of institutions is to support practices because only within a practice will humans flourish. In that sense, practice is more important than institution, but conversely, practice needs institutional backup to function (ibid. 194). Practices can be of all sorts of deeds, but the defining feature is that they exemplify cooperative human activity.

Hence, according to MacIntyre, farming, biology as a science, and chess playing are all practices. The hard question then is this: Why should co-operation within a business organization be exempt from being a practice in MacIntyre's sense? Moore speculates about this and argues that for MacIntyre, the institution of competition and power (of capitalism) that business practice is embedded within tends to defeat the practice (Moore 2005, 678). Hence, using MacIntyre's virtue ethical theory in the realm of business is a case of appropriation in the derogative sense. Moore denies this and argues that it is possible for a corporation to be a suitable and supportive framework for good business practice (ibid.). This requires that the institution of the firm must be in tune with the virtues. This is done by individuals who possess the virtues because only the virtues are capable of balancing the powers of practice and institution. Responsible, virtuous leaders have the power necessary to institutionalize a culture of support for the business practice to excel (ibid. 676).

There is no justification for the vices to control the institution of the corporate organization by referring to the circumstances of fierce competition in the market (Solomon 2003). Accordingly, Moore concludes that "in capitalist forms of business organization the practice is potentially and continually under threat from the acquisitiveness and competitiveness of the corporation, with its inherent tendency to avarice" (Moore 2005, 679). The argument from virtue that Moore espouses to balance the tendency of the institution to crowd out the practice relies not just on an individual's duties. It also relies on the claim that for any corporation to survive, it needs to be able to sustain its practice. If co-operation is dysfunctional, if the employees hired are not capable of completing their tasks and find no pleasure in doing so either, or if there is no desire in the organization to innovate and reach out to the surroundings – in short, if the business practice is not working – the firm will soon be out of business. So, the argument derives from the internal value of the virtues of the practice and not directly on the (institutional) argument from the financial bottom line (Solomon 1993, 8, supports this kind of argument).

This usage or "borrowing" from MacIntyre's theory of practice and institution makes sense for developing a more complete theory of corporate responsibility. It resembles, to some extent, Habermas's distinction between lifeworld and system, even though Habermas is strict in the dismissal of the feasibility of business ethics as the corporation is deeply embedded within an amoral system. MacIntyre might be in full accordance with Habermas on this point, but Moore draws out an interpretation that makes sense. The weakness of Moore's argument, however, is that it does not fully account for how it is possible to defend the virtues of the benign business practice when the institutional framework of capitalist firms is usually so hostile to virtuous practice. The dualism that Habermas and MacIntyre relate to modern society and its division of labours under the rule of the capitalist economy is difficult to overcome and argue against. However, I think that Moore has succeeded in his argument to show that as a matter of fact, it does make a difference as to how influential people within and outside of the organization exert their virtues (or vices). Some organizations are more successful than others in this regard, and this is often thanks to the efforts made by such virtuous individuals (Brennan 2012).

Leaders and Virtues

It is, therefore, less surprising that the character of the leader is in focus in much recent literature on leadership and corporate responsibility. Leaders are the heroes in many conceptions of corporate responsibility, and much lies on the shoulders of leaders to succeed in establishing not just practices of virtue within the organization but also an institutional framework that sustains it over time. In the leadership literature, Bernard Bass has proposed that leaders must exemplify an authentic moral kind of leadership, making them capable of attracting followers in the organization. Such leaders are transformational and can move an entire organization from one place to another (Bass & Steidlmeier 1999). They are often also charismatic leaders who people look up to and want to identify with. The problem with such leaders is that they can often be manipulative and hence corrupt an entire organization, causing a corrosion of its character (Sennett 1998). Kirkeby (2008) makes a helpful distinction between the manager and the leader, where the former is the archetypal, old-fashioned director of the company based on the theory of scientific management. And the latter is a modern type of co-operative leader who has inculcated virtues and can make a sound judgment of the situation. When the leader has to make tough decisions, the tendency to backslide into old-fashioned dictatorial management is critical. So, there is a general challenge for virtue ethical accounts that are supportive of corporate responsibility to explain how it is possible for virtuous leaders to sustain their moral capabilities and preserve character in times of hardship. Solomon argues that in business, *toughness* can be a particular business virtue (1993, 213–216). Toughness is similar to the Aristotelian virtue of courage.

In business, the general list of Aristotelian virtues is valid (e.g., temperance, magnificence, truthfulness, and justice). Justice is an ultimate value in corporate life according to Solomon (ibid. 231), but the basic business virtues are honesty, fairness, trust, and toughness. The first four of these virtues are needed to make co-operation work and hence to make the corporation a favourable partner in business. In that sense, the virtues are basic and valid in any social co-operative context, business included, and this is what is reflected in Moore's argument as well. However, one virtue stands out as odd: *toughness*. Solomon mentions that toughness as *perseverance* is key in business but is also often misunderstood to be callousness or indifference (cold-heartedness). Toughness is needed when the market gives you setbacks, even though you gave it an effort and provided a good service. It insulates against weakness of the will, as Aristotle warned against as well (*akrasia*). Toughness should not be confused with being smart or able to negotiate in a persistent way because this is a skill that one can obtain without holding the virtue. Importantly, toughness entails emotionally painful consequences as it can be necessary to do "something wrong in order to do what is right" (ibid. 214). The problem of *dirty hands* known from politics showcases that the leader must often face difficult dilemmas (ibid. 215). Even though it is painful, it can be necessary to let good employees go simply because this is what the situation requires. As such, toughness is a problematic and difficult virtue because it must surface in dire circumstances when opinions are divided about the proper thing to do. Toughness may even require that the leader sacrifices him- or herself, so toughness has no necessary connection to self-interest and can better be seen as an altruistic virtue (ibid.). In empirically based research, there is some evidence that leaders can succeed in internalizing moral values to face up to difficult situations and dilemmas (Skubinn & Herzog 2016).

Solomon's addition of toughness to the virtues might seem controversial. Conceding that toughness is a term with a particular American significance that cannot easily be translated into other languages, Solomon might have a point but a point limited to the American business context. It is less plausible that toughness can be considered a virtue as such in, for instance, a Scandinavian setting, where norms of leadership tend to reflect less individualistic and more democratic forms of governance. However, if taken to mean *perseverance* or *courage*, it makes sense to say that this is a virtue one needs to have to develop the virtues in general and thus a personal character in which the virtues become a habit (*hexis*). So, it seems problematic to argue that perseverance is a virtue mostly, or only, needed in the world of business – life in general cries out for such a virtue, one might argue. But Solomon is right that perseverance and courage have their own names in the particular practice that business is, and toughness surely is common parlour in some business quarters.

Epistemic Injustice Inside the Business Organization

Key to establishing a supportive culture in the organization for the virtues to flourish is leadership. However, equally important is that the employees, leaders included, are skilled at communicating with each other. In the theory of social virtue epistemology, Miranda Fricker proposes a theory about *epistemic injustice* (Fricker 2007). The theory focuses on speaker–hearer situations in the *credibility economy*, where prejudices such as gender or racial stereotypes distort communication and are therefore harmful to individuals who are rendered less credible than they deserve. In particular, Fricker is seeking to cast light on the hearer side of communication to reveal how important it is for a virtuous hearer to have the right epistemic skills and virtues in place. The practical backdrop for epistemic injustice goes along with the saying that we hear what we want to hear. And much of philosophical epistemology considers abstract notions of propositions and truth value of the speaker as detached from actual epistemic practice. Moreover, there is a bias in much social epistemology to forget about power relations and how epistemology connects with ethics. Fricker discusses a case based on interviews in the corporate world in her book about a woman who experiences that men do not listen to her when she is in a meeting.

> One Egyptian women, working in Cairo, said that when she is at a meeting and wants to make a suggestion about policy, she actually writes down the suggestion on a little piece of paper, surreptitiously passes it to a sympathetic male colleague, has him make the suggestion, watches it be well received, and then joins in the discussion from there.
>
> (Fricker 2007, 47)

According to Fricker, the underlying prejudice against the credibility of women as speakers of truth is harmful to the Egyptian woman in this example. She experiences what Fricker calls *testimonial injustice*. The defective epistemic virtues are most clearly discovered in such cases where discrimination and prejudice are obvious (at least to the outsider). Less clear are cases where a speaker is seen as less credible than deserved but for no obvious reason that can be attached to the speaker as a person. For instance, the organizational hierarchy distributes roles and powers of decision-making among employees. These are both formal and informal. Some of the roles are expert roles and rely on employees having special epistemic insights in their fields of expertise. If generalist leaders do not show sufficient acknowledgment of expert speakers based on identity prejudice (e.g., gender), they fail as epistemic hearers and can damage the virtuous practice of expertise in the organization. The credibility of speakers is also dependent on the status of role of the speaker, rendering lower-positioned employees less credible compared to higher-placed employees, all other things being equal. The problem for creating a supportive culture for the virtues is if such biases rig communication in the organization and this rigging is unknown by employees. In such a case, the organization will fail at being a responsible corporation, according to the virtue epistemological account.

Other reasons that cause epistemic injustice in organizations are ideological and can concern the structural and political contexts of the organization. Elizabeth Anderson (2012) proposes supplementing Fricker's individualist account with a structural account in which the cause of epistemic injustice is found in the pervasive structures of society that prevent particular speakers from being heard sufficiently or at all. The problem in structural injustice is not reducible to identity prejudice that the individual hearer suffers. Rather, the problem concerns the distribution of power in society at large. Anderson favours an epistemic democracy that gives each an equal saying or vote (ibid. 172). However, the business organization is not a public space to be governed by democratic rules, as such, and hence remedies are needed to compensate for structural epistemic injustice within organizations. Anderson suggests that "[i]n employment contexts, for example, structural remedies to prevent employment discrimination include institutional requirements that hiring, firing, and promotion decisions be based on explicit, objective measures rather than subjective assessment" (ibid. 168). Hence, according to Anderson, it is important that there are "institutionalized principles" that ensure "giving hearers enough time to make unbiased assessments, this is what it is for the organization itself to be testimonially just" (ibid. 169).

Even though this is an abbreviated presentation of epistemic injustice with regard to organizations, I think it is clear enough how the theory is relevant to understanding the underpinning of corporate responsibility and how questions of epistemic injustice have the potential to be further developed in research and practice.

I have included the somewhat foreign concerns of epistemic virtues in this chapter about virtue ethics and business. The main reason for taking the epistemic issue into account is that it reveals the impact of the problem if the internal affairs (practices to remain in the language of virtue ethics) of the corporate organization are dysfunctional. The strength of virtue ethical business approaches is the ability they have to insist on the pivotal role of the micro level: how significant the thinking and behaviour of the employees and leaders are. If a theory about corporate responsibility is to be grounded in the life of an organization, virtue ethics contributes with helpful theory. A theory of corporate responsibility detached from the virtues and the inner life of organizations, and questions of leadership and virtuous communication, remains an abstract notion with little motivational content and little relevance for practitioners in the field.

My main objection to the virtue ethical account is that it is too critical about liberal ideas of individual rights. Somehow, these concerns get lost in the unfolding of the virtue ethical story. I do not think that liberalism is incompatible with virtue ethics. In fact, any political ideal would need the virtues to be realized. And therefore, a comprehensive theory of corporate responsibility, if it aims at being feasible for business practice in a liberal society, must also consider virtue ethics. But, it should also seek to balance the inherent conservatism of virtue ethics. Thus, the social liberal corporation needs the virtues to be realized, but simultaneously, it also needs to safeguard individuals' rights, and therefore it is in tension with a virtue ethical conception of corporate responsibility.

References

Anderson, E. (2012) Epistemic justice as a virtue of social institutions. *Social Epistemology*, *26*(2), 163–173

Aristotle (1976) *Ethics: The Nicomachean ethics*. Translated by J. A. K. Thompson. London: Penguin Books

Aristotle (1997) *Politics*. Translated by Peter L. Phillips Simpson. Chapel Hill: The University of North Carolina Press

Bass, B. M., & Steidlmeier, P. (1999) Ethics, character, and authentic transformational leadership behavior. *The Leadership Quarterly*, *10*(2), 181–217

Bennedsen, M., & Van der Heyden, L. (2010) *When MBAs meet Henokiens: What can we learn from long-lived family firms?* Working paper, Insead

Brennan, J. (2012) For-profit business as civic virtue. *Journal of Business Ethics*, *106*(3), 313–324

Ciepley, D. (2018) Can corporations be held to the public interest, or even to the law? *Journal of Business Ethics*, 1–16

Flew, A. (1976) The profit motive. *Ethics*, *86*(4), 312–322

Fricker, M. (2007) *Epistemic injustice: Power and the ethics of knowing*. New York: Oxford University Press

Kirkeby, O. F. (2008) *The virtue of leadership*. Copenhagen: Copenhagen Business School

MacIntyre, A. (1985) *After virtue – A study in moral theory*. London: Duckworth

MacIntyre, A. (2016) The irrelevance of ethics. In A. Bielskis & K. Knight (Eds.), *Virtue and economy: Essays on morality and markets*, 7–21. New York: Routledge

McDowell, J. (1979) Virtue and reason. *Monist: A Quarterly Magazine Devoted to the Philosophy of Science*, *62*(3), 331–350

Melé, D. (2009) Integrating personalism into virtue-based business ethics: The personalist and the common good principles. *Journal of Business Ethics*, *88*(1), 227–244

Moore, G. (2005) Corporate character: Modern virtue ethics and the virtuous corporation. *Business Ethics Quarterly*, *15*(4), 659–685

Sennett, R. (1998) *The corrosion of character: The personal consequences of work in the new capitalism*. New York: W. W. Norton & Company

Skubinn, R., & Herzog, L. (2016) Internalized moral identity in ethical leadership. *Journal of Business Ethics*, *133*(2), 249–260

Solomon, R. C. (1992) Corporate roles, personal virtues: An Aristotelean approach to business ethics. *Business Ethics Quarterly*, *2*(3), 317–339

Solomon, R. C. (1993) *Ethics and excellence: Cooperation and integrity in business*. New York: Oxford University Press

Solomon, R. C. (2003) Victims of circumstances? A defense of virtue ethics in business. *Business Ethics Quarterly*, *13*(1), 43–62

5 Market Liberalism, the Firm, and the Market Failures Approach

Ever since Milton Friedman's famous rejection of CSR in the *New York Times Magazine* article "The Social Responsibility of Business is to Increase its Profits" (1970), the market liberal's view – in which I include that of current libertarians – has been a recurring source of dispute. According to Friedman, the state should not interfere with the free market, except to hinder criminal activities such as fraud and collusion. Corporations, on the other side, should not take on state responsibilities for social welfare or the environment. The problem with corporate responsibility, according to Friedman, is that it not only turns the corporate manager into a civil servant doing the job of the welfare state but one that is badly informed and incompetent in doing it (Friedman 1962, 134). More seriously, it also violates stockholders' legitimate and lawful property rights. This is assuming that owners have invested capital to get maximum returns and that CSR projects by definition will detract from profits. Hence, the fiduciary responsibility of the manager to the owners of the corporation is sidestepped by CSR. Managers who pursue CSR projects seek their own (private) interests at the expense of the owners. In literature on corporate governance of the firm, the potential conflict of interest between managers and owners is framed as the *principal–agent* problem (Jensen & Meckling 1976). Managers have control over the corporation, and stockholders want to ensure that managers exercise this control in their interest. Stockholders and their property rights are the primary ethical concerns for Friedman. This is often neglected when Friedman is portrayed as a cold-hearted and neoliberal critic of corporate responsibility and a defender of unbridled and inhuman free market forces. Actually, Friedman also cares about the free market, but his main concern in the rejection of CSR is corporate structure and the principal–agent issue.

In this chapter, I will approach market liberalism and corporate responsibility from three perspectives. First, I will discuss the notion of the corporation as market liberals see it. This is basically a dispute about whether the corporation or the firm is best seen as a market in itself or if it has an existence and type of governance over and above the market.

The question about the theory of the firm is critical to market liberals as they prefer to see it as an aspect of the market and not as a non-market entity in itself. Second, I will provide the outline of a market liberal typology of CSR theories to illustrate the variety of theories available currently. The distinctive feature of market liberal theory is its emphasis on the *voluntary* aspect in being responsible for reflecting the value of *individual* liberty (Friedman 1962, 13; cf. Brennan 2012b). And, the divisive feature among varieties of market liberalism can be seen in the differing commitment to the *separation thesis* (Freeman 1994, 412), which claims that economics and ethics are separate issues. Even stakeholder theory, in some versions, although critical about the separation thesis, is compatible with market liberalism in its emphasis on voluntariness. Last, I will discuss the view of the market entertained by market liberals as they have wide-ranging confidence in the market's ability to solve social and environmental problems. To do this, I introduce and discuss the market failures approach, as developed by Joseph Heath. This approach remains committed to the market liberal view that markets are competitive games that allocate resources in effective ways, but it also departs from amoral views of the market that render market activities value neutral in the sense that the separation thesis claims it should be.

Market Liberalism and Theory of the Firm

Friedman's economic theory of the market belongs to the Chicago school of neoclassical theory, later associated with neoliberalism, although Friedman did not subscribe to this contested term nor to an excessive libertarian marketization of the public sphere, for example, in his defence of public state-funded schools and basic social welfare (Friedman 1962, 1966). The ideal theory of the free market, according to Friedman, would allocate resources in the most efficient way as Adam Smith also alluded to by the metaphor of the *invisible hand*, which was later relaunched by Friedrich Hayek as *spontaneous order* – both are key theoretical references for Friedman. Hence, he holds an idealized view of the market in which free buyers and sellers meet on a *voluntary* basis and make an exchange of goods for a price on which they have settled. As Joseph Heath mentions, due to the historical period Friedman belonged to, he did not consider market failures such as information asymmetries and market externalities such as pollution as serious problems (Heath 2014, 15). In fact, Friedman was convinced that the capitalist free market produces wealth, but it also makes the individual politically free. The link between economics and politics is strong, and a free society is conditioned by the chance individuals have to exercise their freedom in the market. Friedman and the Chicago school considered the social democratic regulation of the market and the economics of John Maynard Keynes underpinning public expenditure and the regulation of the market as an infringement on liberty (Friedman 1962, 11). The market is, in most cases, the best arbiter to allocate resources effectively and certainly much more adept than a centralized planning economy of the state. Thus, the idea that business ethics should provide some soft regulation of the market is considered critical to effectiveness and liberty and on a par with taxation of the firm and "unadulterated socialism", according to Friedman (1970, 253).

The neoclassical Chicago school, therefore, provides the theoretical backdrop for understanding Friedman's libertarian view of the firm (Heath et al. 2010). As already mentioned, his main concern about the corporation is that it is a *private* and *free enterprise* (Friedman 1962, 14), but with regard to the internal affairs within the corporation, he considers it to be "an instrument of the stockholders who own it" (ibid. 135). The legal fiction of the corporation separates ownership from control, which might endanger the stockholder's interest, as stated in the theory of the principal–agent. Friedman does not oppose the separation of ownership and control, but if managers pursue corporate responsibility at the expense of stockholders and without their approval, Friedman does admit that this is a bad consequence of the separation of ownership and control (ibid.). Friedman's view of the firm, by adherence to the primacy of stockholders, is placed somewhat squarely between Ronald Coase's theory of the firm and Jensen and Meckling's *nexus of contract* view. According to Coase (1937), the firm is perceived to be an alternative to a market transaction only if the type of direct authority exercised in a firm is more cost-effective compared to a market transaction. Hence, the firm is justified on the grounds of economic outcome effectiveness operating by the logics of management and hierarchy. Jensen and Meckling take Coase's theory of the firm one step further and argue that the firm is a nexus of contracts among individuals, and thus "the 'behavior' of the firm is like the behavior of a market; i.e., the outcome of a complex equilibrium process", which renders ideas about the objective of the firm or CSR "seriously misleading" (Jensen & Meckling 1976, 311).

Arguably, Friedman subscribes to the principal–agent view of the firm, or some sort of paternalism rendering the stockholders, to be the morally responsible parents of the company. His theory of the firm in that respect can be argued to be different from the prevailing economic theories. However, because owners are in the business for profit, according to Friedman, and usually not with "ulterior" motives of doing good, his theory resembles Coase's theory with regard to the admission of authority of the principal over the agent. But it also resembles Jensen and Meckling's theory of a nexus of contracts by conceding that principals voluntarily enter into contract with agents to create a firm. Abraham Singer, in his reading of Friedman's position on the theory of the firm places him in opposition to the prevalent theories of economics and law (Singer 2016, 99). Friedman opposes anti-trust policy and theory of corporate governance and business ethics, and – according to Singer – this is due to his commitment to the principal–agent view:

> The underlying claim that Friedman asserts – since he does not really offer an argument for it in the 1962 or 1970 pieces – is that the very idea that the corporation is a "structure" is nonsense. For Berle and Means the modern corporation represented the dissolution of liberal and individualistic ideas of property, in which to own means the ability to control, and therefore created new forms of power. For Friedman, this development was not anything new or revolutionary. The corporation was not a new system of property, but simply an arrangement where some people worked for others. Put simply, it is a principal-agent relationship.
>
> (ibid. 112)

Principals, in Friedman's view, are free to contract with agents and cannot, with regard to this contract, be constrained by concerns of business ethics and the rule of corporate governance. They are free to go about maximizing their economic interests in contracting with agents (managers). This, however, does not rule out that principals should not comply with ethical custom and the law. There are basic normative limits to contracting. Besides this, there are no duties beyond the law and basic ethical conduct of not cheating or manipulating.

But Friedman considers ethical duties to be explicitly *private* individual ones (Friedman 1962, 12, 134). So, there is nothing in the notion of ethical duties that Friedman opposes other than the idea that there are corporate social responsibilities that can be translated only as being an agent's moral duty to deliver profits and be loyal to the interests of the principals.

The Separation Thesis and Degrees of Market Liberalism

From the previous section, it should be clear that Friedman considers corporate responsibility to be a subversive doctrine to capitalism and hence to political liberty. But it is less clear to what extent Friedman considers the corporation as on a par with the market or whether he would also endorse a view of the corporate unit being independent from the market. The contracting between principal and agent presumably occurs within the market, but does this entail that the corporate unit is, *in toto*, an instance of the market? Answering this question has consequences for market liberal stances in business ethics and on the issue of corporate responsibility because those who defend the corporation as an example of the market tend to also believe that there are no corporate responsibilities because the market is a norm-free sphere (Gauthier 1982). Those who oppose this believe that even though the corporation acts on the market, it is still different from the market being a sphere of managerial authority (which does not follow the rules of the market, although some believe it ought to) and also a sphere of meeting among stakeholders (Freeman 1994). Friedman is not so easy to place here, and I would argue that in fact, he is usually portrayed as belonging to the market camp, although he should more likely be placed somewhere between (or beyond) the camps. His adherence to the principal–agent view of the firm can be seen as a concession to non-market concerns such as the ethical concern of where an investor should place his or her money. On the other hand, Friedman certainly would not allow the manager to sidestep duties to owners by taking the interests of other stakeholders into account. This reading of Friedman gives rise to the question about market liberalism and whether or not ethics is part of the market. Some market liberals would be happy to concede this, whereas others would oppose it. Thus, I suggest a typology of a range of market liberal views of how far ethical concerns can be compatible with the market. I call them libertarians because they all see the market as a means to achieve liberty and wealth, but they differ in their views on corporate responsibility.

1. *Super-libertarians*: The market is a *norm-free zone*. This conception would deny that corporate responsibility makes sense or is justified because it projects ethics onto the market, which is wrong. Super libertarians will argue that perfect markets of free competition are the most efficient means to create wealth in society. Moreover, they perceive the corporation as an instance *of* the market, a nexus of contracts, and not as a separate unit in itself (Gauthier 1982; Jensen & Meckling 1976).
2. *Principal–agent libertarians*: The market is an ideal system of exchange, and as such, it is norm free and an instrument to achieve collective and individual wealth, *but* individuals can freely pursue and promote their *private ethical* preferences as buyers and sellers if they want to. The corporation is dependent on the market and must obey the rules of the market to survive. However, the corporation is also an autonomous sphere; at least it is directed and controlled by managers by means of non-market instruments (management authority and hierarchy). And, the corporation is a private arrangement between the principal and the agent. Hence, stockholders will rule but also wrestle with managers for control. CSR is rejected based on the claim that it is in conflict with the principal's interest and it is also a subversive doctrine in a liberal society (Friedman 1962, 1970).
3. *Moderate libertarians*:

   a. *Stakeholder and contractualist libertarians*: The market is infused with ethics and values and is not a norm-free zone. The market is an expression of free choice and collaborative ventures among individuals and collectives in a liberal society. They believe in free collaboration among stakeholders, often illustrated by use of philosophical contract theory, and consider this to be the constitution of the firm. Hence, moderate libertarians endorse corporate responsibility in some form. This position ranges from instrumental views of ethics (Porter & Kramer 2011) to those who argue for ethical constraints on contracting (Freeman 1994; Donaldson & Dunfee 1994).

b. *Market failure-correcting libertarians*: This category is moderate because it also sees the market as infused with values, but the market failure-correcting libertarians also believe that the market suffers from imperfections, which they aim to correct. Market failures regard skewed competition, information asymmetries, collusion, and negative externalities such as pollution as imperfections of markets. Hence, not only the government but also corporations are argued to have a corporate responsibility to counteract and avoid market failures. They are moderate libertarians because they believe in the need for business ethics in the corporate sphere, although they also believe that markets should not be regulated beyond the correction of market failures. Moreover, they believe that the corporate agent is not simply an instance of the market but rather is best seen as an autonomous unit separated from the market. They subscribe to the principal–agent theory of the firm (Heath 2014; Brennan & Jaworski 2016).

The typology allows for a variety of market liberalisms/libertarianisms with regard to understanding corporate responsibility. Admittedly, I am not certain that stakeholder theorists (Freeman 1994), the contractualists (Donaldson & Dunfee 1994), or those proposing a shared value-creation approach (Porter & Kramer 2011) will agree that they are libertarians in the common understanding of this word (see, e.g., Jason Brennan 2012a). And, certainly there are huge differences with regard to normativity and the tradition of theory they adhere to among these theories lumped together in category 3. The influential typology or mapping of CSR theories suggested by Garriga and Melé (2004) does not use the market liberal typology. So, the typology suggested here differs significantly from mainstream views expounded by CSR researchers. The justification is to provide a political philosophical perspective on corporate responsibility, and hence the CSR theories can be distributed in new categories. However, the point of mentioning them and placing them in this category merely serves the purpose of showing that market liberalism comes in degrees and cannot be reduced to the view of Milton Friedman. The aim is not to give an account of those theories here but to illustrate a point they have in common. I assume that they will all agree to be champions of the liberal understanding of the market and in this regard consider themselves as market liberals if not libertarians. With the further qualification that there are degrees of libertarians, they would recognize their views as represented by the category. However, they differ on the view they have of corporate responsibility. The hard-core libertarians in categories 1 and 2 reject it, whereas the moderates of category 3 allow it or go further and promote it, as the stakeholder theory does. Now, the reason for their differing views of corporate responsibility regards both the view of the market (as either a norm-free zone or morally infused) and the view of the corporation (as either an example of the market or an autonomous unit). Those who combine the norm-free zone view of the market with the corporation as an example of the market view are therefore the most hard-core deniers of corporate responsibility.

It is possible to review this typology of market liberalisms in the light of the *separation thesis*. According to Freeman, "The discourse of business and the discourse of ethics can be separated so that sentences like, 'x is a business decision' have no moral content, and 'x is a moral decision' have no business content" (Freeman 1994, 412). The varieties of market liberalisms suggested here differ in their allegiance to the separation thesis. The views of the super and the principal–agent libertarians can be seen as committed to this thesis. Conversely, the moderate libertarians will not agree that a business decision has no moral content. Of course, it could be argued that even Friedman would not endorse the separation thesis as he thinks a corporation should comply with ethical custom (not committing fraud) and that managers are in fact ethically bound to shareholders. But as corporations, there are no social responsibilities according to Friedman (besides maximizing profits for the shareholders; cf. Sandberg 2008, 222). The separation thesis is used by Freeman to show how meaningless and ethically unhelpful the contrasting of the shareholders' interests with those of the stakeholders are. He argues in a liberal pragmatist vein inspired by Quine, Dewey, Rorty, and the late Rawls that "we can tell many more, and more interesting, stories about business" (ibid. 410). So, being a defender of stakeholder theory, Freeman rejects the stalemate situation that the separation thesis elicits. This means that he opposes "stories which depict the firm as either (1) the private property of owners; (2) the necessary arrangements if we are to maximize the greatest good for the greatest number; or, (3) the result of a voluntary contracting process, all appeal to the Separation Thesis to rule out certain effects of the firm on other stakeholders" (ibid. 415). This involves a Rortyan *redescribing* of the corporation because "we cannot divorce the idea of a moral community or of a moral discourse from the ideas of the value-creation activity of business" (ibid. 419). Freeman considers this an ad hoc approach to solving problems, and therefore the stakeholder theory is deliberately vague on some key aspects of how it can be considered a version of market liberalism as suggested in this chapter (Sandberg 2008 is critical about the inherent vagueness of Freeman's critique of the separation thesis). Because Freeman subscribes to the late Rawls and political liberalism, there is a link to market liberalism in the moderate sense of including concerns for social justice. Nonetheless, the lesson to draw is that the separation thesis can be used to describe the hardliners of market liberalism but less so the moderate versions.

The Market Failures Approach

Among moderate libertarians (as I call them), the market failures approach to business ethics proposed by Joseph Heath is particularly promising in my view. And, I will explain why after giving a short presentation of this approach. The main idea is to assign moral duties to firms for upholding fair market conditions. These are quite demanding duties. The duties are thought to be related to the market in an ideal conception (the standard view dating back to Adam Smith's invisible hand). And, hence the duties are not owed to the corporation's stakeholders as is typically assumed in theory of CSR. This elicits duties such as the following:

> Minimize negative externalities (e.g. pollution), compete only through price and quality (e.g. avoid misleading advertising), reduce information asymmetries between firm and customers (e.g. if consumers are not experts about the technology of the product), do not oppose regulation aimed at correcting market imperfections.
>
> (Heath 2014, 37)

The reason why Heath constrains the list of duties to those that counter market failures is because he considers the market as capable, in its ideal version, to actually solve problems such as pollution from corporations and the exploitation of consumers. He also admits that the market is never perfect, and this is a reason for discharging duties on market agents to comply with the "rules of the game". Heath furthermore agrees that if a corporation in the real world unilaterally respected the duties, it "would be quickly eliminated from the marketplace" (ibid.). To defend the approach as relevant in the context of real competition, he derives a distinction between moral obligations and justification for noncompliance. If every other competitor firm exploits market imperfections (as many do), the firm on Heath's account still has a duty to seek to correct market failures – Heath here gives a reply to Jason Brennan (2016), who raises this objection. For instance, they can engage in industrial networks of collaboration to raise awareness of and promote respect for the rules of the capitalist game (ibid. 38). So, these are positive duties to be discharged by the corporation.

Heath is referring to *fair play* in his analogy between the rules of sports and the market, which share the feature of being adversarial (competitive) games. According to Heath, business ethicists are much opposed to this analogy because they perceive the market as corrupted by powerful firms and therefore, by definition, in need of being corrected – either by means of government regulation or by voluntary corporate ethics such as CSR policies and business codes (ibid. 6). Hence, Heath's position is market liberal as it highlights the positive aspects of the market for business ethics and corporate responsibility and does not participate in the widespread rejection of the market as the key cause of all problems. To carve out the details in Heath's argument, he maintains that the price mechanism is necessary to ensure effective allocation of goods in society. And, profits are earned by firms when they deduct costs from the price (where taxes are part of costs). According to standard economic theory, market agents are motivated by rationality and self-interest, which translates into the incentive to maximize profits. However, the conflation of self-interest and profits is a problem in the context of the firm. Because corporate responsibility is exercised by managers within firms, the responsibility they have is to maximize profits for the owners, regardless of the manager's own self-interests. Hence, in the corporate context, on this account, there is no simple association between a manager's self-interests and profits (ibid. 25). So, even though the profit motive is identical with the self-interest of the stockholders (assuming they are investing for that sole reason), it does not follow that a manager's self-interest is profit maximizing according to this description of the firm because managers have motives that might counter profits, such as concern for their own careers. Heath, therefore, is subscribing to Friedman's principal–agent theory of the firm in his understanding of what business ethics and corporate responsibility is about. Heath provides another argument from analogy to support the principal–agent ethics he wants to base business ethics on: In the legal context, the lawyer is duty bound to defend the client with all legal means available, regardless of whether the client is guilty. This is the rule of the legal game, and the reason for considering it ethically justified is because it is a central feature of the rule of law in a well-ordered state. Similarly, the agent must "defend" and serve the interest of the stockholder to comply with the liberal capitalist rules of the game (ibid. 28).

According to Heath, there are three profit-maximizing strategies, of which the first is the *acceptable* (lowering price and improving quality), the second the *immoral* (pollution and deceptive advertising), and the third the *illegal* (fraud, theft, and false advertising) (ibid. 35). Friedman is in accordance with the general categories suggested by Heath, even though he does not, at least in his writing, believe that pollution is a serious problem. The question is whether this categorization of corporate responsibilities regarding profit maximization is exhaustive of possible corporate duties. The mentioned duties tend to be mainly *negative* ones of avoiding polluting or advertising deceptively. Heath is quite optimistic about the sufficiency of the negative duties to avoid undermining the market:

> In my opinion, if all companies fully internalized all costs, and charged consumers the full price that production of their goods imposed upon society, it would be impossible to make the case for any further "social responsibility" with respect to, for example, the environment.
>
> (ibid. 36)

Hence, there is nothing inherently wrong with the market as such, although the market cannot solve all kinds of problems that concern the public. It could be that the market in Heath's sense (which is the idealized version that neoclassical economy subscribes to) could mitigate carbon emissions. But it is not evident that the market is an effective means to actually solve the problem of climate change. Considering that climate change has been argued to be the greatest example of a market failure in history (Stern 2007), it is difficult to see how the market is capable of self-correction to the extent of solving the climate crisis. Similar difficult issues such as gender discrimination, poverty, exploitation, and not to mention the provision of genuine public goods such as basic social welfare, basic medical treatment, and education, and so on are hard cases that the market failure approach would need to provide feasible answers to.

Nonetheless, the market failures approach to business ethics, if one accepts the claimed attractive and benevolent features of the market, does provide a productive theory for a market liberal (re)construction of business ethics and corporate responsibility. The theory might be critical about the stakeholder conception due to its internalist focus on the principal–agent relationship. But it is not a *debunking* theory like Friedman's theory often is, and to some degree unfairly, assumed to be. In fact, Heath suggests onerous prescriptions for businesses to follow. In that sense, the theory is ambitious and a real challenge to the kind of social liberal theories that I would defend with reference to the idea of the social liberal corporation. So, the challenge for the market failures approach is to give an account of the possible duties a corporation might have towards its stakeholders that are not created by market interaction but arise from other kinds of relationships: political and ethical, for instance. It seems to be a real challenge for Heath to avoid the super libertarians' claim that excessive exploitation is permissible because exploitation is not easily definable in terms of the market. For instance, the exploitation of sweatshop workers can be caused by non-market structural factors (Zwolinski 2012; Brennan & Jaworski 2016). In what sense is sweatshop exploitation, given that it can be defined as infringing on basic human rights, for instance, to be seen as an example of a market failure? Maybe such cases are to be taken care of by the state, and thus the state should ensure that the rules of the market are fair and not exploitative. However, if so, then the market failure approach has no remedy for cases of non-market caused exploitation. I return to the issue of exploitation in Chapters 8 and 9.

So, if the market liberal relies on the state to intervene and set the rules of the game to solve difficult issues such as exploitation, it follows that market liberals are in dire straits when the state is too weak, illegitimate, or absent. The next chapters devoted to social liberal views of corporate citizenship and political CSR dispute the assumption that the state sets fair rules of the market. In fact, oftentimes the state is absent and duties fall on non-state agents such as corporations and civil society to compensate for government failure. This is now addressed in the next two chapters.

References

Brennan, J. (2012a) *Libertarianism – What everyone needs to know*. Oxford: Oxford University Press

Brennan, J. (2012b) For-profit business as civic virtue. *Journal of Business Ethics*, *106*(3), 313–324

Brennan, J. (2016) Morality, competition, and the firm: The market failures approach to business ethics by Joseph Heath (review). *Kennedy Institute of Ethics Journal*, *26*(1), E-1–E-4

Brennan, J., & Jaworski, P. M. (2016) *Markets without limits – Moral virtues and commercial interests*. New York: Routledge

Coase, R. (1937) The nature of the firm. *Economica*, *4*, 386–405

Donaldson, T., & Dunfee, T. W. (1994) Toward a unified conception of business ethics: Integrative social contracts theory. *Academy of Management Review*, *19*(2), 252–284

Freeman, R. E. (1994) The politics of stakeholder theory: Some future directions. *Business Ethics Quarterly*, *4*, 409–422

Friedman, M. (1962) *Capitalism and freedom*. Chicago: Chicago University Press

Friedman, M. (1966) The methodology of positive economics. In *Essays in positive economics*. Chicago: University of Chicago Press

Friedman, M. (1970, September 13) The social responsibility of business is to increase its profits. *The New York Times Magazine*, 122–126

Garriga, E., & Melé, D. (2004) Corporate social responsibility theories: Mapping the territory. *Journal of Business Ethics*, *53*(1–2), 51–71

Gauthier, D. (1982) No need for morality: The case of the competitive market. *Philosophic Exchange*, *13*(1), article 2, 41–54

Heath, J. (2014) *Morality, competition and the firm – The market failures approach to business ethics*. Oxford: Oxford University Press

Heath, J., Moriarty, J., & Norman, W. (2010) Business ethics and (or as) political philosophy. *Business Ethics Quarterly*, *20*(3), 427–452

Jensen, M. C., & Meckling, W. H. (1976) Theory of the firm: Managerial behavior, agency costs and ownership structure. *Journal of Financial Economics*, *3*(4), 305–360

Porter, M. E., & Kramer, M. R. (2011, January–February) The big idea: Creating shared value – How to reinvent capitalism – And unleash a wave of innovation and growth. *Harvard Business Review*, *89*(1–2), 62–77

Sandberg, J. (2008) Understanding the separation thesis. *Business Ethics Quarterly*, *18*(2), 213–232

Singer, A. A. (2016) *The form of the firm: A critical and normative account of the corporation*. PhD thesis, Department of Political Science, University of Toronto. https://tspace.library.utoronto.ca/handle/1807/73167

Stern, N. (2007) *Stern review: The economics of climate change*. Cambridge: Cambridge University Press

Zwolinski, M. (2012) Structural exploitation. *Social Philosophy & Policy*, *29*(1), 154–179

6 Republicanism and Corporate Citizenship Theory

First Aspect of the Social Liberal Corporation

This chapter and the next are devoted to the political approach to corporate responsibility within the broader family of social liberalism, or *left* liberalism, if compared to market liberalism as right-wing liberalism. In the present chapter, the focus will be on corporate citizenship theory (Moon et al. 2005), and the next chapter will take up the deliberative democratic approach to corporate responsibility called *political CSR* (Scherer & Palazzo 2007). In different aspects, both chapters provide the grounding for what I have called the *social liberal corporation* because the orientation in those political approaches is supportive of – and also an expression of – social liberalist political theory. They both have a normative stance on the question of rights as they support liberal democracy and take issues of social justice into consideration. Moreover, they are friendly critics of the market and can therefore be seen as liberals who want the market to be regulated to avoid market failures. As social liberalism is mostly a theory about the state, the suggestion that corporations should be part of the social liberal purview is controversial. Rawls and Habermas, who are both supporters of social liberal views with regard to the market, exclude the corporation from the moral scope of their theories as seen in Chapter 2. However, both the theory of corporate citizenship and political CSR challenge this scope restriction. Crane et al. (2008, 32) argue for a *reconfiguration* of citizenship because today it is both transformed and shaped by corporations. Corporations are influential actors, not just on the market but also in the sphere of civil society. Similarly, the theory of political CSR builds on Habermas, despite the dismissal of corporations in his political philosophy (Scherer & Palazzo 2007).

The idea of the social liberal corporation defended in this book *is* therefore mainly based on what the theories of corporate citizenship and political CSR argue. However, I will suggest that a few shortcomings need to be addressed to provide a more solid foundation for the social liberal corporation. These shortcomings are regarded to be the contested premise of weak state governance shared by both theories, the claimed ability of private corporations to provide public goods, and the tendency of proponents of political CSR to abstain from normative justification by relying on theories of metaphors and pragmatism. These concerns should be addressed by the theory of social liberalism applied to the corporation, and I will give some provisional responses in the next two chapters as to how the shortcomings could be addressed. Admittedly, these issues are all comprehensive issues that pertain to any theory of corporate responsibility, so I do not pretend to have final answers to solve these issues. However, I try to make it clearer in my reading of social liberal theories how they could defend themselves and give replies to their critics. The social liberal corporation is not a fully defined theory of corporate responsibility but rather an outline that needs to build on the premises provided by the theorizing found mainly in corporate citizenship and political CSR literature. This may sound too weak and defensive, but considering the widespread disagreement about, and distrust of, any notion of corporate responsibility, I believe this is the level of ambition appropriate for the task at hand.

Before returning to the social liberal corporation (in Chapter 7), here follows first my reading of and commentaries to corporate citizenship theory as a key aspect of the social liberal corporation. My reading seeks to tease out the more philosophical features and questions of corporate citizenship and thereby aims at bridging between the more philosophical readings and the mainstream conception in business and CSR literature.

Corporate Citizenship and Republicanism

The republican tradition of emphasizing the importance of political participation, leading back to Aristotle's notion of virtue ethics of citizenship as the capacity for *ruling and being ruled* is pivotal to the kind of corporate citizenship proposed by Andrew Crane et al. (2008, 201). Corporations, besides their economic role in sustaining a competitive market, also play a political role in society. The political role is usually conceived of as lobbyism – *corporate political activity* – but the perspective of corporate citizenship theory is different. Corporate citizenship theory does not deny that firms are often involved in politics as lobbyists that seek to influence regulation in their own interests. However, the variety of political roles adopted by corporations can better be understood through the lens of corporate citizenship eliciting a normative view on corporate responsibility. For instance, the republican perspective sees the firm as committed to the notion of the *common good*:

> While corporations normally are willing to participate in governing when it is in their self-interest . . . a republican perspective would ground the normative basis of citizenship in participation that is enacted for the common good, even if it is not in their immediate self-interest. Indeed, under this model, a "corporate citizen" would

> be expected to readily and actively participate in lobbying and governance for the civic good across a reasonable span of its operations and influence.
>
> (Moon et al. 2005, 440–441)

The normative imperative to work for the common good is sufficiently clear to distinguish corporate citizenship theory from the market liberal imperative of Friedman's "to maximise profits". What the common good is, however, is not made entirely clear by proponents of corporate citizenship theory, besides a general reference to the republican idea of *res publica*: what is of concern to the public as opposed to the merely private. Moon et al. (2005) argue that corporate concern for the common good, for instance, means that corporations should not curtail regulation of carbon emissions designed to curb climate change nor regulation that protects consumers from the health risks of their products (ibid. 441). In that sense, the moral perfectionism is quite minimalistic and is primarily concerned with negative duties not to harm. I will return later in Chapters 7 and 10 to the related idea suggested by corporate citizenship theory and political CSR that corporations should provide for *public goods*.

The notion of citizenship traditionally has two aspects. One is republican and concerns civic duties of participation in the political process and of being a good citizen acting out of civic duty (ibid. 440). The other aspect is liberal and concerns the rights and entitlements the individual citizen enjoys. Both republican and liberal notions of citizenship are typically conceived of as membership of a nation state. Cosmopolitan citizenship, as suggested by the stoics, ascribe this status to any individual independent of national belonging, and the resurgence of cosmopolitan political theory is also embraced by Crane et al. (2008) in the admission of global corporate citizenship. A main reason for the resurgence of citizenship as a topic in political philosophy can be traced to the political atmosphere of post-Cold War optimism about liberal democracy in the 1990s. In political philosophy, the debate between communitarianism and liberalism ended in a stalemate, and republicanism appeared attractive in its ability to connect the concern for community and individual rights; hence, republican citizenship reconciles individualist liberalism with liberal nationalist communitarianism (Kymlicka 2002, 284). Republican political theory has been further developed, for instance, by Philip Pettit (2010) arguing for republican freedom as non-domination. The upshot of notions of citizenship (and deliberative democracy) in the business ethics literature of the 2000s therefore reflects the mainstream of political theory in the 1990s and the optimism associated with a belief in the supremacy of liberal democracy and free markets to alternative political regimes. Crane et al. (2008) do not directly consider this context as motivating their suggestion to choose a republican theory and citizenship as their key approach. They acknowledge the attractiveness of the republican tradition in itself and then dedicate their efforts to connecting the notion of citizenship to the corporate sphere instead. This connecting is controversial, for obvious reasons, and the proponents have some reservations in their method and approach to cater for this challenge of connecting.

The Corporation as Citizen, Government, and Stakeholder Arena

According to the trio, Moon, Matten, and Crane – here taken as proponents of the corporate citizenship theory – there are three key roles for the corporation to adopt with regard to citizenship: First, corporations can *be like citizens*; second, they can *function like a government or state*; and third, they *can be a community or an arena of stakeholders* (Crane et al. 2008).

Corporations can be seen as similar to ordinary citizens because they too enjoy the right to own property, have freedom of expression, and have a duty to pay taxes. Moreover, they also actively engage in politics by lobbying or participating in developing policy together with a public administration or with a nongovernmental organization (NGO). Corporations are also influential as sellers of goods and services that have strong political impacts such as infrastructure, banking, and social media. For instance, a media outlet like a newspaper decides which political views it wants to promote and which to suppress and thus acts like a politically engaged citizen. However, this is merely a comparison with ordinary citizens, and corporations are also different because they do not enjoy all rights of citizenship. For instance, they do not have the right to vote in public elections, nor can they campaign for public office. Furthermore, corporations are not assumed to be morally comparable to ordinary citizens either because they are not seen as having a moral conscience or the capacity for feelings of empathy – they cannot fully qualify to be moral agents and hence also do not enjoy human rights (see also Chapter 3 for a discussion about corporate moral agency). However, the point of employing the lens of citizenship to understand corporate political involvement is to highlight *the fact* that corporations do behave like ordinary citizens in a surprising number of ways. Therefore, the citizenship lens also provides insights into the political aspects of corporate behaviour that the comparable theory of CSR is missing.

> Like the term "legal person", that of "corporate citizen" is designed to draw our attention to thinking about corporations in other ways than simply as a nexus of contracts, intermediaries between demand and supply, and makers of profit and losses and so on.
>
> (Crane et al. 2008, 8)

Corporations acting citizen-like therefore are more morally and politically minded creatures compared to the market liberal view of the corporation that for instance, Friedman suggests. However, if one admits that the type of citizenship corporations qualify for is merely a quasi-citizenship, a *metaphor*, how can the status of normativity be understood? Do corporate citizens have a real moral duty, and not just a metaphorical one, to act citizen-like? The answer seems to be affirmative. Moon et al. state, "The concept of citizenship is appraisive", and "thus . . . would not be a value-free description" (Moon et al. 2005, 434). And further, corporate citizenship entails "certain conditions" to be respected and "certain obligations to be met" (ibid. 448), rendering corporate citizenship an approach that "goes beyond a mere voluntaristic view of CC [corporate citizenship]" (ibid.) so "that all people affected *should* be treated as bearers of rights and responsibilities, or, as *if* they were citizens" (Crane et al. 2008, 9).

In particular, the rejection of corporate responsibility as *voluntary* makes corporate citizenship normatively demanding and places it in opposition to the widespread view that because CSR is "beyond the law", how to respond must be at the discretion of the corporation. Its non-voluntarism also is in contradiction to the instrumental market liberal views of corporate responsibility. Corporate citizenship, therefore, is normatively demanding by suggesting seeing an analogy between the duties of individual citizens and corporations (ibid. 47). The tension with market liberal views makes it clear that critics see corporate citizenship as too normative and demanding and not in tune with the profit motive as a predominant feature of the corporation (Whelan 2012). Critics from the left, however, blame corporate citizenship for its inherent tendency to cover up the realities of the market in the pursuit of ideology (Edward & Willmott 2008; Fleming & Jones 2013).

Even more controversial than seeing corporations as citizens is the suggestion that *corporations can function like a government or a state* (Matten & Crane 2005). In situations of state failure, the corporation can be a substitute for the state and take care of "the administration of a bundle of . . . citizenship rights – social, civil, and political – conventionally granted and protected by governments" (ibid. 166). These are the kinds of rights a social liberal would also endorse. So, although the approach is republican, it is also an endorsement of social liberal rights. This is seen in the explicit reference to the social liberalist T. H. Marshall's idea of citizenship rights (ibid. 170).

Therefore, the corporation *as government* is not itself a citizen but an enabler and provider of features related to citizenship. Matten and Crane explicitly, and surprisingly, take a stance that is purely non-normative and descriptive to this phenomenon (ibid. 170, 174). They give no reason for this, and this leaves the reader of corporate citizenship theory with some confusion about whether or not the theory is normative. However, because all three mentioned authors are explicit about the normativity inherent to corporate citizens in their joint work in 2005 and 2008, I assume that this is the right understanding. It could be that the reason for adopting the descriptive approach with regard to the government role that corporations can take is that the corporation is, in this context, not a citizen-like actor itself but rather provides for other citizens to enjoy this status. Furthermore, given the fact that the neoliberal privatization and marketization of public services has engendered much controversy, it can be difficult to outline the proper role for corporations with regard to being a quasi-government. Corporations can have this role in many possible ways that they did not intend, and Matten and Crane also refrain from guessing about the motivation behind corporations taking over the administration of citizen's rights, although they "suggest a range of motivations might be evident, from altruism to enlightened self-interest or plain self-interest" (ibid. 173). What is clear enough from the descriptive stance is that globalization has caused the nation state to weaken with regard to securing citizens' rights: "Our premise is that corporations enter the arena of citizenship in circumstances where traditional governmental actors fail to be the 'counterpart' of citizenship" (ibid. 171). This premise can, of course, be contested, and it has been (Djelic & Etchanchu 2017).

Matten and Crane do specify three ways of how government and corporation shift roles: "(1) where government ceases to administer citizenship rights, (2) where government has not as yet administered citizenship rights, and (3) where the administration of citizenship rights may be beyond the reach of the nation-state government" (Matten & Crane 2005, 172). These are equivalent to the three tenses – past, present, and future governance of citizenship rights – and they show the variety of ways that the state leaves a governance gap for corporations to fill. Moreover, there are three degrees of taking over from government: Either the government is *absent* and there is no administration of rights, leading to a governance vacuum; or corporations *substitute* for government by taking over all administration; or corporations merely *complement* government administration (Crane et al. 2008, 10).

Regarding the first example of ceasing to administer rights, the case of funding the welfare state under pressure from global competition and lower wages abroad is instructive. In fact, corporate citizenship can be incurred by welfare reform and the privatization of welfare goods such as education and public health. However, there is also a difference between corporate citizenship as an outcome of privatization of the public sector and situations in which there has been no deliberate intention to leave rights administration to private corporations. Hence, it is wrong to imply that corporate citizenship is a foreseeable outcome of neoliberalism, although it can be, in the case of welfare reform. The second and third examples of *not yet administering* and *beyond the reach* might apply to cases such as privacy protection on digital social media, protecting citizens against harms from climate change, or securing their human rights. In these cases, corporations can be called on to fill governance gaps where the state in incapable.

Finally, besides acting like a citizen or a government, the corporation can also facilitate an *arena of stakeholders as citizens*. Corporations, for instance, can offer the public a space for realizing the political rights of freedom of expression and community. Initially, Facebook perceived its role as an arena for users to participate in expressing their opinions, which could be positively framed as an online democracy. Also, the enabling of consumers to buy fair trade products or the facilitation of pension savers to divest and avoid investment in fossil fuels are examples of corporate citizenship as arenas. And, corporations can make workplaces arenas for employees' citizenship. Hence, corporations can facilitate, enable, or block access to citizenship rights due to the power and influence they have. Because liberal democracy is currently under pressure globally, the demand for corporate citizenship to provide democratic arenas is presumably on the rise. Moon et al. (2008, 8–9) contend that corporate citizenship is generally called for due to "political systems that are variously unrepresentative, unresponsive, illiberal or centralised where there is no rule of law or independent judiciary". The idea of citizenship as an arena is built on stakeholder theory. It therefore reflects the view that organizations are not autonomous entities in control of their surroundings. Rather, seeing an organization as an arena invites different metaphors of the network or co-creative venture. When this is the case, it can be more difficult for the corporation to ensure that processes are also conducted in a responsible way because there is a lack of control in such processes, as evidenced by the more recent history of Facebook and the failure to protect its users from being exploited and its infringement on their right to privacy of personal information.

In addition to the three aspects of corporate citizenship (corporations as citizens, governments, and arenas), there are other ways that citizenship is reconfigured. Citizenship is also shaped by culture and *identity politics*, which concern the rights of women, minorities, and marginalized groups. For instance, the LGBT movement's involvement in corporate activities is a case in point (ibid. 128). Moreover, the example of *ecology* raises difficult questions about how to include the environment into the essentially anthropocentric notion of citizenship. I will return to this question with regard to climate change in the final chapter.

In the next chapter on political CSR, the idea of corporate citizenship as arena is addressed by Scherer and Palazzo (2007) through the perspective of deliberative democracy.

Corporate Citizenship in Need of Clarification?

Corporate citizenship has been argued to need further clarification. One aspect of the need for clarification is the definition of the scope of corporate citizenship, what criteria must be satisfied for an agent to be a corporate citizen, or whether the notion would be better abandoned because it does not add to older concepts such as stakeholder theory and CSR (Van Oosterhout 2008). There seems to be a consensus in the literature that corporate citizenship can be understood as *minimalist* – typically requiring corporations to only comply with the law and be philanthropic – versus the *maximalist* understanding, which requires far more from corporations in terms of engaging in corporate social responsibility activities, taking care of negative externalities, and observing how they engage in lobbyism (Néron & Norman 2008a). The term *citizenship* also evokes different connotations with regard to political history as it can be understood as either *bourgeois* or *citoyen* (Aßländer & Curbach 2014). The bourgeois is the private citizen who can act in the market to pursue self-interests, whereas the citoyen is bestowed with a status in political society reflecting not only citizenship rights but also a duty to contribute to the public good. The sort of corporate citizenship referred to in the literature considered here certainly reflects the citoyen aspect of citizenship. But the question is whether liberal citizenship as bourgeois, which is the kind of citizenship institutionalized in most nation state conceptions, challenges the understanding of citizenship in the business ethics literature.

Nonetheless, the aim of seeking clarification is also in regard to the justification of corporate citizenship. As mentioned, Moon et al. (2005) claim that the citizenship of corporations is merely a metaphor. But to what extent are corporations then citizens? Moon et al. refer to Gareth Morgan's metaphor theory of organization to argue that corporate citizenship is a metaphor for "community membership and participation" (ibid. 433). Furthermore, the usage of this metaphor can involve the risk of transferring problematic understandings from politics to business organizations. Moon et al. concede that this must be so because the notion of corporate citizenship is already *essentially contested*. It satisfies the criteria, originally proposed by Gallie, for essentially contested concepts: The concept must be *appraisive* and *internally complex*, and "their rules of application are relatively 'open'" (ibid. 434). Corporate citizenship is surely something to be appraised – it is internally complex because it links up with other features of the corporation and its activities, and there are no clear rules of application either. However, Moon et al. defend the contested notion of citizenship by referring to T. H. Marshall's understanding of the concept as an "image" that activities can aspire to and be measured against (ibid.). This is the *ideal theory* interpretation of corporate citizenship. However, there is also a more *pragmatic* understanding of justification at stake to complement the idealist aspiration. According to Néron and Norman (2008b, 64), corporate citizenship as a concept "might improve our chances of encouraging a community of scholars and citizens to think about a range of normative and political issues. This is a pragmatic justification that is also overtly political".

And, the pragmatism alluded to also finds expression in the openness of rules of how corporate citizenship can be applied in practice because corporations "combine roles which might in other contexts appear incompatible" (Crane et al. 2008, 13). They can be economic profit maximizers and still also take norms of citizenship into consideration. This gives the impression that the pragmatist spirit can turn into a relativist understanding, as for instance in the following longer quote:

> Rather than acting like a lens, citizenship offers a kaleidoscopic view of the corporation that helps to reveal different characteristics at different times and for different purposes. Corporations are not citizens, they are not governments and they are not arenas of citizenship – but in some respects, and under certain conditions, there is a close enough resemblance to each for us to be able to consider corporate roles and responsibilities in new and at times quite powerful ways. We suggest that ultimately this prefigures the need for a redefinition of the corporation to take account of its ambiguous political role.
>
> (ibid. 202)

Hence, the role of being a corporate citizen is *ambiguous* and involves difficult dilemmas. This is the price for seeing the corporation as a political actor, but would not the normative aspect, if taken seriously, require corporations as citizens to choose the moral side in difficult situations? It seems as if Crane, Matten, and Moon want the theory to remain descriptive to encompass the plurality of situations real business faces and at the same time provide normative guidance to solve moral dilemmas in real situations.

In the next chapter on political CSR, the question of justification is discussed to further develop the prospect of justifying the social liberal corporation.

References

Aßländer, M. S., & Curbach, J. (2014) The corporation as citoyen? Towards a new understanding of corporate citizenship. *Journal of Business Ethics, 120*(4), 541–554

Crane, A., Matten, D., & Moon, J. (2008) *Corporations and citizenship*. Cambridge: Cambridge University Press

Djelic, M. L., & Etchanchu, H. (2017) Contextualizing corporate political responsibilities: Neoliberal CSR in historical perspective. *Journal of Business Ethics, 142*(4), 641–661

Edward, P., & Willmott, H. (2008) Corporate citizenship: Rise or demise of a myth? *Academy of Management Review, 33*(3), 771–773

Fleming, P., & Jones, M. T. (2013) *The end of corporate social responsibility – Crisis and critique*. London: Sage Publications

Kymlicka, W. (2002) *Contemporary political philosophy – An introduction.* 2nd edition. Oxford: Oxford University Press

Matten, D., & Crane, A. (2005) Corporate citizenship: Toward an extended theoretical conceptualization. *Academy of Management Review, 30*(1), 166–179

Moon, J., Crane, A., & Matten, D. (2005) Can corporations be citizens? Corporate citizenship as a metaphor for business participation in society. *Business Ethics Quarterly, 15*(3), 429–453

Néron, P., & Norman, W. (2008a). Citizenship, Inc. do we really want businesses to be good corporate citizens? *Business Ethics Quarterly, 18*(1), 1–26

Néron, P., & Norman, W. (2008b) Corporations as citizens: Political not metaphorical: A reply to critics. *Business Ethics Quarterly, 18*(1), 61–66

Pettit, P. (2010) *Republicanism – A theory of freedom and government.* Oxford: Oxford University Press

Scherer, A. G., & Palazzo, G. (2007) Toward a political conception of corporate responsibility: Business and society seen from a Habermasian perspective. *Academy of Management Review, 32*(4), 1096–1120

Van Oosterhout, J. (2008) Transcending the confines of economic and political organization? The misguided metaphor of corporate citizenship. *Business Ethics Quarterly, 18*(1), 35–42

Whelan, G. (2012) The political perspective of corporate social responsibility: A critical research agenda. *Business Ethics Quarterly, 22*(4), 709–737

7 Political CSR and the Second Aspect of the Social Liberal Corporation

Following the argument from corporate citizenship, this chapter further develops the idea of the corporation as a political agent – thus contributing to the political theory of the firm in general and the idea of the social liberal corporation in particular. The theory of political CSR (or PCSR) was coined mainly by Andreas Scherer and Guido Palazzo in a series of articles (especially 2007, 2011). Their approach is close to corporate citizenship in the sense that political CSR also views the corporation as a political actor with the ability to act morally in certain situations. Often, this is expressed in the alleged move from the stockholder firm to the appearance of the stakeholder firm, that is, a democratizing of the corporation (Freeman 1994). However, political CSR is not stakeholder theory as it is concerned with the complex political processes of globalization, political governance, and regulation, in particular multi-stakeholder processes along the supply chain, where the corporation takes the lead in enacting governance and regulation (often as soft law, such as the Forest Stewardship Council, the UN Global Compact, John Ruggie's UN guidelines for business and human rights, the Protect, Respect and Remedy framework, and similar initiatives). The basic premise for the position is the assumption, shared with corporate citizenship theory, that the state has been weakened due to the pressures of globalization. In this situation, civil society, NGOs, social media, critical citizens, employees, consumers, governments, and politicians can act collectively to exert pressure on corporations to help solve social and environmental problems. The moment the corporation responds to such pressures by entering into a public dialogue, it becomes *entrapped* in an argumentative process of democratic deliberation (Scherer & Palazzo 2007, 1111). This process leads to a more optimistic interpretation of corporate responsibility as resembling deliberative democracy. The view is controversial for several reasons, not least due to the normatively ambitious level of expectation towards business corporations. Political CSR also challenges commonly shared assumptions of the political arena, which qualifies for deliberative democracy and do not usually consider private business organizations as suitable partners in deliberation (Sabadoz & Singer 2017). Moreover, as shown in Chapter 2, Habermas's political philosophy would not allow corporations to be legitimate agents of deliberative democracy. Hence, the project of political CSR is controversial in the sense that it, as a self-pronounced Habermasian theory, not only opposes Habermas's own understanding but also the taken-as-given market liberal understandings of the corporation.

In this chapter, the focus is on political CSR as a social liberal theory devoted to promoting liberal democracy, and hence it provides an important argument for the idea of the social liberal corporation. The main aspect addressed will be the question of how political CSR can find justification in a theory of organization. As seen in the prior chapter on corporate citizenship, matters of justification are disputed. A weak justification referring to the metaphorical status of corporate citizenship seems in need of further support to render it a credible theory. In the case of political CSR, a similar challenge appears. Political CSR bases its justification on a reference to deliberative democracy, but the conception is pragmatist and avoids strong commitment to institutional and organizational levels. In this chapter, I will address this weakness in the theory to connect political theory to the topic of corporate moral agency (Chapter 3) and a system view of institutional embeddedness.

Hereafter, I turn to the notion of the social liberal corporation to draw out its main features and how the theories of corporate citizenship and political CSR provide support.

Connecting Political CSR and the Organization

In the literature on political CSR emanating from Scherer and Palazzo, what sort of organization is required to satisfy the theory of political CSR is seldom discussed. Part of the literature does raise this question, for example, by pointing out that *symbolism* in organizational theory fits with the political CSR concept (Heugens & Scherer 2010), criticizing the implicit neo-institutional premise (Banerjee 2010), arguing for decision-making procedures of corporate moral agency (Dubbink & Smith 2011), questioning corporate accountability (Hussain & Moriarty 2018), or revising the theory of the firm (Scherer et al. 2006). Proponents have suggested that the political CSR organization contributes to enacting regulation, that it provides public goods, and that it has an ability to be a democratic agent participating in and promoting deliberative democracy in society (Scherer & Palazzo 2007, 2011; Scherer et al. 2016; Scherer 2017).

However, the theory of political CSR suffers from a *paradox in its justification* because, on the one hand, it predicts that the nation state is subsiding, leaving a vacuum of governance for corporations (the shared assumption with citizenship theory), and on the other hand, this absence of institutions subsequently creates serious challenges as deliberative democracy needs a basic institutional framework to function. I, therefore, argue that given the systemic embeddedness of the political CSR organization, the democratic functionality of the wider political system must be taken into consideration as well because it will be insufficient if the wider systemic context does not provide the conditions for deliberative democracy. The systemic context is composed of the organization itself as well as the surrounding institutions.

As mentioned in the introduction to this book, there is a resurgence of debate on the nature and role of the corporation in political contexts and in political philosophy. The corporation has been interrogated from various angles, but the underlying question is whether or not such an organization can be accepted as a genuine political actor carrying a moral responsibility (Moriarty 2005; Heath et al. 2010; Ciepley 2013; Heath 2014; Landemore & Ferreras 2016; Orts & Craig Smith 2017; Hasnas 2018). The theme is redolent of earlier debates on corporate moral persons and corporate moral agency. In this chapter, I will take issue with an overlap between the philosophical debate on the theory of organization and current discussion on political CSR. In general, there is a research gap between the topic CSR/business ethics and organization theory, often based on the assumption that these are best approached as distinct areas of research. However, Heugens and Scherer in their review article "When Organization Theory Met Business Ethics" (2010, 644) state that "we believe that business ethicists could benefit substantially from closer liaisons with organization theory scholars". Helpfully, they point out that republican political CSR is best understood as being in harmony with a *constructivist* kind of organization theory (ibid. 648). In support of bridging between CSR/business ethics theory and organization theory, Frynas and Stephens (2015), in a comprehensive review of the literature on political CSR, make a plea for further integrating different perspectives of the micro, meso, and macro levels pertaining to organizational aspects of political CSR. Thus, this chapter is an attempt to follow up on these observations and recommendations to investigate further the particular connection between political CSR and the organization to answer the question: What sort of organization does political CSR require to fulfil the norms of deliberative democracy?

To grasp the connection between political CSR and organization theory, the link can be spelled out as a conditional, as in the formal sense of what are the *necessary* and *sufficient conditions* that must be satisfied for political CSR to be possible.

The necessary organizational conditions for the possibility of political CSR are assumed to be the basis of the theory, which are the following: corporations are contributors to the *rule making* of soft law, primarily in the international realm, due to the lack of state governance caused by the market forces of globalization; corporations also provide *public goods* in this situation; and corporations exhibit the ability to participate in and also promote *deliberative democracy* as envisaged by Jürgen Habermas (1994; Scherer et al. 2006; Scherer & Palazzo 2007, 2011; Scherer et al. 2016; Scherer 2017). Thus, these necessary conditions should be obtained as minimal requirements for the political CSR theory to be validated.

From these basic and necessary requirements, it follows, according to Scherer and Palazzo, that the *organizational capacity* to satisfy political CSR must exhibit the following abilities: The organization must have a democratic pluralist type of organizational governance, an organizational ability to manoeuvre in the void or grey zone between the public and private domains, and it must be accountable to relevant stakeholders defined and selected by a *social connection model* understanding of responsibility (Young 2006, 2011; Scherer & Palazzo 2011).

Moreover, these demands of political CSR theory posed to the organization are both descriptive/empirical and normative/ethical. The mixture of the descriptive and normative feature of political CSR is caused by its reliance on Habermas's deliberative democracy, which based normative legitimation on real support from civil society (cf. Scherer & Palazzo 2007; Scherer 2017).

Even when the basic requirements of political CSR's necessary conditions for organizations are satisfied – that is, the capacity for democratic governance and the ability to operate in the public-private sphere and relate to stakeholders selected by a social connection model – it could be questioned when *sufficient* conditions of political CSR are satisfied. Sufficient conditions should be satisfied for political CSR to be fully possible. Perhaps, however, it is possible that no theory of corporate responsibility, as a *non-ideal theory*, can expect to have all its conditions satisfied in the real world of *business*, and one must therefore settle with the partial satisfaction of having some or most of the necessary conditions fulfilled. Only examples of ideal theory in the Rawlsian sense (Rawls 1994) can find such confirmation of the complete satisfaction of criteria because they operate in the context of normative theory, whereas in the more realistic non-ideal domain of CSR theory, it is – by definition – less easy to confirm that all criteria have been met. A main objection of political CSR theory is that the normative ideal of deliberative democracy is simply too far from the reality of private business corporations ruled by the profit motive (Sabadoz & Singer 2017). This objection is addressed later.

However, given that the basic necessary conditions of political CSR theory have been fulfilled, what is meant by sufficient conditions? Let me give the main example that I have in mind: What if the organization is democratized according to deliberative democratic values but operates in an *undemocratic* social and political context? Even though this seems to be the situation that Scherer and Palazzo have predicted for the typical MNC in the age of globalization, when the rule of law and robust democratic institutions are absent in many parts of the world – not to mention the examples of failed regulation of climate change and migration witnessed in fairly well-ordered societies – the theory of political CSR seems to presuppose that the social political context of institutions is viable for democratic deliberation, hence resulting in the paradoxical situation previously mentioned above. It seems as if Scherer and Palazzo presuppose that the kind of organization favoured by political CSR theory is embedded in, or maybe even extended into, the wider social and political context of a society amenable to deliberative democracy.

However, the belief that the global context is benign for deliberative democracy, even in the modified sense, could be an echo of the post-political optimism of the 1990s, when liberal democracy seemed to be the most likely end station of political history. In the survey and update article on political CSR 2.0 (Scherer et al. 2016), however, it is conceded that political CSR needs to reconsider this optimism about democracy in light of the rise in anti-liberal nationalist politics, populism, and religious fundamentalism. What this means for deliberative business organizations is not answered by the proponents of political CSR 2.0, but it is fair to argue that these currents of global politics pose serious challenges to the realism of political CSR theory (cf. Anker 2017). One bold conjecture in the defence of the future of political CSR could be that anti-democratic developments in world politics merely intensify the politicizing of the corporation, and that the normative bar for democratic deliberation should be raised even higher to ensure that democratic deficits are compensated for by corporations.

Assuming this to be a likely conclusion to draw about political CSR's criteria for the organization, it invites questions about the limits and nature of such an organization that will be addressed at the end of the chapter through the consideration of a *systems* view of the organization, elucidated in recent works by Banerjee (2010), Hussain and Moriarty (2018), Sabadoz and Singer (2017), and Djelic and Etchanchu (2017).

Before addressing the wider political and systems context of political CSR organizations of sufficient conditions (the ideal theory so to speak), I will first present the basic layout of how political CSR perceives organizations, that is, their necessary conditions.

Democratic Pluralism of Organizational Governance

A first step in clarifying and reconstructing the possible connection between political CSR and the organization is to look for sources in the literature that address the organization as a democratic community exhibiting a pluralist culture and governance. As mentioned, Heugens and Scherer (2010) suggest that political CSR belongs to the "symbolist" and "constructivist" paradigm in organizational theory (ibid. 648). Philosophically, constructivism is opposed to realism, and thus a pluralist outlook can be seen as more compatible with constructivism because – according to realism – facts of the world are merely given truths beyond the human capacity for making judgments. Constructivism allows for human judgment to decide what is true and what is not, allowing some space for justified disagreement about the facts. The kind of democratic pluralism that political CSR commits to therefore requires an epistemology that allows for a multiplicity of judgments to be truth apt. A main reason for holding pluralism as a credible epistemology is due to the fallibility of human rationality – it is unlikely that one person alone holds the truth. Rather, truth is the outcome of a collective process of questioning and mutual openness for critique, that is, ideally what should happen in a democracy, epistemically speaking (cf. Rawls 1994 about the burdens of judgment).

In constructivist organization theory, the theory of "sensemaking" (Basu & Palazzo 2008) is prevalent. Sensemaking as epistemic constructivism is the process whereby a person projects perceptions and assumptions onto the world and thereby enacts a certain meaning of how things are. CSR can be seen as an enactment of sensemaking in which employees, managers, and consumers project their ideas of what corporate responsibility is onto the organization and its stakeholders. If rigid frames and ideas dominate the sensemaking process, it is myopic and runs the risk of having so-called ethical blindness (Palazzo et al. 2012). Ethical blindness occurs when a person, for example, a manager in an organization, arrives at the organization with a myopic worldview (e.g., that business life is all about making money), and subsequently the organizational culture supports his view, making this view seem right. Even worse, if the surrounding society of the organization also supports myopic and intolerant views inherent in its political and moral culture, ethical blindness can become entrenched in an organization. Hence, for a democratic organization to succeed, it requires that individuals as leaders and employees have a democratic mindset and a social institutional context that supports deliberative democratic values. The impact of the social context on the ethical and democratic aspirations of organizations is significant (Gonin et al. 2012). Metaphorically, in the case of dysfunctional organizations, the relationships among the individual, the organization, and society are pictured as those among an apple, the barrel, and the larder. The problem is not the single rotten apple nor even the barrel (as mainstream organizational theory tends to imply). Rather, it is the larder (i.e., society) that is the ultimate problem:

> To help organizations enlighten their dark side and regain legitimacy in the eyes of the broader society, not only must the organizations change, but foremost the institutional framework on which they rely when defining their identity, objectives and behavior norms must also change.
>
> (ibid. 40)

So, for an organization to live up to political CSR or any other moral aspiration, the question of the institutional framework of the organization and its public legitimacy moves to centre stage. The organization is no longer passively decoupled and neutrally related to the surrounding society. It has a mission of promoting democratic values in the proximal environment of institutions in its sphere of influence, and it should seek support from broader society in executing this policy. The space that the organization occupies shows a dialectic. On the one hand, the organization is functionally differentiated as an independent unit of its own (bounded by features of an individual identity, legal status, and culture). On the other, the organization is also deeply integrated into its institutional surroundings and cannot be ultimately differentiated from its institutional context.

This brings up the question of the organization's place in the public-private dichotomy, which is another basic feature relevant to political CSR theory.

Political CSR, the Public-Private Distinction, and the Theory of the Firm

Political CSR (Scherer & Palazzo 2007, 2011; Néron 2010; Whelan 2012; Scherer et al. 2016; Mäkinen & Kasanen 2016) and theories of "corporate citizenship" (Matten & Crane 2005) dispute the standard liberal perception of the public-private distinction (and the underlying state-market distinction), according to which the sphere of the business corporation is purely private. As mentioned, both theories presuppose that the process of globalization has weakened the state and left a governance gap and a regulatory vacuum for other agents to address. In the wake of absent and weak states, the corporation takes over state functions like delivering health, education, and infrastructure to the public. According to Scherer and Palazzo (2011), the separation between a purely private and a public domain in society is under pressure, and the public demand for corporate responsibility can be seen as a sign of transgressions between the public and the private spheres. This description, however, is also valid for a neoliberal view, where the public administration is governed by the logic of the market and conversely the private corporation is politicized to provide public goods on a market basis. Civil society as a third sector is empowered by social media and NGOs and exerts a pressure on corporations to comply with stakeholders' needs. The rise in such multi-stakeholder types of governance (of the state, business corporations, and civil society organizations) makes the public-private distinction shaky – a business can act like an NGO or a state and vice versa. Hence, it is a basic requirement of the organization, according to political CSR, that it is sufficiently flexible and can manoeuvre beyond or in between the public-private spheres.

Current debates in political philosophy about the role and status of the corporation also address and question the purely private nature of the corporation (McMahon 1995; Moriarty 2005; Heath et al. 2010; Heath 2014; Anderson 2017). David Ciepley (2013), as mentioned in the introduction to this book, has argued that business corporations are not merely private institutions, but in fact they should be seen as *franchises of the government* because they are authorized by the state to own property and to contract and manage employees. And they have the state-granted privileges of *limited liability* and *entity shielding*. Ciepley is critical about the dichotomy between the private market and the public state in the case of the firm because it does not fit nicely into either of these two categories as a government franchise. A similar debate about the public-versus-private nature of the corporation is found in debates over workplace democracy (Landemore & Ferreras 2016; Anderson 2017) and meaningful work (Arneson 1987; Michaelson et al. 2012), where it is argued that the corporation has to adopt the political ideals of democracy, otherwise perceived as the domain of the state and civil society.

However, the public-private distinction runs deep in liberal political philosophy. The conventional area of political philosophy, at least since the 19th century, as seen in Chapters 1 and 2, includes the role of citizens, civil society, the state, and the market but not the corporation. The exclusion of the private business corporation from the domain of political philosophy was found, for instance, in John Rawls's definition of the basic structure of society in assessments of justice (1971). Similarly, Jürgen Habermas excludes the corporation from the realm of ethics as it belongs to the system of bureaucracy and the market (Habermas 1987). The Rawlsian and Habermasian rejections of the corporation as a genuine moral and political agent clash with recent developments in CSR, especially the theories of corporate citizenship and political CSR. Considering the *pervasive impact* of corporations on peoples' lives (Rawls 1971) and the fact that corporations are a significant part of the *system of co-operation* that produces goods for distribution (ibid.), it seems almost counterintuitive that Rawls excludes corporations from his theory of justice by denying them status as part of the main social institutions in society. The impact of business on people's lives provides an empirical argument against Habermas's and Rawls's exclusion of the corporation from their theories. Furthermore, since MNCs comprise the pillar of international trade and regulation, according to Nien-he Hsieh (2009) and Iris Marion Young (2006), the exclusion of the corporation from the purview of justice can be challenged, even on liberal grounds. So, on this account, the corporation and corporate responsibility should not be seen as merely private.

Thus, it is a basic requirement of the organization, according to political CSR, that it must be able to operate beyond or within the spheres of the public and private by creating partnerships with civil society organizations and, when required, by taking on the role of the state in solving social and environmental problems and providing public goods. Moreover, it must accept being the object of moral and democratic evaluation and critique – it cannot and should not escape such assessment by appealing to its private status as a corporation; it is a politicized kind of organization, and therefore it shares features with the public organization, which in a genuine democracy, is open for public contestation and critique.

The Social Connection Model

In the theory of political CSR, it is a basic premise that the scope of corporate responsibility with regard to the supply chain should be determined by the *social connection model* developed by Iris Marion Young (2006; Scherer & Palazzo 2011, 913). In her 2011 book, Young claimed that "for thinking about issues of responsibility and structural injustice, however, it seems helpful to focus on one system at a time rather than on global capitalism in general, so that actors can be identified along with their actions and how this might be altered" (133).

Young suggested the social connection model as an alternative to the legal and contractualist *liability* model, which determines responsibility for the supply chain according to responsibility for direct causal harm and, in her opinion, is individualist and backward looking, lacking the capacity for conceptualizing structural harms. Instead, Young proposes a *forward-looking*, collective, and preventive kind of moral responsibility that distributes a *political responsibility* along the supply chain to be carried by all complicit agents, ranging from the individual producers to retailers and eventually the consumer. Responsibility is therefore not only attributed to individual agents like the corporation but is a shared kind of responsibility in which the corporation participates. This moralized *social connection* view of corporate responsibility creates a situation in which the limits of corporate responsibility are not as easily settled as in the legalist liability model. The risk of letting the social connection model determine the scope of corporate responsibility is that critical NGOs, consumers, media outlets, and other agents gain a tremendous power to name, shame, and blame corporations. Hence, with the social connection model follows the risk that justified corporate responsibility cannot be separated from the currents of the populist mind. The boundaries of the corporation in terms of its scope of responsibility are, therefore, extended to the global level, and it is up to society at large to decide where the limit of responsibility is. So, the corporate organizational boundaries become volatile. The philosophical reason for restraint in the lack of scope can be traced back to Young's (and hence also political CSR's) dismissal of the contract as an appropriate model for delineating responsibility.

The outcome of political CSR can be seen in Schrempf-Stirling and Palazzo's (2016) use of the social connection model to highlight what they call *full producer responsibility*, which entails that corporations now become responsible for problems in the entire chain of production, sub-suppliers included. Hence, corporate responsibility is owed to agents with whom they have no direct contractual or legal responsibility.

However, the advantageous feature of the philosophical social contract is that it presupposes voluntary acceptance and therefore ensures that people entering it are relatively equal in knowledge and power. This entails that duties are acknowledged by subscription to the contract, and it is implausible that anyone would enter a contract that discharges duties without clear limits. The price of rejecting the contract is high, and it is difficult for the social connection model to provide an alternative to the contract in determining the limits to the duties a corporation can carry.

However, Young's pivotal point is that social connections are neither plainly global in scope nor confined to the individual nation state, corporation, or individual citizen. Young's position is better seen as a multi-level, many-tiered approach that runs across levels spanning the individual, the corporate, the nation state, and the global level. Hence, it is a shared responsibility, and duties are not unilaterally ascribed to individual corporations but are rather shared among many agents through the supply chain. I return to this question about the supply chain and matters of exploitation in the sweatshop in Chapter 9. The outcome for the political CSR theory and its organization adopting the social connection model to determine the scope of responsibility is critical. The organization seems destined to be pictured as a network of connections of actors involved in the supply chain – each being vulnerable to the ascription of duties to compensate for harms in the supply chain about which it did not necessarily have knowledge nor any control to prevent.

Political CSR and Levels of Justification

The basic necessary conditions of organizations to satisfy political CSR theory have been identified as democratic governance, operating in between the public and private spheres, and adopting the social connection model. However, the political CSR's method of justification and its appeal to philosophical theory is also relevant to understanding the connection with the organization. To get an overview of how corporate responsibility theories have justificatory levels, the representation that follows compares three levels (see Table 7.1): the political reality (empirical level), organization theory (science level), and philosophical theory (philosophical level).

Connecting political CSR to the organization can thus be seen as seeking justification by creating *coherence* among three levels: that of political reality, organization theory, and philosophical theory. I concede that the levels are not always possible or advisable to separate because claims about reality depend on theoretical perspective, and I would also assume

Table 7.1 Justificatory levels of CSR theory

	Social liberal		*Market liberal*	*Conservative virtue ethical theory*	*Neo-Marxist critique of ideology*
	Political CSR	*Corporate citizenship*			
Political reality	Absent states Corporations provide public goods and regulation Politicization of the corporation Multi-stakeholder	Absent states Corporations administer citizens' rights Privatization of public goods Stakeholder democracy	Rule of law exists Maximizing profits Shared value creation Stakeholder engagement	The good corporation Purpose driven Business virtues Excellence and leadership virtues	Corporations exploit and alienate Hegemony of the capitalist system Capitalist appropriation Commodification
Organization theory	Constructivism Symbolism Sensemaking	Metaphor theory	Rational choice Principal–agent	The virtuous corporation Anti-individualism Corporation as community	Critical management studies Discourse analysis
Philosophical theory	Deliberative democracy (Habermas) Priority of democracy to philosophy (Rorty)	Republicanism Citizenship theory (Aristotle)	Classical liberalism Utilitarianism Libertarianism Contract theory (Locke, Smith, Bentham, Friedman)	Virtue ethics Perfectionism Personalism (Aristotle, Aquinas)	Marxism (Marx)
Main objections	Contested organizational boundaries Contested public-private spheres Presupposes a benign democratic context	Corporations are not citizens Corporatization of the political sphere	Presupposes wrongly that the rule of law exists Amoral corporations	Romanticism about the organization and the virtues Needs individual rights and complex division of labour	Needs a positive theory of the corporation, e.g., cooperatives Needs an explicit normative theory of justice and ethics

that any scientific organization theory would not be possible without making some philosophical assumptions. Furthermore, to make theories true and valid, they should be able to describe and predict reality, at least in some minimalist sense.

My point in drawing attention to the justificatory levels, and political CSR in particular, is that the levels are often confused. In the case of political CSR, and corporate citizenship as well, it has been notoriously difficult to figure out when the theory is merely descriptive (about reality) and when it is prescriptive about what corporations ought to do according to a normative standpoint (Frynas & Stephens 2015, 3). For instance, when is political CSR a theory about lobbyism (corporate political activity), and when is it about a normative ideal of how corporations participate as legitimate political agents? According to a recent review article, Andreas Scherer makes it clear that political CSR is a normative theory but that it can also be used instrumentally. Moreover, he argues that any CSR theory should make its own value preferences explicit; there is no value-free CSR theory (Scherer 2017, 16). Due to the inherent complexity of how normativity, rules, institutions, and agents interact, political CSR is especially prone to creating confusion about levels of justification. And, I would add that CSR theories that aim at being normative are not explicit about what the normative standard for assessment is. There is a difference among being transparent about the values a theory subscribes to, employing normative theories like Habermas's deliberative democracy to theorize about corporate responsibility (without clear and explicit normative recommendations), and being explicit about how to do an assessment in practice by, for instance, offering a method or a normative standard applicable to practice. In that sense, little theory of corporate responsibility, although targeting practitioners as well, is easy to use in business. Being aware of the *levels of justification* issue raised here should be a bulwark against the inherent tendency to confuse and conflate the levels. So, how does political CSR seek justification from the philosophical level, considering Scherer and Palazzo's (2007, 1102) appraisal of Richard Rorty's dictum – *priority of democracy to philosophy*?

The "Priority of Democracy to Philosophy"

In their 2007 article on the political conception of CSR from a Habermasian perspective, Scherer and Palazzo explicitly reject a philosophical justification of the theory: "It does not start with philosophical principles but with a political analysis of the changing interplay of governments, civil society actors, and corporations, and the institutional and cultural consequences of that dynamic" (1098). This mirrors the commitment to a pragmatist justification that avoids philosophical foundationalism. This, however, does not mean that political CSR is avoiding philosophical justification; it merely signals that it avoids a particular kind of philosophical justification, that is, a foundationalist, presumably metaphysical, justification. This resembles Rawls's (2004) *political and not metaphysical* approach of political liberalism. Corporate responsibility should not be based on any religious, metaphysical, or moral comprehensive view but should be the result of a democratic decision procedure – in particular a consensus reached by means of public deliberation. This is what is meant by invoking the Rortyan dictum of the "priority of democracy to philosophy". By presenting corporate responsibility as deliberative democratic and thus *dialogical*, they create a stance to dismantle the competing so-called *monological* theories of business ethics, for example, Kantian, Aristotelian, and utilitarian theories (Scherer & Palazzo 2007, 1097).

By referring to deliberative democracy, political CSR also relies on *equality* as a foundational value because it presupposes that dialogue is not rigged by asymmetrical power relations between the corporation and its stakeholders. Moreover, it also presupposes, as Habermas does, that reason and the better argument should prevail in the dialogue (see also Chapter 2 on Habermas and discourse ethics). Both assumptions are stated as *normative yardsticks*: "[I]n the context of political CSR, the ideal conditions of a power-free discourse are rather taken as a normative yardstick for the democratic quality of existing regulatory activities of private actors" (Scherer & Palazzo 2011, 916). So, given that such norms are yardsticks for dialogue, the *priority of democracy* imperative must be understood as including deontic requirements of the ideal dialogue. This distinguishes the process in political CSR from competing accounts like those found in market liberalism, such as the instrumental stakeholder theory, which subscribes to voluntary agreements (Freeman 1994, 415, does rule out that normative Kantian stakeholder theory is completely voluntary but should rather account for fairness and Rawlsian impartiality). The difference then is between deontic political CSR and the voluntary contractarian approaches of market liberalism. This is a reason for seeing political CSR as an example of a social liberalism, or rights-based liberalism, in the Kantian tradition mediated by Habermasian discourse ethics and deliberative democracy.

As political CSR theory seeks to avoid contentious justification in deeper philosophical and metaphysical foundations, the "priority of democracy to philosophy" approach resembles the view endorsed by anti-perfectionist liberalism, the ideal of *liberal neutrality*.

According to John Rawls, liberals need not, and should not, base their liberal convictions on metaphysical or religious comprehensive doctrines (Rawls 1994). They should instead plead *neutral* about metaphysics and pursue a *method of avoidance* with regard to deep and contested justifications; that is, they should "apply the principle of toleration to philosophy itself" (Rawls 1985, 231). The reason for this advice is that deep metaphysical and religious views tend to create conflict and disagreements among people from different communities and cultures and therefore should be avoided in a liberal society where the ideal is a pluralist consensus based on basic liberal values such as basic human rights. According to the liberal neutralist view, the corporation as a political actor should not seek its own metaphysical foundation in a theory of the organization because this will only create division among its stakeholders and diminish legitimacy.

Moon et al. (2005) also seem to commit to liberal neutrality about justification when they emphasise that the personhood of corporate citizens is merely meant as *metaphorical* (see Chapter 6). We should not think of a corporate citizen as a real person capable of being conscious or having the capacity for a moral conscience and feelings of guilt. Citizenship regards only rights and duties assigned to the role of acknowledged individuality in a nation state and does not connect to deeper metaphysical justifications of moral personhood. So, from the viewpoint of corporate citizenship, there is a profound *discontinuity* between theories of corporate responsibility and metaphysical theories of the organization (cf. McMahon 1995).

However, I would question the discontinuity view held by corporate citizenship but also PCSR theory's commitment to liberal neutrality. It seems overly cautious to avoid philosophical justifications in the field of corporate responsibility because why should a theory about the metaphysics of organizations and the theory of corporate moral agency as has been explored in Chapter 3 evoke serious political disagreement or threaten the public legitimacy and support for corporations? People in general have strong feelings and often disagree about the metaphysics of political and religious ideas, but why should they have similar strong feelings about any philosophical justification *per se* and in particular the admittedly more theoretical philosophical theorizing about justifying corporations as morally responsible for what they do?

Moreover, a revival is seen in attempts to restate and challenge the discontinuity view of how business ethics connects to the philosophy of the organization. For instance, Lisa Herzog's *Reclaiming the System* (2018) challenges the Habermasian relegation of the corporation to the "amoral" system. Liberal neutrality and the avoidance of seeking deeper justifications and understandings of the organization, as seen in both political CSR theory's giving "priority of democracy to philosophy" and the metaphorical talk of corporate citizenship, need not block the road of inquiry to reach a better and more comprehensive understanding of the corporation and how it can be morally responsible.

After having discussed the basic features of optical CSR theory – the necessary conditions – I now turn to the *sufficient conditions* that an organization must satisfy to be deliberative and democratic, as political CSR wants it to be.

Democratic Systems and Political CSR

For political CSR to be feasible and realizable, it follows that the organizational context of institutions and the socio-political system is also capable of *democracy*.

Even though an organization might succeed in becoming internally democratized by fulfilling the minimal and necessary conditions demanded by political CSR theory, for example, by realizing workplace democracy (Michaelson et al. 2012), it will not be fully successful if the social and political context is undemocratic and not capable of deliberative democracy (Sabadoz & Singer 2017). However, why does the internal democracy of the organization depend on the outside context?

Take, for example, the firm operating with its own production facility in an undemocratic country. Consider that this firm is fully democratized from within. It has successfully made employees co-determinates in democratic decision-making, and it even seeks to promote the values of democracy and democratic institutions in the undemocratic society where it operates. However, according to the theory of political CSR, even though the firm can be described as deliberative and democratic, in particular due to its democratic aspirations, it still needs to *actually* succeed as a liberal democratic firm. Assuming that the employees are recruited from local communities where traditionalist authoritarian political values are inculcated, how can they truthfully participate in the democratic decision-making process of the firm? They would, at least, need some training and time to adapt to and internalize a culture of democracy. Moreover, it would not be easy for a firm to succeed in establishing deliberative democratic processes in this undemocratic society. Media would be under censorship, there would be no free choice of unions, and freedom of speech in general would be suppressed by the state. Human rights would not be protected by the local government, and it would be unadvisable to make partnerships with the authorities as this would lend them undesirable international legitimacy. This could render the corporation complicit in various harms as well.

Political CSR considers this to be a typical situation for the globalized corporation. Political CSR is designed to step in and provide answers for how corporations actually do and should act in situations of state failure and argues that corporations enter into multi-stakeholder collaboration and that this contributes to public rule making and to public goods:

> In a nutshell, political CSR suggests an extended model of governance with business firms contributing to global regulation and providing public goods. It goes beyond the instrumental view on politics in order to develop a new understanding of global politics where private actors such as corporations and civil society organizations

> play an active role in the democratic regulation and control of market transactions.
>
> (Scherer & Palazzo 2011, 901)

Political CSR theory argues that the corporation compensates for the state's failure to provide for regulation by filling out the *regulatory vacuum* (ibid. 900). Various motivations drive this process, ranging from instrumental economic reasons and soft law requirements to institutional pressures from civil society and global organizations.

However, for this prediction or argument to work, it requires that it is also possible that the political context is benign to deliberative democracy. Political CSR theory, I will argue, therefore presupposes an institutional and political context that is benign to deliberative democracy or at least open to a process of democratization. This interpretation of political CSR theory is in contrast to the core assumption that the corporation compensates for the absence of state regulation and governance. The absence of the state also translates into an absence of the rule of law. But the example of the democratic firm operating in an undemocratic society shows that absence of the rule of law could, in fact, be caused by an authoritarian oppressive state. The local state is absent from positively governing and securing the rule of law, but its absence can also lead to a negative presence in its oppression of the population.

For the political CSR theory to have successful predictive power, normatively as well descriptively, it must therefore presuppose that the local political system, where the corporation operates in collaboration with international society, can be compatible with a reasonable level of deliberative democracy.

Before considering whether the assumption of a democratically benign context is plausible, I will first consider the consequences it has for the boundaries of the organization to perceive it as contextually dependent.

The kind of organization that political CSR theory needs is destined to be caught in the flux among several poles of powerful attractors. On the one hand, it should manoeuvre between private individualist libertarian shareholder-maximizing market liberalism and public collectivist stakeholder-maximizing social liberalism. On the other hand, the organization should negotiate its legitimate boundaries by deliberating with the stakeholders of its social connections. However, such a process does not result in a clear-cut definition of organizational boundaries because these are constantly contested, challenged, and negotiated. Another way to phrase the situation of blurry organizational boundaries can be found in Heugens and Scherer (2010), who argue that the political CSR organization is best reconciled with the symbolist paradigm in organization theory, and therefore it is situated in the middle ground between modern and post-modern conceptions of the organization. The modern conception does not allow for democratic governance but prefers rational control and authoritarian governance of the managerial bureaucracy. The post-modern conception, conversely, is critical about power and domination and tends to imply that organizations are always in a state of flux (Morgan 1997). The symbolic conception of the political CSR organization carries features from both the modern and the post-modern organization. This explains why its boundaries are grounded in soft power and soft law and not in the modernist preference for causal mechanistic power and hard binding law. Modern organization theory prefers power that is clear and visible, whereas the post-modern organization is evasive about the existence of power; this type of organization drifts along with the forces of the process. Both organizational drifts are at stake in the political CSR organization's adherence to symbolism in the organization theory, if following Heugens and Scherer. Only legitimacy created by democratic deliberation will provide a stable equilibrium in the tension between the forces of modernist brute power and post-modern *noumenal* power (Forst 2015).

According to Djelic and Etchanchu (2017), the political CSR organization is, in fact, not as flexible as Scherer and Palazzo think as it is configured on the basis of the classical liberal distinction between the public and the private; hence, even political CSR falls short of distancing itself from instrumental CSR of the neoliberal kind. However, for the organization to be truly political and historically informed, political CSR theory should acknowledge that only if it is accepted that "business and state responsibilities are tightly interconnected, often blurred, difficult to disentangle, and always being negotiated . . . [could we] develop a more radical view of stakeholder democracy for the proper governance of business activities" (ibid. 658). Djelic and Etchanchu blame political CSR for presupposing the liberal distinction of the public and the private for the critique of instrumental CSR of the neoliberal kind (Friedman). However, in my reading of the political CSR theory, it may be true that it is partially historically neutral about the entanglement of business and state, but the theory actually predicts the kind of organization capable of radical deliberation with stakeholders that Djelic and Etchanchu are calling for. So, this objection misreads political CSR theory, on this account, I would argue.

What then is the positive vision of the political CSR organization if it embraces the *system view* of the organization as caught in a balanced flux between the forces of the political context?

The political CSR need for organizations to be a part of, or co-enacting, a political system amenable for deliberative democracy has sparked much debate in the literature on PCSR (Hsieh 2009; Banerjee 2010; Néron 2010; Dubbink & Smith 2011; Whelan 2012; Landemore & Ferreras 2016; Djelic & Etchanchu 2017; Hussain & Moriarty 2018). For instance, Hussain and Moriarty (2018) argue that political CSR should retreat from its promotion of corporate involvement in the political democratic process and thereby acknowledge that corporations are better seen as *functionaries* and not as *supervising authorities* (525).

In a recent critique of political CSR, Sabadoz and Singer (2017) claim that corporations are not an appropriate *forum* for deliberative democracy. Even when managers are genuine in their attempt to deliberate, the locus of the corporation is so fraught with the logic of competition and economy that norms of deliberative democracy will be curtailed. Instead, Sabadoz and Singer suggest that recent and more *pragmatic* versions of deliberative democracy that acknowledge *power asymmetries* and emphasise a *system view* could work better for political CSR (Mansbridge et al. 2013). If, for instance, the board consists of democratically well-qualified people, but these are also representative of people from a diversity of ethnic, religious, gender, and class backgrounds, they could promote deliberative democracy even when other parts of the organization would not be able to (ibid. 204). Lowering the bar for inclusion in the deliberative democracy by allowing representatives to deliberate on behalf of the organization is therefore one possible avenue for developing political CSR and the organization. There is nothing in Scherer and Palazzo's theory to deny a pragmatic understanding of political CSR. Rather, the opposite is true. Critics could argue that political CSR is a misapplication of Habermas's normative theory to the corporate sphere, and this is only possible because the normative bar has been lowered to fit actual practice. In that sense, Sabadoz and Singer's critique misconstrues political CSR as in need of further modification to fit into the practices of business.

Another suggestion to reinterpret political CSR and the political context is to look at the global system for *translocal democratic governance* (Banerjee 2010). Even if political CSR is considered too "corporate" in its orientation and may ignore the interests of weak and marginal stakeholders, or if it might contribute to increasing corporate power by securing public legitimacy through deliberations with stakeholders of civil society, one could still, according to Banerjee, shift attention to the *demand* side of CSR (ibid. 272) and ask how people as corporate stakeholders could be empowered to exercise their democratic rights. The question, of course, is if the critical perspective on political CSR is compatible with the social liberal acceptance of the market as an efficient means to solve allocation problems (Scherer et al. 2006, 524). According to Banerjee,

> the governance of translocality has less to do with how corporations can penetrate civil society or enter into dialogue with civil society actors but more to do with how marginalised and impoverished communities who are non-corporate, non-state and often non-market actors can ensure their rights are protected in a democracy.
>
> (2010, 272; cf. Young 2001)

Liberal democracy is more about including all affected, the worse off and marginalized, and less about entrenched corporate interests that rig the democratic system to their own advantage. Chiapello (2013) joins Bannerjee's critical reading of CSR. Global corporations embark on CSR because this creates the sort of *level playing field* that accrues a competitive advantage over companies from countries that cannot comply with the CSR norms of human rights and high environmental standards. Moreover, Chiapello considers CSR as an investment that *recuperates* on making profits in neutralizing activist criticism, which eventually exemplifies the resilience of the capitalist system and how it can integrate social and ecological criticism, and turn it into a viable business.

Political CSR, however, seeks to focus on certain political *fora* of *multi-stakeholder initiatives* such as the Forest Stewardship Council (FSC) or the United Nations Global Compact. These are suitable for corporate participation in deliberative democracy, Scherer and Palazzo argue (Scherer & Palazzo 2007, 1110). The democratic legitimacy of such institutions can, of course, also be contested (Banerjee 2010, 267–268; Ehrnström-Fuentes 2016). Similarly, the FSC has been criticized for being undemocratic (Moog et al. 2015).

Assuming that the argument for a system view of the political CSR organization is convincing, the organization not only has to be internally democratic and have the capacity for participating in deliberative democracy, but it also needs to be part of a political system amenable to deliberative democracy.

This sufficiency condition raises the bar considerably for the credibility of the political CSR theory, perhaps even to the level of ideal theory, because only within *well-ordered* democratic societies will political CSR organizations find the proper deliberative institutional context. The demanding sufficiency condition is not imposed on political CSR from the outside. Rather, it is inherent to the necessary conditions of political CSR theory itself: the demand for organizational democratic governance, the capacity to move beyond private interests and contribute to the public good, the acknowledgment of responsibility in the social connections of the supply chain, and the avoidance of non-democratic justifications. The combined force of these demands imposed on the political CSR organization requires that the organization is situated in an institutional context amenable to deliberative democracy. Only when this context is in place will political CSR be substantiated as a justified political theory of the corporate organization.

The debate on political CSR and its relation to Jürgen Habermas's philosophy invokes the concern that despite the relative success of political CSR in finding adherents among academic researchers, it is not in tune with Habermas's own understanding of democracy nor the role of the corporation that resides in the system (see Chapter 2). Thus, notions of corporate responsibility in general are examples of a colonization of the lifeworld (of civil society), as Habermas would allegedly see it (Habermas 1987). Deliberative democracy, as crafted by Habermas, is thought to ensure that the law-making process is public and morally legitimate, and corporations have no place in this political process (Habermas 1994). This reading of Habermas resonates in much of the critique of political CSR. However, Scherer and Palazzo's usage of Habermas's deliberative democracy shows that the dualism of system and lifeworld is under pressure and is often transgressed by the political forces of globalization (Scherer & Palazzo 2011). Currently, the forces of populist nationalism and religious fundamentalism reconfigure political CSR and create new understandings of how the lifeworld seeks to reclaim power over the system (Scherer et al. 2016). Thus, a too static view of the dualism between the system and the lifeworld misses the essential insight that deliberative democracy is also a political experiment. And, in some cases, the alternatives to corporate participation in democracy, besides the worst cases of harmful lobbying, may be even worse when the state is absent. Political CSR is inspired by Habermas's theory of deliberative democracy, but it is also a proposal to revise the inherent dualism that curtails corporate engagement by relegating it to the amoral system and ostracizing it from the lifeworld of morality and civil society. Hence, I contend that political CSR is compatible with my "co-evolutionary" reading of Habermas in Chapter 2.

Prospects for Political CSR and the Social Liberal Corporation

To build an argument for the social liberal corporation, I have taken the two theories of corporate citizenship and political CSR to provide the grounding. In the landscape of corporate responsibility theories under scrutiny here, the market liberal (see Chapter 5) and the critical Marxist-inspired approaches are debunking corporate responsibility (see Chapter 8). The conservative virtue ethical approach is supportive of corporate responsibility, but it is dismissive about core liberal values such as the importance of securing individuals' rights (see Chapter 4). This is the *negative* argument for the social liberal corporation. However, I presuppose that liberal values and the basic tenets of liberal democracy are considered significant and worth defending (or promoting, for that matter), and thus, I give preference to the social liberal approaches in comparison to virtue ethical approaches. I admit that, but I do not intend to argue that corporate citizenship and political CSR theory is decoupled and possible to realize without a conception of the virtues (as also mentioned in Chapter 4). So, the social liberal corporation, so conceived, depends also on virtuous character and organization. The defence of the social liberal corporation, then, is circular to the extent that the preference for social liberal values is taken for granted when compared to the conservative virtue ethicists.

So, this is the general and abstract argument for the social liberal corporation.

The more concrete argument then relies on the credibility and robustness of the two social liberal theories presented and discussed here in Chapter 7 and the preceding chapter on corporate citizenship.

To recollect, I have pointed out that both theories are committed to a normative and ethical understanding that underpins corporate responsibility. And both theories are explicit about the political nature of corporate responsibility and, in fact, also the corporation (which equates a normative and "political" theory of the firm).

Corporate citizenship is focussed on substantial issues about rights and duties (being adherent to republicanism), whereas political CSR is more focussed on the process of deliberative democracy and a procedural understanding of the political. This is significant in the search for a "political theory of the firm". And both theories also have answers to the question of what corporate responsibilities hold in situations of government, and market, failure. This is a shortcoming in many of the rivalling theories (except for Heath's "market failure approach" presented in Chapter 5).

These features taken together constitute a theory of corporate responsibility crafted to address a number of the challenges and problems of current global society. I return to how this is done in Part III, which addresses "contemporary issues" and in which the notion of the social liberal corporation is applied to issues of the supply chain, digital and financial firms, as well as the environment and climate change.

Notwithstanding these "advantages" of the social liberal conception, spelled out in the notion of the social liberal corporation, the weaknesses addressed also show that it might be premature to celebrate.

I found the following weaknesses:

First, corporate citizenship and political CSR theory are too unclear about the status of normativity. Clearly, both commit to a moral understanding of corporate responsibility, but they simultaneously include a descriptive element in the theory. It is not clear what level of demandingness and what responsibilities follow from the theories when looking at practice. Part of this is due to confusing the levels of justification in the theory as demonstrated in Table 7.1 in this chapter. So, a further clarification is needed to render the social liberal corporation workable for practice. I have suggested a means to increase awareness of how justification proceeds and avoid confusing the levels, as advisable, to amend the theory.

Second, both theories commit to weak and supposedly neutral justifications. Corporate citizenship is to be conceived only metaphorically, and political CSR gives priority to democracy. I have argued that the need for weak and thus politically uncontroversial justification is inherently liberal. However, looking at the corporate realm in society, there is no particular political reason to abstain from seeking deeper and perhaps more metaphysical justifications because why should notions of corporate agency divide people in the same way as political doctrines would? To make full sense of the idea that corporate agents are also morally responsible, some justification of agency is needed – thus, I refer to the corporate moral agency discussed in Chapter 3.

However, the focus in this chapter, was the claim that for political CSR to succeed, it required a political context of institutions amenable to deliberative democracy. And this is precisely the premise most disputed because a main assumption in political CSR, and corporate citizenship, is the absence of the rule of law and a democratic, well-ordered state system. The weakness of the state seems to be the prime mover for both theories. So, if this assumption is questioned as it has been, then it seems as if this is a serious objection to both theories. I have not tried to defend the theories by pointing out the empirical facts in favour of the claim that globalization marginalizes the state, nor have I taken into consideration facts that undermine the claim. This is an empirical question dealt with by, for instance, Knudsen and Moon (2017), that surely has consequences for the empirical credibility of corporate citizenship and political CSR theory.

My contribution is instead to argue that the type of organization envisaged by political CSR – as democratic in its culture and decision procedure and responsive to the curtailment of the public-private spheres in society is apt for the situation in which the political context is open to deliberative democracy but might not yet have enacted institutions to realize it. My argument in this chapter was to point to the philosophical understanding of the "*system view* of the organization as caught in a balanced flux between the forces of the political context" as stated previously. I argue that this ability is required of the organization to satisfy the theory of political CSR. And, it is exactly this ability that makes the corporation able to sway its surrounding context towards deliberative democracy, provided that the surrounding society and political culture allows it. If it does not, the entire political CSR project is a non-starter. In that sense political CSR conceives of the corporation as an enabler of deliberative democracy along with the state and civil society. What is missing in the rivalling theories is this ability because they exempt the corporation from being part of political life in this sense.

As this might appear to be a lofty ideal, there is good reason to suspect that the rivalling theory of Marxist criticism of corporate responsibility will be able to articulate relevant objections. Hence, this is the focus of the following chapter.

References

Anderson, E. (2017) *Private government: How employers rule our lives (and why we don't talk about it)*. Princeton: Princeton University Press

Anker, T. B. (2017) Corporate democratic nation-building: Reflections on the constructive role of businesses in fostering global democracy. *European Management Journal*, *35*(1), 1–7

Arneson, R. (1987) Meaningful work and market socialism. *Ethics*, *97*(2), 517–545

Banerjee, S. B. (2010) Governing the global corporation: A critical perspective. *Business Ethics Quarterly*, *20*(2), 265–274

Basu, K., & Palazzo, G. (2008) Corporate social responsibility: A process model of sensemaking. *The Academy of Management Review*, *33*(1), 122–136

Chiapello, E. (2013) Capitalism and its new criticisms. In P. Du Gay & G. Morgan (Eds.), *New spirits of capitalism? Crises, justifications and dynamics*, 60–81. Oxford: Oxford Scholarship Online

Ciepley, D. (2013) Beyond public and private: Toward a political theory of the corporation. *American Political Science Review*, *107*(1), 139–158

Djelic, M. L., & Etchanchu, H. (2017) Contextualizing corporate political responsibilities: Neoliberal CSR in historical perspective. *Journal of Business Ethics*, *142*(4), 641–661

Dubbink, W., & Smith, J. (2011) A political account of corporate moral responsibility. *Ethical Theory and Moral Practice*, *14*(2), 223–246

Ehrnström-Fuentes, M. (2016) Delinking legitimacies: A pluriversal perspective on political CSR. *Journal of Management Studies*, *53*(3), 433–462

Forst, R. (2015) Noumenal power. *The Journal of Political Philosophy*, *23*(2), 111–127

Freeman, R. E. (1994) The politics of stakeholder theory: Some future directions. *Business Ethics Quarterly*, *4*, 409–422

Frynas, J. G., & Stephens, S. (2015) Political corporate social responsibility: Reviewing theories and setting new agendas. *International Journal of Management Reviews*, *17*, 483–509

Gonin, M., Palazzo, G., & Hoffrage, U. (2012) Neither bad apple nor bad barrel: How the societal context impacts unethical behavior in organizations. *Business Ethics – A European Review*, *21*, 31–46

Habermas, J. (1987) *The theory of communicative action*, vol. 2. Boston: Beacon Press

Habermas, J. (1994) Three normative models of democracy. *Constellations*, *1*(1), 1–10

Hasnas, J. (2018) Should corporations have the right to vote? A paradox in the theory of corporate moral agency. *Journal of Business Ethics*, *150*(3), 657–670

Heath, J. (2014) *Morality, competition and the firm*. Oxford: Oxford University Press

Heath, J., Moriarty, J., & Norman, W. (2010) Business ethics and (or as) political philosophy. *Business Ethics Quarterly*, *20*(3), 427–452

Herzog, L. (2018) *Reclaiming the system: Moral responsibility, divided labour, and the role of organizations in society*. Oxford: Oxford University Press

Heugens, P. P. M. A. R., & Scherer, A. G. (2010) When organization theory met business ethics: Toward further symbioses. *Business Ethics Quarterly*, *20*(4), 643–672

Hsieh, N. (2009) Does global business have a responsibility to promote just institutions? *Business Ethics Quarterly*, *19*(2), 251–273

Hussain, W., & Moriarty, J. (2018) Accountable to whom? Rethinking the role of corporations in political CSR. *Journal of Business Ethics*, *149*(3), 519–534

Knudsen, J. S., & Moon, J. (2017) *Visible hands: Government regulation and international business responsibility*. Cambridge: Cambridge University Press

Landemore, H., & Ferreras, I. (2016) In defense of workplace democracy: Towards a justification of the firm-state analogy. *Political Theory*, *44*(1), 53–81

Mäkinen, J., & Kasanen, E. (2016) Boundaries between business and politics: A study on the division of moral labor. *Journal of Business Ethics*, *134*(1), 103–116

Mansbridge, J., Bohman, J., Chambers, S., Christiano, T., Fung, A., Parkinson, J., Thompson, D. F., & Warren, M. E. (2013) A systemic approach to deliberative democracy. In J. Parkinson & J. Mansbridge (Eds.), *Deliberative systems*, 1–10. Cambridge: Cambridge University Press

Matten, D., & Crane, A. (2005) Corporate citizenship: Towards an extended theoretical conceptualization. *Academy of Management Review*, *30*, 166–179

McMahon, C. (1995) The political theory of organizations and business ethics. *Philosophy and Public Affairs*, *24*(4), 292–313

Michaelson, C., Pratt, M. G., Adam, M. G., & Dunn, C. P. (2012) Meaningful work: Connecting business ethics and organizational studies. *Journal of Business Ethics*, *121*(1), 77–90

Moog, S., Spicer, A., & Böhm, S. (2015) The politics of multi-stakeholder initiatives: The crisis of the forest stewardship council. *Journal of Business Ethics*, *128*(3), 469–493

Moon, J., Crane, A., & Matten, D. (2005) Can corporations be citizens? Corporate citizenship as a metaphor for business participation in society. *Business Ethics Quarterly*, *15*(3), 429–453

Morgan, G. (1997) *Images of organization*. London: Sage Publishing

Moriarty, J. (2005) On the relevance of political philosophy to business ethics. *Business Ethics Quarterly*, *15*, 455–473

Néron, P. Y. (2010) Business and the polis: What does it mean to see corporations as political actors? *Journal of Business Ethics*, *94*, 333–352

Orts, E. W., & Craig Smith, N. (2017) *The moral responsibility of firms*. Oxford: Oxford University Press

Palazzo, G., Krings, F., & Hoffrage, U. (2012) Ethical blindness. *Journal of Business Ethics*, *109*(3), 323–338

Rawls, J. (1971/1999) *A theory of justice*. Revised edition. Cambridge, MA: Harvard University Press

Rawls, J. (1985) Justice as fairness: Political not metaphysical. *Philosophy & Public Affairs*, *14*(3), 223–251

Rawls, J. (1994) *Political liberalism*. New York: Columbia University Press

Sabadoz, C., & Singer, A. (2017) Talk ain't cheap: Political CSR and the challenges of corporate deliberation. *Business Ethics Quarterly*, *27*(2), 183–211

Scherer, A. G. (2017) Theory assessment and agenda setting in political CSR: A critical theory perspective. *International Journal of Management Reviews*. doi: 10.1111/ijmr.12137

Scherer, A. G., & Palazzo, G. (2007) Toward a political conception of corporate responsibility: Business and society seen from a Habermasian perspective. *Academy of Management Review*, *32*, 1096–1120
Scherer, A. G., & Palazzo, G. (2011) The new political role of business in a globalized world: A review of a new perspective on CSR and its implications for the firm, governance, and democracy. *Journal of Management Studies*, *48*, 889–931
Scherer, A. G., Palazzo, G., & Baumann, D. (2006) Global rules and private actors: Toward a new role of the transnational corporation in global governance. *Business Ethics Quarterly*, *16*(4), 505–532
Scherer, A. G., Rasche, A., Palazzo, G., & Spicer, A. (2016) Managing for political corporate social responsibility: New challenges and directions for PCSR 2.0. *Journal of Management Studies*, *53*, 273–298
Schrempf-Stirling, J., & Palazzo, G. (2016) Upstream corporate social responsibility. *Business and Society*, *55*(4), 491–527
Whelan, G. (2012) The political perspective of corporate social responsibility: A critical research agenda. *Business Ethics Quarterly*, *22*(4), 709–733
Young, I. M. (2001) Activist challenges to deliberative democracy. *Political Theory*, *29*(5), 670–690
Young, I. M. (2006) Responsibility and global justice: A social connection model. *Social Philosophy & Policy*, *23*(1), 102–130
Young, I. M. (2011) *Responsibility for Justice*. Oxford: Oxford University Press

8 Debunking Corporate Responsibility – Critical Theory and Market Ideology

This chapter presents a discussion of critical views on corporate responsibility. The philosophical heritage is Marx and his critical view of capitalism and the market (see Chapter 1). Hence, any notion of corporate responsibility is ideological, a veneer that *masks* the exploitative and alienating nature of capitalism (Fleming & Jones 2013, 99). Paradoxically, for different reasons, the critics agree with libertarians that corporations can have no social responsibility. However, libertarians are against corporate responsibility because it undermines the market, whereas Marxist critics believe that corporations are one of the root causes of capitalist harm and therefore cannot be trusted – they are "corporate psychos" (Bakan 2004). Corporate scandals, the periodic financial crises, pollution of the environment, and exploitation of workers are all facts that disprove corporations' ability to be responsible in spite of the proliferating CSR agenda (Shamir 2008). Denying the neo-Marxist stance to corporate responsibility is on a par with denying the harmful consequences that capitalism as a system has, as proponents of the critical approach to corporate responsibility would argue. So, the debate about corporate responsibility as situated in the vicinity of Marxism is more about *political economy* and less about the internal organizational workings addressed in the previous chapters (Polaney 2001; Hanlon 2008; Fleming & Jones 2013, 98; Djelic & Etchanchu 2017).

However, this macro-perspective predicts certain analytical approaches to the corporation that aim at revealing the contradictions inherent to projects of corporate responsibility. These are the sorts of contradictions between a corporation saying that it wants to be responsible, but in reality, the corporation acts contrarily. The ideology of a humanized capitalism (Porter & Kramer 2006) leaves the impression that capitalism can be renewed into a more responsible version, but the history of political economy shows differently: that the conjunction between humanism and capitalism remains a contradiction in terms, an *oxymoron*. The critical take on corporate responsibility makes the neo-Marxist approach a *via negativa*, mostly concerned with all the failures of the corporate responsibility of the firm. However, as in the chapter on Marx, the critique of capitalism also harbours its own positive vision of what corporations should do. Marx did have a vision of a communist society in which people gathered in free association and took over control of the means of production to regain autonomy. The worker-controlled co-operative figured as a promising means to realize this vision, although Marx was also in doubt about it.

In this chapter, I will first present and discuss two aspects of the critical approach to corporate responsibility in the Marxist tradition. The first aspect regards the macro-political level. Here, I will focus on Eve Chiapello's (2013) diagnosis of the *New Spirit of Capitalism* to show that corporate responsibility is but an example of capitalist resilience. The second aspect, much related to the first, regards the meso and micro levels of the firm. To highlight the second aspect, I will use literature from *critical management studies* (CMS) (Fleming & Banerjee 2016), which has developed into a research paradigm of its own that targets the organizational level. Even though the philosophical frame of reference is quite broad in CMS, encompassing post-structuralism – Derrida and deconstruction, as well as discourse theory based on Foucault and Mouffe, to mention the main sources – Marxist ideology critique looms large in CMS and critical business ethics (Jones et al. 2005). For that reason, I will also discuss the inspiration from Slavoj Žižek (2008) on current CMS approaches (Hanlon 2008; Fleming & Jones 2013; Cederström & Marinetto 2013). In the end section of the chapter, I will address the theory of exploitation to look for a positive theory to underpin current critical approaches. I do this for the main reason that Marxism has influenced two philosophical traditions: the continental – which CMS mostly commits to – and the analytical – which is absent in current theorizing of critical Marxist-inspired approaches to corporate responsibility.

I have earlier suggested providing a positive grounding to the critical approach through an understanding of exploitation in informing the theory of corporate responsibility (Toft 2015). I derive this understanding mainly from *analytical Marxism* (Kymlicka 2002). My motivation for infusing an analytical clarification of exploitation into the debate on corporate responsibility is twofold. First, the concept of exploitation has not received explicit attention from the mainstream of CMS. This is likely due to the Hegelian influence on the continental tradition – especially existentialism – that CMS subscribes to, which is more concerned with alienation than exploitation (ibid. 190). Second, by suggesting a positive contribution with a clarified normative understanding of exploitation, it is possible to supplement and counteract the pervasive scepticism about ethics and justice inherent to CMS. It has long been a contested issue whether or not Marx had a positive theory of justice (ibid. 168). Marx had good reason for being abstinent about embracing liberal justice and human rights, but this does not necessarily licence moral abstinence today. I assume that liberal thinking today is much more self-critical about the gap between ideal norms and less ideal reality, and hence there is less reason to suspend normativity and its linking with notions of corporate responsibility.

Resilient Capitalism

Looking at corporate responsibility historically, it appears that capitalism evolves in phases. The phases are interrupted by crises in the political economy to which capitalism responds and adapts. According to Max Weber, the Protestant ethic is deeply connected to the capitalist spirit. Hence, the early political economy of capitalism relies on a particular religious outlook that values hard work and abstinence. Eve Chiapello, together with Luc Boltanski, proposes a *new spirit of capitalism* to account for the phases that capitalism has been undergoing. Here, I rely on Chiapello (2013) as she addresses CSR. The internal engine of change is the Marxist, and basically Hegelian, idea of a dialectic that dissolves contradictions in the political economy. The first serious contradiction of capitalism is poverty and exploitation, as Marx and Engels so well described as the *rabble* and the *reserve army*. Capitalism is increasing general wealth and prosperity in society, but this is contradicted by the fact of the destitute. So, for capitalism to remain trustworthy and not raise indignation, but also maintain law and order, the critique of capitalist-engendered poverty is responded to by instigating measures of private conservative philanthropy and public social welfare – hence, conservative and social criticism evokes new normative orders of responsibility for the poor and marginalized. According to Chiapello, the conservative criticism is also virtue ethical and reflects the *noblesse oblige*, so the "firm owner should have a duty to live on the same territory as his workers, so that he . . . will retain a permanent concern for their living conditions and safety" (ibid. 70). The notion of a moral capitalism is reminiscent of conservative criticism and the paternalistic view of corporate responsibility (Djelic & Etchanchu 2017).

Similarly, the capitalist response to the alienation of workers in meaningless jobs, and consumers drowning in the commodification of all life's aspects, is to appropriate from the arts to invigorate an authentic experience in the workplace and the market. The spirit from 1968 of the hippie movement and the revolutionary left was appropriated in the 1970s and 1980s by firms to show innovation and a tolerant mindset. The downside of the new authentic work life has been the rise in project workers, resulting in short-term contracting and the precariat. Corporate responsibility during this phase is characterized by an increased focus on the corporate culture and the corporate narrative as well as increased focus on employees' genuine passion and commitment. Work must be meaningful, and the corporation must be purpose driven.

Chiapello argues that the most recent ecological criticism is different from former kinds of criticism as it now concerns the survival of human civilization (ibid. 74). Ecological criticism is foremost evoked by the bleak future scenarios of climate change, and it can be responded to by capitalism with help from a diversity of mutually incompatible political ideologies. Critical deep ecology and libertarians can both offer solutions to respond to the ecological crisis, and democracy is no longer needed. Rather, democracy might be a barrier to solving ecological problems, so this sort of critique could be a call for more authoritarian governance. Chiapello also believes that social democrats (social criticism) are under pressure to adapt to the ecological crisis because it might be necessary to decrease economic growth (de-growth) to avoid exacerbating climate change, and this will be costly to workers in developed countries. So, how can the "third way" respond to this dilemma?

Interestingly Chiapello claims that *green capitalism* and *CSR* are current responses to the ecological crisis. The notion of green growth and sustainable development are built on the premise that economic growth is compatible with sustainability and environmental concerns. CSR and green capitalism have support from conservatives who trust in the "elite's good intentions" and considers responsible corporations as substitutes for "powerless governments" (ibid. 77). The resurgence of the co-operative as a viable alternative to the capitalist firm. Chiapello also considers a systemic response to the ecological crisis (ibid. 78). Hence, in this "Hegelian" reading of capitalism, corporate responsibility is a mere symptom of a deeper crisis, and it is a response with the ulterior motive of saving capitalism.

Critical Management Studies and CSR

The view held by proponents of CMS of corporate responsibility is critical, and debunking ranging from a *reformist* stance to disruptive *interventionist* approaches with the aim of dismantling the discourse of the corporation in its current form exist (Fleming & Banerjee 2016). The aim is *emancipatory* to show an ethical care for marginalized stakeholders in the current hegemonic discourses of corporate responsibility that permeate liberal democracies (Banerjee 2008, 74). The interests dividing marginalized stakeholders and the firm is considered as *agonistic* and therefore cannot be dealt with by means of consensus seeking in a deliberative model, as political CSR hopes for (Dawkins 2015).

Often, CSR programmes are adopted in the firm to solve this agonism of interests. But CSR programmes and codes of ethics tend to translate difficult agonisms into easy fixes that eventually silence opposition from the outside. For instance, the idea that it is possible to have stakeholder dialogue with parties of unequal standing in terms of power is illusory, according to Banerjee (2008).

> In my work with two indigenous communities in Australia I sought "stakeholder input" about the presence of a mine on indigenous

> land. The response was unanimous: both communities wanted the mining company (a very, very, very large multinational company) to "clean up, pack up, leave and never come back", to quote the words of one traditional owner. The company's response was to hire an anthropologist to "consult" with communities on how best to expand its operations. The fact that these "consultations" take place under drastically unequal power relations remains unaddressed.
>
> (64)

As Hanlon (2008, 167–168) remarks about Banerjee's report of this failed attempt at dialogue, the notion of pluralism is celebrated by liberal business leaders but only as long as *the other* is willing to communicate and agree to solutions compatible with corporate interests. If the parties in a stakeholder dialogue are not willing or capable of joining the conversation, they are considered as "too different, as fundamentalist, extreme, traditional, behind the times, etc.". The idea that deliberative democracy is compatible with capitalism ignores that they are built on "mutually exclusive institutional logics" (Fleming & Jones 2013, 87). By ignoring power asymmetries and mixing up ethics and economics, adherents to CSR and stakeholder theory eventually harm those whom they want to save.

CSR is, therefore, a tool to conduct risk management and has nothing to do with genuine ethical concern for anyone but the shareholder. Slavoj Žižek (2008) has inspired some of the critical approaches through his notion of *liberal communism*, which makes a caricature of the politically correct who believe that contradictions can be overcome in the attempt to be responsible. According to Cederström and Marinetto, Žižek's liberal communist has three deeply held views:

> (1) that there is no opposition between capitalism and the social good; (2) that all problems are of a practical nature, and hence best solved by corporate engagement and (3) that hierarchies, authority and centralized bureaucracies should be replaced by dynamic structures, a nomadic lifestyle and a flexible spirit.
>
> (ibid. p. 416)

These views sum up the worldview of corporate leaders who deny conflicts of interest between capital owners and those who work for them. The view that capitalism can be a force for good and create value shared between business and society is an influential view often associated with Porter and Kramer (2006). This view has had a huge influence in business, and governments have also embraced the win-win thinking in their promotion of corporate responsibility as a cutting-edge competitive advantage. The idea that corporations are better than governments at solving problems, and that there are no structural and systemic problems, only practical ones, is typical for the liberal communists, according to Žižek:

> They [the liberal communists] hate a doctrinaire approach. For them there is no single exploited working class today. There are only concrete problems to be solved: starvation in Africa, the plight of Muslim women, religious fundamentalist violence. When there is a humanitarian crisis in Africa – and liberal communists really love humanitarian crises, which bring out the best in them! – there is no point in engaging in old-style anti-imperialist rhetoric. Instead, all of us should just concentrate on what really does the work of solving the problem: engage people, governments, and business in a common enterprise; start moving things, instead of relying on centralised state help; approach the crisis in a creative and unconventional way.
>
> (2008, 18–19)

The sarcasm is evident, and the argument is *ad hominem*, but Žižek is raising the point that the appearance of benevolence is masking the real underlying problems of the capitalist system. He invokes the distinction between *subjective* and *objective* violence, where the former is the sort of harm that horrifies the liberals, although the real harm is done by the invisible social and economic structures that distribute powers in an unequal way globally. So, the cultural and innovative self-image permeating the elites devoted to "corporate responsibility" is shallow and self-serving. Alvesson and Spicer (2016) diagnose this tendency to be a case of *functional stupidity*. CSR is functional because it provides guidelines and answers to how to solve the difficult problems of the corporation, but CSR is also stupid in the sense that it prevents people from thinking critically about a problem.

Exploitation: Towards a Positive Critical Theory of Corporate Responsibility

The question remains, is it possible to provide a positive theory of corporate responsibility on the basis of the critique directed at shallow notions of corporate responsibility? And, is it appropriate to ask for a positive theory considering that the diagnosis of the systemic problems in political economy calls for more radical change? The founding father of critical theory, Theodor W. Adorno, is famous for saying that it is a bourgeois prejudice to demand positive alternatives to critique (Jones et al. 2005, 110). Hence, the structure of the global capitalist system must be dismantled first before any viable alternatives can be fully considered. This is, of course, a fairly radical view, and I think it is problematic for a number of reasons. It does block the road of inquiry to finding alternatives to systemic problems, of which corporations, especially the big multinationals, are a part. But more troubling is that normativity tends to be considered with suspicion in much of CMS and critical business studies. This makes it difficult to clarify, beyond the obvious, what makes, for instance, exploitation morally wrong. The critics all agree that exploitation is massive and permeates the entire capitalist system, and that it is an obvious wrong. But are all aspects of "taking advantage" of another to be considered exploitation, or are there clear criteria of when exploitation is wrong and not just circumstantial?

In this section, I will assess understandings of exploitation suggested in the literature of mainly analytical Marxism, to clarify what makes exploitation wrong. Moreover, what can be derived from such clarification to inform a theory of corporate responsibility (besides the obvious critique already mentioned)? Even though it might be possible to reach a fair understanding of exploitation, it is not a given that it can be of any use to a theory of corporate responsibility.

First, the standard definition of exploitation is that "A exploits B when A takes unfair advantage of B" (Snyder 2010, 188). However, the classical Marxist definition is not so general as it situates exploitation of the worker in the context of capitalist production. Here, according to the labour value theory, the worker is the source of value creation, which in the Marxist account, is called surplus value, or profits. The worker is exploited because he or she is not getting a wage that is equivalent to the value of the work in return for the work done. Hence, the worker is working part time for free, which is a *theft* of the worker's labour (Cohen 1995, 197). Now, if the worker could simply choose to leave this job to pursue another one that paid the equivalent of the work contributed to the production, there would be less of a problem. At least, to Marx, the fact that there is no other job to get makes it a forced choice to work and be exploited; the worker did not *voluntarily* enter the contract. Capitalism also manages to keep unemployment sufficiently high to sustain a *reserve army* of unemployed so that wages are kept at a minimum and the threat of being fired is daunting (Kymlicka 2002, 177–178). Hence, the Marxist account of exploitation makes wage labour wrong, and it is therefore impossible to defend the capitalist private firm as it relies on hiring workers. Subsequently, this spills over to why it is a non-starter, in the Marxist account, to take the notion of corporate responsibility seriously. However, it has been argued that the concept of exploitation should not be seen only in the rather limited context of the Marxist labour theory of value (Zwolinski & Wertheimer 2017). Exploitation also has meaning in the non-labour contexts of everyday life (Wolff 1999, 110). And, the labour value theory has difficulty in accounting for why the value of products is often independent of work as, for instance, the value of land shows.

In the broader understanding of exploitation, the distinction between micro-level *transactional* and macro-level *structural* exploitation can be made (ibid.). When a firm is relying on exploiting workers in the supply chain, this can be an example of transactional exploitation because the firm is the direct cause. However, if one considers the supply chain to be an aspect of the global capitalist system, the exploitation can be seen as structural. As consumers, we are all unwillingly, and often even more unknowingly, part of global value chains that are exploitative in nature (Young 2006). The problem shows that the background conditions of exploitation have significance, which points to the difference between exploitation with regard to *fairness in distribution* or *access to the means of production* in capitalism. The structural version of exploitation considers access to control over and ownership of the means of production. Hence, even if workers are paid the fair equivalent of the work they put into the production, they might still suffer from a lack of access to the means of production.

Moreover, exploitation can be seen as wrong because it infringes upon norms of justice, equality, fairness, or respect for the person. Various moral theories could, in principle, explain the wrong-making property of exploitation (Wolff 1999, 112). The obvious candidate is Kantian duty ethics' formulation of the Categorical Imperative, which would say that to exploit people is to treat them as a means to an end and not as an end in themselves (ibid.). However, other possibilities are open, although less intuitive. For instance, Rawlsian social justice theory would predict that if an exchange of work and wages resulted in not being of benefit to the worse-off, it would be exploitative.

Now, to return to the context of corporate responsibility, what can be derived from this sketch of exploitation theory? First, as mentioned, if accepting that wage labour is inherently exploitative by definition, it will debunk corporate responsibility because firms rely on wage labour. With regard to workers then, the more relevant question, if accepting that wage labour is *not* inherently exploitative, is what terms of labour are acceptable and explicitly non-exploitative? Given that the background conditions of society are not excessively unfair, responsible corporations should pay a wage that makes a decent standard of living possible. And, they should comply with basic labour rights and human rights as well. However, as Jonathan Wolff points out, it might not be so simple to escape exploitation because Marx's insight into the essence of *capitalism as mutual exploitation* tells us about the degrading aspect of being forced to trade on those terms (ibid. 119–120).

So, to unpack the content of corporate responsibility designed to avoid or minimize the exploitation of workers, the salient and much-debated case of the sweatshop is discussed in the next chapter on responsibility in the supply chain.

References

Alvesson, M., & Spicer, A. (2016) *The stupidity paradox – The power and pitfalls of functional stupidity at work*. London: Profile Books Ltd

Bakan, J. (2004) *The corporation: The pathological pursuit of profit and power*. London: Constable

Banerjee, S. B. (2008) Corporate social responsibility: The good, the bad and the ugly. *Critical Sociology*, *34*, 51–79

Cederström, C., & Marinetto, M. (2013) Corporate social responsibility a´ la the Liberal Communist'. *Organization*, *20*(3), 416–432

Chiapello, E. (2013) Capitalism and its new criticisms. In P. Du Gay & G. Morgan (Eds.), *New spirits of capitalism? Crises, justifications and dynamics*, 60–81. Oxford: Oxford Scholarship Online

Cohen, G. A. (1995) *Self-ownership, freedom and equality*. Cambridge: Cambridge University Press

Dawkins, C. (2015) Agonistic pluralism and stakeholder engagement. *Business Ethics Quarterly*, *25*(01), 1–28

Djelic, M. L., & Etchanchu, H. (2017) Contextualizing corporate political responsibilities: Neoliberal CSR in historical perspective. *Journal of Business Ethics*, *142*(4), 641–661

Fleming, P., & Banerjee, S. B. (2016) When performativity fails: Implications for critical management studies. *Human Relations*, *69*(2), 257–276

Fleming, P., & Jones, M. (2013) *The end of corporate social responsibility: Capitalism, crisis and critique*. London: Sage Publishing

Hanlon, G. (2008) Rethinking corporate social responsibility and the role of the firm – On the denial of politics. In A. Crane, A. McWilliams, D. Matten, J. Moon, & D. Siegel (Eds.), *Oxford handbook of corporate social responsibility*, 156–172. Oxford: Oxford University Press

Jones, C., Parker, M., & Ten Bos, R. (2005) *For business ethics*. London: Routledge

Kymlicka, W. (2002) *Contemporary political philosophy: An introduction*. 2nd edition. New York: Oxford University Press

Polaney, K. (2001) *The great transformation – The political and economic origins of our time*. Boston: Beacon Press

Porter, M. E., & Kramer, M. R. (2006) Strategy & society – The link between competitive advantage and corporate social responsibility. *Harvard Business Review*, *12*, 78–92

Shamir, R. (2008) The age of responsibilization: On market-embedded morality. *Economy & Society*, *37*, 1–19

Snyder, J. (2010) Exploitation and sweatshop labor: Perspectives and issues. *Business Ethics Quarterly*, *20*(2), 187–213

Toft, K. H. (2015) Liberal CSR and new Marxist criticism. In S. Idowu, C. Frederiksen, A. Mermod, & M. Nielsen (Eds.), *Corporate social responsibility and governance: CSR, sustainability, ethics & governance*. Heidelberg: Springer

Wolff, J. (1999) Marx and exploitation. *The Journal of Ethics*, *3*(2), 105–120

Young, I. M. (2006) Responsibility and global justice: A social connection model. *Social Philosophy and Policy*, *23*, 102–130

Žižek, S. (2008) *On violence*. London: Profile Books

Zwolinski, M., & Wertheimer, A. (2017, Summer) Exploitation. In E. N. Zalta (Ed.), *The Stanford encyclopedia of philosophy*. https://plato.stanford.edu/archives/sum2017/entries/exploitation

Part III

Applications of Corporate Responsibility – Contemporary Issues

9 Who's Responsible for the Supply Chain? Iris Marion Young's Social Connection Model

The next three shorter chapters apply the theory of corporate responsibility and the social liberal conception of the corporation to contemporary issues of the supply chain, financial and digital firms, as well as to climate change. The focus is to clarify how the *social liberal corporation* is to respond to these issues. My method of applying the philosophical theory of corporate responsibility to these issues follows the general outline of Rawlsian *reflective equilibrium* (Rawls 1971/1999). Hence, I aim at integrating concerns based on the weight of moral intuitions, theories, and principles as well as empirical evidence as provided by scientific theory. The idea, therefore, is not to apply philosophical theory top down but rather to seek coherence among the best materials available. I am not going to follow any strict procedure but will seek to take the theory of the social liberal corporation, as it was spelled out in Chapters 6 and 7 on corporate citizenship and political CSR, and apply it in the context of contemporary issues. I have argued that the social liberal corporation is emerging in current academic literature on CSR and that it is superior to the competing theories of market liberalism, conservative virtue ethics, and critical approaches in terms of providing better answers to current challenges in a globalized world. It acknowledges that the rule of law is not always a given or sufficient to provide helpful answers. It acknowledges that the state might fail to deliver on pivotal goods such as basic rights, and it also acknowledges that corporations in general do have a moral responsibility to solve problems in society at large. For anyone who believes that corporations should carry a responsibility besides complying with the law, the idea of the social liberal corporation is a good place to start. Hence, let us start with a look at how it fares with regard to problems in the supply chain.

Historically, stories of child labour and poor working conditions at the bottom of the supply chain have given rise to demands for more responsible behaviour on the part of corporations. The rise of CSR is parallel to the rise in media reporting about the corporate scandal of hiding horrible working conditions in the supply chain. In particular, child labour has been a critical issue. Currently, the issue of slavery in the supply chain has become a key topic for corporations to address (Crane 2013).

However, to what extent can the corporation be responsible for human rights violations in its supply chain? Developments since the 1990s show that corporations have been increasingly assigned responsibility for their supply chains by the media and NGOs (Schrempf-Stirling & Palazzo 2016). Iris Marion Young made a significant contribution to addressing this issue with her writings on the *social connection model* about how to distribute responsibility for poor working conditions in the supply chain, notably issues pervading the *sweatshop* debate (2006, 2011). As seen in Chapter 7 on political CSR and the adoption of Young's model, it is no longer enough to limit moral responsibility in the supply chain to an individualist, backward-looking legal type of responsibility, that is, what Young calls the *liability model* of responsibility. Now, to respond to harms done in the global supply chain, we need a *forward-looking* and *political* kind of *shared responsibility* to tackle *structural injustice*. Not only corporations, but also individual consumers who, for instance, buy a T-shirt produced in Bangladesh, become responsible for preventing *future* harms and rights violations in the production process. Thus, responsibility entails a duty to promote political awareness of bad working conditions in the far-flung worksites of supply chains, and then act collectively to prevent further harms in the future. Political CSR adopted Young's social connection model in its argument for why corporate moral responsibility has become a *political* and shared kind of responsibility (Scherer & Palazzo 2011). This rendered the organization vulnerable to external and often unfounded claims of what the corporation should take responsibility for, regardless of the level of its complicity. In fact, as argued in Chapter 7, the social connection model resulted in difficulties in limiting the scope and content of corporate responsibility. In this chapter, I am going to explore the possibility of finding justified limits to the corporate responsibility of the social liberal corporation. To define such limits, I will take up the sweatshop debate and discuss to what extent corporations are responsible for exploitation in faraway sites of production.

Responsibility for Sweatshop Exploitation

Sweatshops are usually small units of production that deliver to retailers and producers further down the production chain, mostly larger corporations. Sweatshops typically operate in the garment and agricultural industries, where products are labour intensive and employees require limited education. The working conditions are bad, salaries are below minimum-wage (if such exists in the country), and basic human rights are often violated. Sweatshops are typically found in developing countries, although they also exist in the United States and Europe, where they offer jobs to poor people who have no alternative work to find. The moral issue is that it is claimed that workers are being exploited. Not only does the local owner and manager of the sweatshop take an unfair advantage of the workers' bad situation, but corporations in the supply chain benefit from cheap sweatshop labour as well. This is Iris Marion Young's description of a sweatshop:

> The vast majority of workers are female, and often as young as thirteen or fourteen. They are often treated in dominative and abusive ways by bosses, and sexual harassment is common. Typically, they work ten- to sixteen-hour days in peak seasons; if the manufacturer is behind on an order, the workers may be forced to work through the night. They have few bathroom breaks or other opportunities for rest during their long working day. Sick leave or vacation time are generally unavailable; a worker too ill to work is often fired. Violations of the most basic health and safety standards are normal. Factories are often excessively hot with no ventilation, insufficient lighting, excessive noise, little fire-fighting equipment, blocked exits, poor sanitation, unhygienic canteens and bathrooms, and no access to clean drinking water. Typically, workers in these facilities have no freedom to organize unions to bargain collectively with their employers. Workers who complain and try to organize are typically threatened, fired, blacklisted, beaten, and even killed. Local governments often actively or passively support such anti-union activity.
>
> (Young 2006, 108)

Judging from this description of the sweatshop, several moral wrongs can be noted. Clearly, it is not only morally wrong, but also illegal by any account committed to basic human rights, to threaten and kill workers for not complying with the management's authority. Moreover, denying the right to unionize violates citizenship rights to gather freely in political association, and this sorts of discrimination and health threatening-working conditions are not possible to defend in any sane moral account. However, the *prima facie* wrongness of sweatshops has been contested as sweatshops often offer better alternatives to poor people compared to being unemployed or working in traditional sectors. In particular, the wage is often three to seven times higher compared to the alternatives (Zwolinski 2012, 163), even though it remains below a *living wage*, defined as the income required to meet the most basic needs (Arnold & Bowie 2003, 233). Furthermore, due to this advantage in working in a sweatshop, workers themselves choose to work there. Zwolinski argues that all things considered, this suggests a reason for respecting the choice of sweatshop workers by not interfering in their choice (Zwolinski 2007). However, even though this may be true if limiting one's focus to the micro level of sweatshop exploitation, what happens locally, the *choice* argument and the *better wage* argument fare less well in the macro-con ext. The point of the social connection model is to cast light on the institutional background conditions that render the baseline for judging sweatshops morally problematic. Although it is possible that workers freely choose the sweatshops, the constraints on the choice need not be morally acceptable. If, for instance, the wages are far below the living wage, the sweatshop wage remains morally problematic. The same goes for the other wrongs described by Young. If sweatshop workers accept that they cannot unionize or reject a command to work longer hours because the general perception in the country says these are not rights a worker has, it remains wrong to accept such working conditions. Moreover, the sweatshop owners themselves are under pressure to supply products at a low price, so they can rightfully say that they are not solely responsible for paying such low wages.

Hence, it need not be the individual sweatshop that exploits, but rather the reason for exploitation lies elsewhere, namely, in the system that supports sweatshops. The causes behind macro-level exploitation are, by nature, complex, and this is the reason why it becomes difficult to single out what the corporate responsibility is. Surely, if a corporation is engaged locally in sweatshops, it becomes liable for wrongs in the working environment. Often, firms are more closely engaged than they willingly admit. For instance, when garment factory Rana Plaza in Dhaka, Bangladesh, collapsed in 2013, resulting in 1129 dead workers and 2500 injured, some retailers denied responsibility, even though they used the factory as a sub-supplier (Reinecke & Donaghey 2015). There is a grey zone between direct involvement and being complicit caused by the legal definition of being responsible as being liable. Hence, the retailers may have had no direct contractual and legal responsibility for the accident at Rana Plaza, but they were morally complicit by relying on products from the site, or – to stretch the notion of complicity – they participated in an industry in Bangladesh that made it possible for such an accident to occur. Stretching corporate responsibility beyond legal liability makes it clear what Young has in mind with her social connection model and hence what political CSR theory considers the relevant notion of responsibility.

Now, what can be said to define and possibly limit this sort of political responsibility for structural injustice?

According to Jeremy Snyder, the scope of CSR necessarily grows wide if one takes complicity in sweatshop exploitation into consideration (2010, 206). However, just as individuals have other duties and limits in resources, corporations by analogy are also limited in what they can and should do to prevent sweatshop exploitation by engaging politically to change the economic and legal background conditions. Moreover, if corporations are to compensate for state failure in creating fair background conditions for workers in a country, they need to "work with other corporations to self-regulate their actions through industry-wide codes of conduct" (ibid. 207). But such collaboration suffers from a general collective action problem because what if the individual corporation stands alone and the rest of the industry prefers to profit from the situation? In that case, the moral responsibility must be limited, and the corporation cannot be blamed for failing to change the structures.

Lisa Herzog addresses the collective action problem related to *sector responsibility*. Here, she finds that "[i]ndividual companies can make an important difference by breaking through an implicit consensus that bans moral questions from the conversation" (Herzog 2017, 144); they might be "moral pioneers" (ibid. 145). And, according to Herzog, there are ways to overcome or mitigate the inherent collective action problem by, for instance, entering alliances with like-minded corporations to change the institutions that make exploitative sweatshops possible. This is in alignment with Young's suggestion that responsibilities are collective and political. Young also suggests a number of *parameters of reasoning* about responsibility that can provide limits. And she admits that the idea that social connections, as such, bring obligations of justice "seems too enormous" without taking "our abilities and our particular circumstance" into consideration (Young 2011, 143). The first parameter is *power*. The more influence an organization has on structural processes, the more it becomes responsible. The second is *privilege*, rendering the beneficiaries of sweatshops responsible. The third is *interest* in promoting justice. This is obviously in the interest of the victims, the exploited workers. However, some corporations committed to selling ethically responsible products, such as fair trade, share this interest with the workers and are therefore responsible. The fourth and last parameter suggested by Young is *collective ability*, which asserts that an organization that commands the ability to motivate larger groups of agents, such as the stockholder organization (ibid. 147), carries more responsibility. As such, Young does not propose any moral standard or theory to limit responsibilities and instead relies on pragmatics.

Business and Human Rights

However, the idea of the social liberal corporation is committed to the value of human rights. So, what about finding limits to corporate responsibility in human rights? The UN special representative of the secretary-general on the issue of human rights and business, John Ruggie, issued the UNs' *Guiding Principles on Business and Human Rights* (UNGP 2011). Accordingly, businesses have a duty to *respect* human rights, which is less burdensome than the state's responsibility to both protect and sustain human rights. The term *respect* primarily elicits a negative duty on the corporation to avoid harming people's human rights. But the guiding principles also refer to corporate duties to "prevent or mitigate adverse human rights impacts linked to their operations, products or services . . . even if they have not contributed to those impacts" (ibid. 19). Hence, corporations should conduct *due diligence* to reveal potential negative impacts on human rights. The UNGP explicitly mentions the workers' rights of the International Labour Organization (ILO) as part of human rights. Without going into the details of the limits to corporate responsibility found in core human rights documents, the conclusion to draw is that limits do exist. Ruggie explicitly refers to Young and the social connection model's preference for forward-looking and shared responsibility. This is particularly so in his considerations about how to define corporate complicity and the sphere of influence (Ruggie 2007).

The social liberal corporation, because it bases its concept of responsibility on political CSR and thus Young's, and also Ruggie's, definition, finds its orientation in current liberal human rights regimes. This is one way to scope and settle the limits of what the corporate responsibilities are in the supply chain. Because the business and human rights agenda is still evolving and expanding its scope, the limits of responsibility are not final and fully settled. Importantly, corporations should have an ongoing concern about how they impact on human rights throughout the supply chain. A process and policy should be in place as part of the corporate decision-making procedure. Hence, a due diligence of human rights is a requirement of the UNGP. The duty to conduct due diligence is not merely a risk management procedure to avoid complicity in scandals. The negative duty to merely respect human rights stated in the UNGP should not be taken as a minimalist and managerialist duty. In fact, the duty to respect human rights might be far-reaching and have moral content. For instance, a corporation has a positive duty to conduct a proper risk assessment of its human rights impact. It also has a positive duty to prevent acting and becoming complicit in human rights violations. Thus, the wording of *respect* for human rights in the UNGP does not necessarily entail that there are no positive duties to discharge for the corporation. Furthermore, the UNGP makes it clear that the full list of human rights is relevant, and therefore, social and economic rights of social justice cannot be neglected. This signals that the social liberal corporation matches the requirements of the UNGP, based on the understanding of corporate citizenship and the duty to administer and protect social and economic rights (see Chapter 6). The UNGP is also clearly stating that the failure of the state to protect and uphold human rights within its jurisdiction is no excuse for the corporation not to take on its share of responsibility. The duty to respect cannot be appealed to in this situation because corporate responsibilities remain regardless of whether or not the state is succeeding.

It is a clear fact that rivalling conceptions of corporate responsibility found in the market liberal, the conservative virtue ethical, and the critical approaches are not at all capable of giving support to the human rights regime in the business realm. Only the social liberal corporation based on corporate citizenship and political CSR are able to do this because they are social liberal and rights-based theories. Consequently, the rivalling theories of corporate responsibility are less qualified with regard to responding in practice to difficult cases such as exploitation found in the supply chain.

References

Arnold, D. G., & Bowie, N. E. (2003) Sweatshops and respect for persons. *Business Ethics Quarterly*, *13*(2), 221–242

Crane, A. (2013) Modern slavery as a management practice: Exploring the conditions and capabilities for human exploitation. *Academy of Management Review*, *38*(1), 49–69

Herzog, L. (2017) No company is an island. Sector-related responsibilities as elements of corporate social responsibility. *Journal of Business Ethics*, *146*(1), 135–148

Rawls, J. (1971/1999) *A theory of justice*. Revised edition. Cambridge, MA: Harvard University Press

Reinecke, J., & Donaghey, J. (2015) After Rana Plaza: Building coalitional power for labour rights between unions and (consumption-based) social movement organisations. *Organization*, *22*(5), 720–740

Ruggie, J. G. (2007) Business and human rights: The evolving international agenda. *American Journal of International Law*, *101*(4), 819–840

Ruggie, J. G. (2011) *Guiding principles on business and human rights: Implementing the United Nations "Protect, respect and remedy" framework'*. www.ohchr.org/Documents/Publications/GuidingPrinciplesBusinessHR_EN.pdf

Scherer, A. G., & Palazzo, G. (2011) The new political role of business in a globalized world – A review of a new perspective on CSR and its implications for the firm, governance, and democracy. *Journal of Management Studies*, *48*, 899–931

Schrempf-Stirling, J., & Palazzo, G. (2016) Upstream corporate social responsibility. *Business and Society*, *55*(4), 491–527

Snyder, J. (2010) Exploitation and sweatshop labor: Perspectives and issues. *Business Ethics Quarterly*, *20*(2), 187–213

Young, I. M. (2006) Responsibility and global justice: A social connection model. *Social Philosophy & Policy*, *23*(1), 102–130

Young, I. M. (2011) *Responsibility for justice*. Oxford: Oxford University Press

Zwolinski, M. (2007) Sweatshops, choice, and exploitation. *Business Ethics Quarterly*, *17*(4), 689–727

Zwolinski, M. (2012) Structural exploitation. *Social Philosophy & Policy*, *29*(1), 154–179

10 Digital and Financial Firms

The Limits of Corporate Responsibility

Corporate responsibility is born out of concerns for harms done by real productive units that have physical impacts on people's lives. This was seen in the previous chapter on responsibility in the supply chain. Therefore, it is no surprise that the more virtual existence of the internet and capital were not seen as topics of CSR (Scherer et al. 2016; Flyverbom et al. 2017, 6), at least not until the financial crisis in 2008 revealed that irresponsible financial institutions had caused immense harm to the public and – similarly with the internet – not until it became clear that big ICT corporations had exploited their ignorant users' data for commercial purposes. Before these events and related corporate scandals, capital was considered a neutral substance that would be potentially harmful only in the hands of malign corporations, and the internet was conceived of as a *global commons* for everyone to access and benefit from (Ossewaarde & Reijers 2017). This has changed dramatically. So, now, it is no longer possible for a firm in the financial sector or digital sphere to plead neutral about its corporate responsibility. However, still it remains unclear what sort of corporate responsibility is relevant. In this survey chapter, I will explore this question with regard to corporate responsibility in finances and the digital economy. First, I address digital firms and discuss the early perception of the internet as a global commons, a public good with free and equal access for all. The thorny question is whether the use of social media on the internet can be seen as a public good or whether it creates, in fact, a private good. In particular, the right to privacy is under pressure in the digital age, when new forms of surveillance are possible (Zuboff 2015). As the social liberal corporation should be capable of providing public goods and regulation, and as it is also capable of manoeuvring in the grey zone between the public and private spheres, the case of digital responsibility becomes salient and critical (Scherer et al. 2016, 286).

Corporate responsibilities in finance are concerned with two aspects: one as a finance institution (a bank) and another as an investor (e.g., a pension fund). A bank carries more traditional corporate responsibilities for its stakeholders, whereas investors are traditionally exempt from being considered agents accountable for corporate responsibility. In the latter case, the term *responsible investment* has permeated the financial sector. I argue that it is difficult to separate the two aspects of capital in practice because professional banks are sites of capital transfers and hence investments. For instance, banks can be used for the laundering of vast amounts of capital, and thus banks become responsible for capital flows in transit through their accounts. Alasdair MacIntyre (2016) has argued that traders in finance cannot possess virtues due to the rough capitalist culture so deeply entrenched in these institutions. The social liberal, I will argue, partially agrees but will nonetheless claim that the financial sector can be made more responsible by complying with basic liberal values enlisted in core UN human rights documents.

Digital Firms

The digital economy is ubiquitous with terms such as *big data*, the *internet of things* (IoT), and *blockchain*, all of which offer promises for new business models. Online platforms offer services that compete with traditional services in the transport, hotel, and media industries, the upshot of a new *sharing economy* (Ossewaarde & Reijers 2017). Recently, mentions of *data ethics* and *digital responsibilities* have cropped up but often allude to users' digital literacy and less to corporate responsibility. As the internet came into existence in the 1990s in an atmosphere of anarchist tech-savvy liberalism, the standard perception of the internet has been that the World Wide Web is a global infrastructure, a global commons, offering open access to anyone and hence a panacea of transparency (Flyverbom 2019). Hence, as a public infrastructure, it is provided as a *public good* from which no one can be *excluded* and which offers a digital space so abundant that no *rivalry* among users occurs. The idea of open source has been deployed by Wikipedia, for instance. The promise of the internet became a panacea of *digital democracy*, where citizens could freely deliberate and collectively form public opinions about policy issues. Corporations willingly provided the platforms for *citizenship arenas* that enabled people to *voice* their concerns and opinions and hence also challenge powerful institutions in society (Whelan et al. 2013). Soon, social media firms and search engine providers were caught in difficult trade-off situations, as for instance, Google, which was forced to censure criticism of the Chinese government (Brenkert 2009). And, more recently, the undermining of democracy and the spread of so-called fake news through cyberattacks during public elections bear witness to the dysfunctional aspects of the digital arena. Corporations are blamed and made responsible for the content on their digital platforms, although they tend to plead innocent as users are creators of the content.

Hence, the value-neutral infrastructure metaphor lives on in the corporate denial of responsibility – less so when it comes to the tracking and surveillance of user behaviour on the internet and pursuing data extraction and analysis for commercial purposes (Flyverbom et al. 2017, 2; Zuboff 2015, 78–81). Often it is impossible for the individual user to understand the consent given when accessing a social media platform. Who has property rights to surveillance data can be disputed. Therefore, the notion that the internet is a public good provided to citizens at no price can be seriously questioned, and the digital commons seems to be an illusion (Ossewaarde & Reijers 2017). Now, some of the disputes about the responsibilities of private corporations profiting from extracting user data can be resolved as simply illegal. However, because the digital sphere is evolving at a pace beyond the capacity of lawmakers, another part of the dispute is less easy to resolve. One way to perceive corporate responsibilities would be to follow the libertarian conception that the internet is a free market and users tacitly consent to conditions when they enter a digital space. It would be destructive not only to innovation but also to individual freedom, to regulate, for instance, social media too harshly. The virtue ethicist might argue that what is needed is digital literacy to develop a moral character in the young so that they will know how to act online. And, the critical Marxist-inspired response is to reveal the capitalist exploitation of users. The social liberal could agree with all of this, but I think that notions of corporate citizenship and political CSR provide a theoretical framework that offers further guidance to what exactly corporations need to be concerned about and responsible for. As such approaches take their starting point from the fact that regulation and governance is weak or absent, as in the sphere of global supply chains, they could also work in the digital context, which lacks regulation and governance (Flyverbom et al. 2017). For corporations, this is an option for choosing between a strategy of exploiting governance gaps or taking on responsibility to compensate for the consequences of governance and regulatory gaps in the digital sphere. Surely, the latter has been avoided by the major ICT firms in their denial of carrying full responsibility for users' data. It is difficult to single out the exact limit of corporate responsibility in the digital sphere, not least due to the plurality of cases associated with different kinds of technologies and platforms. However, according to the ideals associated with basic political rights to freedom of speech and free access to information, corporations as citizens providing the digital arenas of social media need to be both responsible for the rules governing the arena and also the content. And, if privacy is infringed upon, for instance, if a user profile is stolen and misused, it must also be the platform provider who is responsible. In that respect, the social liberal corporation approaches its responsibility differently than the libertarian market liberal would do.

Now, the sceptic will ask, how it is possible for the social liberal corporation to be a provider of public goods in the digital sphere? Such public goods could, for instance, be open source access to the use of social media platforms or a contribution to institutionalize regulation and governance. The typology of private versus public goods makes the case for why private firms can profit from providing private goods and the government is needed as the provider of public goods because these are impossible to commercialize (being non-excludable and non-rivalrous). The defence offered by proponents of political CSR could be to respond and argue in at least three ways. First, corporations are forced to provide public goods and are under pressure to do so by critical publics. Second, corporations collaborate with NGOs, governments, and other businesses to ensure regulation and governance that is of benefit to their market access, that is, the level playing field argument. Finally, political CSR and corporate citizenship theory offer normative standards of basic liberal values broadly adhered to by liberals but also more demanding norms of social justice and environmental protection that social liberals would demand in this case. This is sometimes framed as *moral legitimacy*. The social liberal corporation derives its orientation from this framework, and it can be assessed by those standards. Hence, corporations *should* provide public goods in addition to securing the financial bottom line. In case the provision of public goods conflicts with the economic interest, there can be the need for a trade-off.

The current theory of political CSR has not yet developed a comprehensive response to how exactly it is possible for a privately owned firm to provide public goods (Scherer et al. 2016; Flyverbom et al. 2017, 10), and the case of digital firms might be an obvious starting place for developing the theory in this regard. One possible future avenue for developing the theory could be to explore the public-private distinction with regard to goods. For instance, besides public and private goods, there are also *common pool resources* (which are non-excludable but are rivalrous) and *club goods* (which are excludable and non-rivalrous). Club goods seem to better correspond with membership in social media platforms. It is possible that the social liberal corporation needs to be more precise about the nature of the goods provided and even give up the ambition to be a public goods provider (or contributor in the more modest version). To use the phrasing of Flyverbom et al. (2017, 8), social media firms "are more akin to shopping malls than public squares". At least, for some digital firms operating in social media, this would call for the more traditional corporate responsibilities of caring for their members' rights and basic interests.

Similar to the call for human rights in the context of supply chains, digital firms perceived through the lens of the social liberal conception could also find orientation in the human rights regime. However, as digital firms and their corporate responsibility is an issue currently in development, it is less clear what conception of responsibility will win out in practice. The notion of the social liberal corporation – and the kind of organization it requires to act politically and morally responsibly – seems well suited to the digital sphere because it is capable of handling difficult dilemmas pertaining to the public-private distinction. One caveat might be relevant because the social liberal corporation not only handles issues that transgress public-private spheres but is also a symptom or a consequence of the breakdown of liberal distinctions of these spheres: That is, there remains the question of whether the social liberal corporation can ensure privacy protection, for instance, as this requires clear compliance with basic liberal norms. This objection seems warranted, although the adherence to basic liberal values and individual rights features in the setup of the social liberal corporation. Digital firms are therefore "hard cases" for conceptions based on political CSR as there is an inner ambivalence or tension in the theory with respect to securing privacy rights. Another way to frame the issue is to say there is a trade-off between the public value of transparency and the private value of having one's life protected from the public eye.

The conception of the social liberal corporation therefore needs further exploration to cater for this issue of rigging digital firms.

Financial Firms

In the aftermath of the financial crisis of 2008, it has become clear that the financial sector carries a major responsibility for the crisis. Complicated loans and mortgages were offered to homeowners, who were indebted for life. Various reasons for the sector's failure to act responsibly and the extent of its complicity in causing the crisis have been proffered. One possibility is that banking professionals were lacking in epistemic competence in dealing with complicated financial products (De Bruin 2015). Alasdair MacIntyre (2016) has gone even further and argued that an "effective education into the virtues would in fact disqualify one for a successful career in the financial sector" (ibid. 16). MacIntyre justifies his pessimistic claim about the nature of the financial sector with a comparison among four key virtues that the virtuous character possesses and other character traits needed to succeed in finance. Hence, one should have a "tempered realism about oneself" and be able to "strike a mean between rashness and cowardice" (ibid. 9), act with regard to "common goods", and have a long-term perspective – meaning that one should "prefer honourable failure to dishonest success" (ibid. 10). These four traits, according to MacIntyre, are negated by practice in finance institutions because traders must be "too self-confident" (ibid.) to succeed and convince investors of their insights. They are bad risk takers, not able to strike the balance between rashness and cowardice, and they incur risk for investors. They do not care for the common good, and the collateral damage from investments is not considered by traders. Finally, traders prefer the short term and the "longer term is professionally precluded" (ibid. 11). Thus, people working successfully in finance fail with regard to the four virtues mentioned. MacIntyre stresses that they are not bad people, and they certainly are acting "virtuously" by the professional standards of finance. So, "it is the financial sector as a whole that is from the Thomistic Aristotelian point of view a school of bad character" (ibid. 12).

There is a longer history leading back to the Enlightenment, according to MacIntyre, of divorcing ethics from economics, which partially explains why the finance sector became resistant to the virtues, eventually leading to the financial crisis. But it is not simply possible to reduce to the financial sector to the individual level, nor is the single finance firm responsible for the faults of the entire financial system. I agree with MacIntyre that his description could very well be true to the facts, but rather than letting finances off the responsibility hook, it makes sense to ask for reform of the institution that is supportive of moral failure. For instance, Herzog (2019) suggests that finance firms together should be collectively responsible in professional associations of fostering a professional ethics among employees. Only through mutual support and pressure will finance firms be able to reform.

Now, adopting the stance of the social liberal corporation, the call for an integrated and collective effort to reform the institutional context of the finance sector can be applauded. According to proponents of political CSR, to initiate a multi-stakeholder network, it is also necessary to include civil society and governmental institutions in reform by following the standards of deliberative democracy. For the finance sector to become not just more transparent, but also open for democratic contestation, there will need to be a fundamental change in the corporate culture. However, what happened to corporations that relied on far-flung supply chains decades ago is now happening in the finance sector. The increased attention on the ethics of investment has led investors to divest from fossil fuels and blacklist investments in the weapons and tobacco industries. This reforming tendency has certainly not happened because financial firms suddenly became morally concerned but is rather due to external pressure from the media and civil society. Subsequently, investors' organizations globally, with support from the United Nations, have agreed to the *Principles for Responsible Investment.* The principles demand that investors incorporate a concern for environmental, social, and governance (ESG) issues in their practice. Moreover, investors and financial institutions should pursue *active ownership* to change the behaviour of irresponsible corporations in which they have invested. Active ownership offers some leeway for investors to keep unethical assets based on the consequentialist excuse that the ethics are better served by exerting a pressure on the corporate culprit.

Certainly, the financial firm can avoid deeper reform by complying with these, and similar, initiatives. However, the call for a more responsible finance sector found in such types of governance and regulations is leverage in support of the social liberal corporation and its adherence to a shared responsibility.

To sum up, the digital sphere and finances pose serious challenges to notions of corporate responsibility of any orientation, the social liberal one included. There is sufficient reason to be sceptical about the prospect for the digital and financial firm to become more responsible. Conversely, as this chapter has discussed, there are also signs that the entire institutional setting is starting to enforce norms on those powerful and influential organizations to make changes. How these firms will react remains to be seen. Nonetheless, the conception of the social liberal corporation could provide normative guidance in the attempt to develop corporate responsibility for digital and financial firms.

References

Brenkert, G. G. (2009) Google, human rights, and moral compromise. *Journal of Business Ethics*, *85*(4), 453–478

De Bruin, B. (2015) *Ethics and the global financial crisis: Why incompetence is worse than greed*. Cambridge: Cambridge University Press

Flyverbom, M. (2019) *The digital prism: Transparency and managed visibilities in a datafied world*. Cambridge: Cambridge University Press

Flyverbom, M., Deibert, R., & Matten, D. (2017) The governance of digital technology, big data, and the internet: New roles and responsibilities for business. *Business & Society*. doi: 10.1177/0007650317727540

Herzog, L. (2019) Professional ethics in banking and the logic of "integrated situations": Aligning responsibilities, recognition, and incentives. *Journal of Business Ethics*, *156*(2), 531–543

MacIntyre, A. (2016) The irrelevance of ethics. In A. Bielskis & K. Knight (Eds.), *Virtue and economy: Essays on morality and markets*, 7–21. New York: Routledge

Ossewaarde, M., & Reijers, W. (2017) The illusion of the digital commons: 'False consciousness' in online alternative economies. *Organization*, *24*(5), 609–628

Scherer, A. G., Rasche, A., Palazzo, G., & Spicer, A. (2016) Managing for political corporate social responsibility: New challenges and directions for PCSR 2.0. *Journal of Management Studies*, *53*, 273–298

Whelan, G., Moon, J., & Grant, B. (2013) Corporations and citizenship arenas in the age of social media. *Journal of Business Ethics*, *118*(4), 777–790

Zuboff, S. (2015) Big other: Surveillance capitalism and the prospects of an information civilization. *Journal of Information Technology*, *30*, 75–89

11 Sustainability and Climate Change

The Case for Corporate Environmentalism

Corporate responsibility for the environment has become a major issue with the advent of concern about climate change. The general public first became aware of environmental pollution from industry as early as the 1960s. Rachel Carson's *Silent Spring* from 1962 disclosed to the public how the agrochemical industry poisoned the farmland with an insecticide called DDT. The industry responded and denied such harmful effects. Much the same happened when scientists working in the oil industry became aware of anthropogenic climate change in the early 1970s or even earlier. The fossil fuel industry not only denied that fossil fuels resulted in harmful climate change, but major companies went further and lobbied against regulation of emissions, even to the extent of undermining the Kyoto Protocol – the first attempt at reaching a global agreement on climate change (Arnold 2016; Shue 2017). Recent research into the sources of historical greenhouse gas emissions has documented that private corporations in the oil, coal, gas, and cement industries bear the brunt of historical responsibility for climate change. In fact, about 90 companies in these industries are on the list of top emitters of those responsible for 63% of the cumulative global emissions of industrial carbon dioxide and methane between 1751 and 2010. And they cannot even be excused from being ignorant about the science of climate change as 50% of total emissions have happened since 1984 (Heede 2014). These facts challenge the ordinary wisdom of the UN climate negotiations that take the nation state to be the agent responsible for climate change. For the first time, the United Nations recently addressed corporate responsibility for climate change in 2015. In a letter to the conveners of the Paris COP 21 meeting, the UN Office of the High Commissioner on Human Rights argued: "Businesses are also duty bearers. They must be accountable for their climate impacts and participate responsibly in climate change mitigation and adaptation efforts with full respect for human rights" (OHCHR 2015, 4).

This chapter will provide an outline for how corporations bear a responsibility for the environment in general but with a particular purview to climate change. To clarify how the social liberal corporation responds to climate change, the case of a collectivist and institutional bottom-up approach adopted by the UN Sustainable Development Goals (SDGs) (2015) is used in the last section of the chapter.

Corporate Environmentalism

In the research literature on corporate environmentalism, several approaches are on offer (Toft & Rüdiger 2020). The mainstream approaches are market liberal in their emphasis on making a business case from the demand in the market for green solutions. The triple bottom line that integrates concern for the environment with the financial bottom line, as well as the supposed market value in reporting on environmental indicators in general, for instance, by use of life cycle assessments, carbon footprints, off-setting, and more, all provide evidence for the huge influence of a market liberal approach (Crane et al. 2008). Business and the market are significant drivers for bettering the environment, or at least, this is what proponents of green capitalism assume. Because the media are constantly publishing stories about corporate *greenwashing*, the whole idea of leaving the care of the environment to corporations who caused environmental deterioration in the first place seems wrong. In fact, the use of environmental resources is often not priced in the market and figures as an *externality* (Arnold 2016, 253). As was mentioned in Chapter 5, Nicolas Stern called climate change the largest market failure in history. Critics of corporate (ir)responsibility also point out that corporations are more often involved in window dressing (greenwashing) when they pose as sustainable and green (Wright & Nyberg 2015). Critics of capitalism have argued that the ecological crisis poses a serious challenge to the integrative capacities of the entire capitalist system (Chiapello 2013). Hence, the feasibility of capitalism as a global system is under threat from the environmental crises. Climate change is one if not the main crisis, which connects to a number of other crises, for instance, the issue of biodiversity. However, the recent dispute about the *Anthropocene* bears witness to the fact that the last 200 years of industrialization have resulted in deeper changes that will eventually pose serious challenges to human civilization. The resurge in debates about *deep ecology* and the anthropocentric worldview is raising the doubts about what role corporations can have with regard to the environment (Schuler et al. 2017). Furthermore, the concept of sustainability – as, for instance, framed in the notion of sustainable development – is also much contested as it can be used for a manifold of purposes, of which some are at the brink of what is basically good for the environment. Hence, the idea of business sustainability can be argued to be inherently contradictory.

More practically, at the corporate level, the pursuance of so-called *eco-efficiency*, which means a more efficient use of natural resources measured by cost, has been questioned. Because even though a business becomes more eco-efficient as it increases the number of units it produces, this might still, due to market expansion, cause a rebound effect. *Rebound effects* occur because the total measured effect on the environment can be negative simply because of the increase in quantity produced. More sustainable products are still more products that eventually deplete environmental resources.

So, these objections to business sustainability have made it clear that a more holistic approach to the environment is required. One such attempt is ecological corporate citizenship (Crane et al. 2008).

Corporate Citizenship and the Environment

A possible avenue for the corporation, and I am here alluding to the social liberal one in particular, is to use the lens of corporate citizenship as an *ecological citizenship*. Crane et al. (2008) argue that this perspective on corporate responsibility towards nature can be helpful in obtaining a more comprehensive outlook. Hence, ecological corporate citizenship shows "that corporations can be located as political actors with obligations to non-humans and future generations (in rethinking the stakeholder set) or to global constituencies within its ecological footprint (in reconfiguring the community of the corporation)" (ibid. 385).

Thus, to rephrase, corporations should discharge duties to non-humans, the environment, animals, and future generations. These duties are constrained by a revised set of stakeholders and the scope of the corporate ecological footprint. These are wide-ranging and demanding duties. For instance, by adopting the lens of corporate citizenship (as presented in Chapter 6), the corporation has responsibilities in at least three roles. It can be a substitute for the government, it can be a citizen itself, and it can be an arena for citizenship. In the first role, it should secure citizens' right to a liveable and clean environment. This is equivalent to an expansion of the social liberal rights core to citizenship suggested by T. H. Marshall to also include environmental rights (ibid. 375). In the second role, the corporation as citizen should comply with environmental duties of good citizenship. The environment is a public good or a common good that no one, corporations included, should deplete or exploit. Hence, the corporation should consider what the *fair share* of resources available for it to use is – for instance, the Science Based Targets initiative operates with the assumption that corporations are entitled to a fair share of the carbon budget available. Hence, guidance can be found in complying with the absolute targets recommended by the climate scientists of the UN Intergovernmental Panel on Climate Change (IPCC) or, at the local scale, in protecting and sustaining the resources needed to sustain local communities. Crane et al. (2008) also argue that adopting the corporate citizenship lens accrues further and more political duties for the corporation. For instance, with regard to climate change, the corporation could have the role of facilitating the political preferences of citizens. And, such responsibility is not merely a negative of avoiding harm to the environment, of which emissions reduction is an example. Rather, such duties can be more comprehensive and positive duties, requiring contribution to institution-building:

> The obligations suggested by ecological citizenship not only go further than simply minimizing one's impact but also extend to participation in the political process with other actors in designing effective solutions to global problems such as climate change.
>
> (ibid. 384)

Being a good corporate citizen is, therefore, imbued with duties that can be classified as both negative and positive. Usually, environmental responsibility is local and easy to limit because the corporation uses its resources from traceable sources. And, if it pollutes, this is often measured at the local site of production. However, in the case of climate change, the issue is more complicated. First, climate change is a result of historical emissions, and the average corporation is not significantly guilty with regard to history. Larger corporations usually rely on substantial emissions from production, transport, and consumption. So, in that regard, even if they have only limited *backward-looking* responsibility for climate change, they could have a significant *forward-looking* responsibility due to emissions now and in the future. According to Henry Shue, we all have forward-looking *negative duties* to avoid harm. And, if we fail to observe this negative duty, we incur *positive duties* to correct and compensate for our previous neglect (Shue 2017). The same goes for big corporations. However, because they both burden the environment more than individuals do, and command financial, political, and technological capacities and power far beyond the individual, their responsibility is substantial. Shue insists that the negative duties to do no harm in the current situation of harmful climate change translates into substantial duties. Corporations therefore, simply due to their negative duty not to harm, should take leadership and lobby for carbon taxes. They should also invest in research to convert to renewable energy sources (ibid. 5).

Recently, attempts have been made to argue that corporations' human rights duties include also a concern for the issue of climate change (Toft 2019). In particular, the carbon majors are considered responsible for their historical emissions and how this has caused harmful climate changes that affect millions of people's lives. Human rights litigation is becoming a common strategy to pursue justice and compensation from the big emitters. A key issue here is what human rights duties can be ascribed to corporations when they are non-state agents. Human rights duties are typically only relevant for the state. So, it is controversial (as seen in Chapter 9) to consider privately owned corporations as bearers of human rights duties – because they should respect only human rights. What is significant here is that the notion of the social liberal corporation is well placed to conceptualize and respond to the claim that business firms have human rights duties relevant in the context of climate change. The rivalling theories of corporate responsibility are less equipped to respond (for the reasons stated in Chapter 9), which counts in favour of the social liberal conception.

Finally, to explore the holistic approach of ecological citizenship that the social liberal corporations should commit to – with regard to climate change – the case of the UN SDGs is examined.

The SDGs and Climate Change

The SDGs of the United Nations, signed by almost 200 countries in 2015, are examples of the recent turn to global *governance of bottom-up* processes also seen in the Paris Agreement on climate change in 2015. Bottom-up governance is supplementary to unilateral, state-led governance as it includes partnerships from civil society and business. Corporations are therefore perceived as contributors to a collective process of promoting the 17 SDGs (Sachs 2012). With regard to this chapter's focus on the environment, several goals are relevant, but most relevant are Goal 7 on *affordable and clean energy*, Goal 14 on *climate action*, and Goal 17 on *partnership for the goals*.

Part of the reason for supporting bottom-up governance is due to the failure of the state system to deliver. Hence, the (now often disputed) premise of the absent or weak state eliciting corporate duties in the social liberal approaches is also confirmed or taken as given in the Paris Agreement and the SDGs.

The SDGs raise several practical questions about how a corporation can contribute to the goals, which cannot be explored here. Instead, the SDGs also raise more theoretical and philosophical questions about corporate responsibility. It is obvious that the SDGs are usually launched as a business opportunity to be pursued voluntarily, and therefore the framework is market liberal. However, the SDGs are also imbued with a social liberal orientation due to the nature of the goals listed. For instance, the issue of eliminating poverty is listed as Goal 1, and the goals on gender and equality are fully aligned with basic human rights. Hence, it is difficult to maintain that the SDGs are possible to defend on a purely market liberal account of corporate responsibility. It makes more sense to see them as compatible with the idea of corporate citizenship and political CSR, as the social liberal approach combines. Corporations as citizens contribute to regulation and to solving problems that concern public goods (health, education, infrastructure, the environment), and they do this in concerted action together with civil society and state agencies. Hence, corporations can be seen through the lens of corporate citizenship, fulfilling a political role by contributing to the SDGs. And, importantly, they are in fact *obliged* to contribute as far as they can within the limits of their financial, political, and technological capacities (Young 2011; Hormio 2017). A further qualification can be added to the argument. I would suggest a distinction between *first-order duties* to contribute to climate change mitigation and adaptation and a *second-order duty* to contribute in a collective process to promote and discharge first-order duties. The first-order duties can be of various sorts, but what is important here is whether or not these can be discharged by the single corporate actor or whether a collective effort is required. The question arises when, for instance, a corporation has responsibility for victims of climate change because it has or will emit excessively and create harms. But this corporation as a single actor has no chance of making any real difference to climate victims; only through large-scale collective initiatives can it reduce harms. In this case, it is clear that the corporation is faced with the second-order duty to contribute to institution-building to mitigate climate harms. Seeing global governance initiatives like the SDGs from this perspective, it makes sense to argue that they facilitate and strengthen second-order duties to act collectively. However, if a corporation cannot find partners for collective action without excessive costs, it cannot be blamed for not discharging its first-order duties, if these are dependent on collective powers to be discharged. Thus, the SDGs raise the probability in general that second-order collective duties to combat climate change fall onto corporations. This conclusion supports the notion of the social liberal corporation defended throughout this book: that only by accepting a political role and the duties associated with it does the corporation stand a chance of responding to global challenges such as the concern for a transition to renewable energy and taking care of the victims of climate change now and in the future.

References

Arnold, D. G. (2016) Corporate responsibility, democracy, and climate change. *Midwest Studies in Philosophy*, *40*(1), 252–261

Chiapello, E. (2013) Capitalism and its new criticisms. In P. Du Gay & G. Morgan (Eds.), *New spirits of capitalism? Crises, justifications and dynamics*, 60–81. Oxford: Oxford Scholarship Online

Crane, A., Matten, D., & Moon, J. (2008) Ecological citizenship and the corporation – Politicizing the new corporate environmentalism. *Organization & Environment*, *21*, 371–389

Heede, R. (2014) Tracing anthropogenic carbon dioxide and methane emissions to fossil fuel and cement producers, 1854–2010. *Climatic Change*, *122*(1–2), 229–241

Hormio, S. (2017) Can corporations have (moral) responsibility regarding climate change mitigation? *Ethics, Policy & Environment*, *20*(3), 314–332

OHCHR (2015) *Submission to the 21st conference of the parties to the United Nations framework convention on climate change*. www.ohchr.org/Documents/Issues/ClimateChange/COP21.pdf

Sachs, J. D. (2012) From millennium development goals to sustainable development goals. *Lancet (British edition)*, *379*(9832), 2206–2211

Schuler, D., Rasche, A., Etzion, D., & Newton, L. (2017) 'Guest editors' introduction: Corporate sustainability management and environmental ethics. *Business Ethics Quarterly*, *27*(2), 213–237

Shue, H. (2017) Responsible for what? Carbon producer CO2 contributions and the energy transition. *Climatic Change*, *144*(4), 591–596

Toft, K. H. (2019) Climate change as a business and human rights issue – A proposal for a moral typology. *Business and Human Rights Journal*, 1–27. doi: 10.1017/bhj.2019.22

Toft, K. H., & Rüdiger, M. (2020) Mapping corporate climate change ethics: Responses among three Danish energy firms. *Energy Research & Social Science*, *59*, 101286. doi: 10.1016/j.erss.2019.101286

UN (2015) *Sustainable development goals*. www.un.org/sustainabledevelopment/

Wright, C., & Nyberg, D. (2015) *Climate change, capitalism, and corporations*. Cambridge: Cambridge University Press

Young, I. M. (2011) *Responsibility for justice*. Oxford: Oxford University Press

Conclusion

Should the corporation then be a relevant topic for current political philosophy to consider? I think that this question can be answered with a qualified yes. However, considering the philosophical views of the corporation held over the last two centuries from the Enlightenment until today, it is clear that its role is marginal and, to some degree, even neglected. There are a number of reasons for the exclusion of the corporation from political philosophy. A key reason is the historical division of labour between economics and ethics. Conceiving of the corporation as an economic functionality, perhaps even as a market in itself, the notion of corporate responsibility – as a moral term – does not make sense. Another reason concerns the distinction between the private and the public spheres. This distinction, together with the notion of citizenship, has occupied political philosophy with the governance of the public sphere and how it can gain legitimacy from the private sphere of individual citizens. The corporation does not have an obvious role to play in political philosophy on those terms because it is not a citizen or a moral person in the ordinary sense, nor does it fit nicely into the dichotomy of the private and the public spheres. The common-sense understanding that the corporation belongs to the private sphere, also partially supported by the legal term of the corporate person, can easily be contested. In fact, it never was a purely private body as it enjoyed the legal privilege of limited liability. Furthermore, corporations today are influential agencies within the public sphere, and to use Rawls's phrasing, they have a pervasive impact on people's lives right from the start. Consider also the main assumption of corporate citizenship and political CSR: that when the state is weakened, unwilling, or absent in situations where globalization has disempowered the nation state, the corporation is called upon to take on a political role. This assumption, the truth of which can be contested as corporations only marginally substitute for the state, still provides reason for why corporations are also relevant to the concerns of political philosophy.

The thread of the argument that has been used to defend a particular conception of corporate responsibility throughout the book – the social liberal corporation – relies much on the premise that the state is either absent, weak or not willing to secure citizens' basic interests and rights. Conceptions of corporate responsibility are diverse, as also demonstrated in this book, but a common feature looming in most thinking about the corporation in society is about the corporate ability to contribute to the common good. Although this is also a disputed notion from the perspective of liberal thinking, in particular versions of liberalism that adhere to neutrality about the good, it is clear that the notion of the common good is at stake in all approaches to corporate responsibility.

However, while acknowledging the relevance of raising the issue of the common good, I have instead argued throughout the book that the market liberal and critical Marxist-inspired conceptions are debunking the notion of corporate responsibility – despite the fact that modified versions of market liberalism, as found in the market failures approach, are supportive of corporate responsibility. Only the conservative virtue ethical and the social liberal conception of corporate citizenship and political CSR are unequivocally supportive. Given that corporate responsibility is held to be a moral duty to provide such goods to the public, there are limits to which theories are eligible. I have argued that even though conservative virtue ethical approaches are supportive of corporate responsibility, they also fail to give full support to the notion of rights, in particular human rights, which are significant in the current global schemes of corporate governance and responsibility. Moreover, the mainstream currents of the virtue ethical tradition are antithetical to commerce and capitalism as political institutions. Hence, I have argued that corporate citizenship theory and political CSR win out in the general argument in support of corporate responsibility appropriate for the challenges currently permeating the world. I have suggested perceiving of such approaches as sharing a social liberal orientation. This is so because they commit to correcting market failures and they are also in support of social liberal rights and values. Even though they tend to be in some tension with the liberal conviction that the private and the public are separate spheres, because this is part of the diagnosis political CSR provides, they still seek to remedy the harms that occur as a result of the politicization of the private as well as the commodification of the public. Moreover, when addressing contemporary issues in Part III (supply chains, digital and financial firms, as well as the environment and climate change), it was shown how the social liberal corporation can respond in a moral way to such issues.

However, despite the support found for a belief in the social liberal corporation, it still makes sense to raise serious doubt about the underlying logic and causal processes driving the responsibility agenda. As it can be a lucrative business to act responsibly and to take on a political role for the good of society (here ignoring lobbyism for unilateral corporate self-interest at the cost for the rest of society), corporations are basically motivated by purely economic incentives; hence, the profit motive is a lingering motivator. This sort of *ad hominem* critique can be made against the bold claims of corporate citizenship. I have not tried to reject this type of critique, apart from the conceptual clarifications proposed. The fact that business corporations are driven by the profit motive need not be disputed. Rather, the question is whether they are also driven by other concerns and how they balance with the profit motive. The theory of corporate citizenship explicitly approaches the corporate sphere with the *lens* of citizenship, meaning that it is looking for behaviour and features *resembling* citizenship. This is certainly no proof of any claim that corporate citizenship is empirically or conceptually justified, but it does provide a way of *framing* aspects of the corporation with regard to its political role.

A second reservation concerns political CSR and the use of deliberative democracy as a model for corporate engagement and communication with the public. Assuming that corporations can be reconfigured or interpreted as organizations amenable to deliberative democracy – which Habermas would deny – it is still difficult to maintain, as I did in Chapter 7, that the political institutional corporate context is compatible with democracy in general. It is possible that the global corporation envisaged by political CSR engages in multi-stakeholder initiatives together with institutions that support liberal democracy. Many NGOs and governments will do that, but in the global context, support for liberal democracy is not a given. And, in raising the bar by demanding a *deliberative* democracy, this makes it all the more difficult for political CSR to render its theory plausible. I am not saying that less cannot work or that the pragmatist stance of political CSR would not enable a dialogue with non-liberals that aimed to turn them into deliberative democrats. The concern is rather that political CSR might be too optimistic about the prospects for deliberative democracy as a model for corporate responsibility. Similarly, the claim that corporations provide public goods might also be overstated. Public goods are, by definition, difficult to commercialize as they are non-exclusive and non-rivalrous. Political CSR needs to qualify further how it is possible for a business corporation to provide public goods. As long as these issues are left unacknowledged and unresolved by proponents of political CSR, they continue to be critical to the social liberal conception proposed here.

With regard to the future prospects for corporate responsibility in general and the notion of the social liberal corporation in particular, there is good reason to maintain some perseverance. The prospect of an overturn of the liberal world order, which is coming under threat from nationalism and non-democratic capitalism, is decisive for the notion of corporations as responsible agencies. I have argued in the introduction to this book that the call for a social liberal orientation in the theory of corporate responsibility represents a concern – and perhaps even a *longing* – for the social liberal state, which is currently under pressure or is withering away. Surely, it might be a cleverer ambition to strengthen the state to regain its status and therefore not to invest too much hope in the notion of the social liberal corporation. However, it is a fault of a *defunct* political philosophy (to rephrase another social liberal, John Maynard Keynes) to think that the state does not need support from responsible corporations. The idea that corporations can be seen only as adversaries to the state is misconceived. The discussion about the social liberal corporation should be seen as a contribution to reconfigure the division of labour between the state and the corporation. Moreover, it is a suggestion to also reconsider corporations as relevant to political philosophy. Hence, this book is supportive of a current, more general tendency among political philosophers to think about the corporation and look for a political theory of the firm. I have aimed at presenting such thinking in a comprehensive philosophical context that includes the philosophical history of corporations, notions of corporate moral agency, the main political theories of corporate responsibility, and an outlook on contemporary issues.

I have argued that the social liberal corporation is supportive of corporate responsibility, whereas market liberal and critical conceptions are not. However, I have also argued that the current theorizing found in corporate citizenship and political CSR theory needs further consideration. Therefore, this book has attempted to cast light on the philosophical tensions and debates that have formed our current understanding of the corporation. And, in doing so, it has stated a positive case for a social liberal theory of corporate responsibility.

Name Index

Subject Index

Kolibri 360 GmbH
Ferdinand-Jühlke-Straße 7
99095 Erfurt, Deutschland
produktsicherheit@kolibri360.de